Ibn Khaldun

♦♦♦

Ibn Khaldun

✦✦✦

AN INTELLECTUAL BIOGRAPHY

Robert Irwin

PRINCETON UNIVERSITY PRESS

Princeton & Oxford

Epigraph to chapter 3 from C. P. Cavafy: *Collected Poems*, revised edition translated by Edmund Keeley and Philip Sherrard, edited by George Savidis. Translation copyright © 1975, 1992 by Edmund Keeley and Philip Sherrard. Reprinted by permission of Princeton University Press.

Excerpts from *The Muqaddimah: An Introduction to History* by Ibn Khaldûn. Copyright © 1958, 1967 by Bollingen. Reprinted by permission of Princeton University Press.

Published by Princeton University Press,
41 William Street, Princeton, New Jersey 08540

In the United Kingdom: Princeton University Press,
6 Oxford Street, Woodstock, Oxfordshire OX20 1TR

press.princeton.edu

Jacket art: Maxfield Parrish, "The City of Brass," from *The Arabian Nights*, ed. 1909. Reproduction courtesy of Art Passions.

Library of Congress Cataloging-in-Publication Data

Names: Irwin, Robert, 1946- author.

Title: Ibn Khaldun : an intellectual biography / Robert Irwin.

Description: Princeton, New Jersey : Princeton University Press, [2018] | Includes bibliographical references and index.

Identifiers: LCCN 2017028272 | ISBN 9780691174662 (hardcover : alk. paper)

Subjects: LCSH: Ibn Khaldun, 1332-1406. | Historians, Arab—Islamic Empire—Biography. | Historiography—Islamic Empire. | Islamic civilization.

Classification: LCC D116.7.I3 I79 2018 | DDC 907.2/02 [B] —dc23 LC record available at https://lccn.loc.gov/2017028272

British Library Cataloging-in-Publication Data is available

This book has been composed in Sabon LT Std

Printed on acid-free paper. ∞

Printed in the United States of America

1 3 5 7 9 10 8 6 4 2

We later civilizations . . . we too know that we are mortal.
—Paul Valéry, "The Crisis of the Mind" (1919)

CONTENTS

✦✦✦

The world historian Arnold Toynbee, who produced a twelve-volume study of the rise and fall of civilizations, described Ibn Khaldun's theoretical treatise on history, the *Muqaddima*, as "undoubtedly the greatest work of its kind that has ever been created by any mind in any time or place."[1] Although the historian Hugh Trevor-Roper was a fierce critic of Toynbee's theories about the cyclical rise and fall of civilizations, he agreed with him about the merits of Ibn Khaldun: "It is a wonderful experience to read those great volumes, as rich and various, as subtle deep and formless as the Ocean, and to fish up from them ideas old and new."[2] The historian of the culture of Muslim societies, Marshall Hodgson described the *Muqaddima* as "no doubt the best general introduction to Islamicate civilization ever written."[3] The philosopher, sociologist, and anthropologist Ernest Gellner declared that Ibn Khaldun was "a superb inductive sociologist, a practitioner, long before the term was invented, of the method of ideal types."[4] As we shall see, Ibn Khaldun's ideas were cited with approval in Bruce Chatwin's novel *Songlines* and they underpinned Frank Herbert's *Dune* cycle of science fiction novels, as well as Naguib Mahfouz's fine novel, *The Harafish*. Ibn Khaldun himself had no doubts about the value and originality of what he had written: "It should be known that the discussion of this topic is something new, extraordinary, and highly useful. Penetrating research has shown the way to it . . . In a way it is an entirely original science. In fact, I have not come across a discussion along these lines by anyone."[5] "We . . . were inspired by God. He led us to a science whose truth we ruthlessly set forth."[6]

Wali al-Din 'Abd al-Rahman Ibn Khaldun (1332–1406) was born in Tunis and in the first half of his life he held various advisory and bureaucratic roles in the service of the Merinid rulers in Fez, the Hafsids in Tunis, the 'Abd al-Wadids in Tlemcen, and the Nasrids in Granada. In 1375 he retired to a remote castle in western Algeria where in the course of the next four years he worked on the first draft of the *Muqaddima*, his book on the principles of history and rise and fall of dynasties. In 1378 he reentered civilization and undertook some teaching in Tunis while consulting its libraries. He also worked on a lengthy chronicle that followed on from his book on the principles of history. In 1382 he left for Mamluk Egypt. There he held the office of chief qadi (judge) of the Maliki rite several times and he continued to work expanding and revising what he had already written. In 1400 he had a memorable meeting outside the walls of Damascus with the would-be world conqueror Timur (also known as Tamerlane). Ibn Khaldun died in Cairo and was buried in a Sufi cemetery.

The *Muqaddima* (Prolegomena) is a lengthy theoretical consideration of the laws of history as well as a general survey of Islamic societies and their arts and sciences. It is divided into six chapters: Chapter one deals with human society in general; chapter two, nomadic society; chapter three, states, caliphs, and kings; chapter four, civilized society and towns; chapter five, trade and ways of earning a livelihood; chapter six, sciences and arts. Though the original aim in writing the chronicle that followed, the *Kitab al-'Ibar wa diwan al-mubtada wa'l-khabar* (The Book of Warning and the Collection of Beginnings and Historical Information), seems to have been to produce a history of the Berber and Arab tribes of North Africa and the dynasties that they established, as he wrote, the scope of his history expanded and became something grander. The theoretical prolegomena to the history, the *Muqaddima*, occupies three fat volumes in its English translation, while the standard Arabic edition of the history, the *'Ibar*, is in seven volumes. The first draft of the *Muqaddima* was allegedly completed in 1377 in five months and it is on this work that Ibn Khaldun's chief claim to fame rests, rather than on the history that followed it.

The first question posed in the *Muqaddima* is why do historians make mistakes? Three things lead to error in writing history. First, partisanship. Secondly, gullibility. Thirdly, ignorance of what is intrinsically possible. It was this third issue that first and foremost he sought to address, since earlier chroniclers had not given any serious consideration to the general laws that govern the formation and dissolution of human societies. They had not studied the *batin* (the interior meaning) of history, but were only compilers of the *zahir* (its externals). Ibn Khaldun scrutinized accounts of past events and sought to assess them on the grounds of plausibility. One needed to take account of cause and effect, then how things work when the situations are similar, and then how things work when the situations are dissimilar. This was an unusual thing for an Islamic historian to do. The '*Ibar* is an even lengthier work, a chronicle theoretically based on the principles outlined in the *Muqaddima*. Another much shorter book, *Al-Ta'rif bi Ibn Khaldun wa rihlatihi sharqan wa gharban* (Presenting Ibn Khaldun and His Journeys in the East and the West), can be misleadingly described as an "autobiography," even though it is somewhat short on self-revelation, for, although Ibn Khaldun had had an adventurous life, he did not present it as such.

During the last two centuries the meaning of what Ibn Khaldun wrote and its significance has been hotly debated. Was he the world's first sociologist? Was he a sociologist at all? Did his theorizing about history owe much or anything to the principles of Greek philosophy? Has his originality been exaggerated? Islam seems to be central to his historical thought, but in what way exactly? Or was he secretly really a rationalist and an atheist? Was he a Sufi? Why did he make so many enemies in the Maghreb and in Egypt? Does his model of the cyclical rise and fall of dynasties apply outside the Maghreb? Did he think it did? Did he think that nomads were a good thing or a bad thing? Insofar as he was a futurologist as well as a historian, was he any good as a prophet?

These are some of the questions that modern commentators have tried to deal with. That there are so many interpretations of Ibn Khaldun may suggest that he did not express himself very clearly. The bibliography on him is huge. Aziz al-Azmeh's *Ibn Khaldun in Modern Scholarship* listed over 850 items and, as the decades have passed, the number must have at least doubled.[7] The University of Chicago online Mamluk bibliography lists 854 books and articles about Ibn Khaldun, though that excludes Maghribi and Andalusian items. If you tried to read everything that has been written about Ibn Khaldun, you would die before you could finish the job.

One may get a sense of half the history of Orientalism just by following the fortunes of Ibn Khaldun in European scholarship from the early nineteenth century onwards. Even so, it took a long time before he was discovered by European scholars, for he wrote in a century when Europeans had given up translating Arabic works. (The heyday for such translations was over by the twelfth century.)

There are already so many books on Ibn Khaldun that I have been hesitant to add yet another to the list. As Ibn Khaldun himself wrote: "It should be known that among the things that are harmful to the human quest for knowledge and to the attainment of a thorough scholarship are the great number of works (available), the large variety in technical terminology (needed for purposes) of instruction, and the numerous (different) methods (used in those works)."[8] As far as he was concerned, there were already too many books in fourteenth-century North Africa.

The above has been a brisk and conventional account of the life and writings of Ibn Khaldun, but it is at best only partially true, for it seems to me that generations of scholars have read Ibn Khaldun with their eyes glazed over and I get the impression that, by the time students of the *Muqaddima* get to its final chapters, they are too weary to take proper account of them. Because the book is so long, it has been selectively sampled and abridged. Its messages have been modernized and rationalized. From the nineteenth century onwards there has been a conscious or unconscious drive to Westernize his thought and to present him as a precursor of such totemic Western thinkers as Machiavelli, Hobbes, Montesquieu, Vico, Marx, Weber, and Durkheim. There is an understandable wish to make him exciting and relevant. But, of course, Ibn Khaldun's world had more in common with that of the Qur'an and *The Thousand and One Nights* than it does with modern historiography or sociology. Ibn Khaldun may have placed monkeys just below men in the Great Chain of Being, but this falls a long way short of having preempted Charles Darwin's closely argued *On the Origin of Species by Means of Natural Selection*. A similar point might be made by comparing Ibn Khaldun's notion of profit as being based on labor with Karl Marx's elaborate exposition of the implications of the labor theory of value.

As Patricia Crone observed: "The civilized societies of the past resemble those of modern times, but in some ways the similarity is deceptive. One cannot come to grips with them without thinking away modernity and working out the consequences of its absence."[9] Although what Ibn Khaldun has to say about the rise and fall of North African dynasties and the circulation of tribal elites is intensely interesting, it is not particularly relevant to modern concerns, since there are few places left in the world where there is a politically significant symbiosis between towns and the tribesmen of the hinterland and there are, I think, no regimes that rely on the military support of nomads. How relevant can Ibn Khaldun be in a world of globalization, digitzation, nation-states, democracies, and dictatorships? So I am not interested in making Ibn Khaldun's writings seem relevant to present-day issues. (Though I have been interested in the reverse process—in making modern writings relevant to him and his world and using those writings to clarify his thought, if only by contrast.) It is precisely Ibn Khaldun's irrelevance to the modern world that makes him so interesting and important. When I read the *Muqaddima*, I have the sense that I am encountering a visitor from another planet—and that is exciting. There have been other ways of looking at the world than the one we mostly take for granted today.

An immersal in the way of thinking of Ibn Khaldun may allow a modern reader access to a premodern and radically different approach to understanding societies and their histories—one in which causation is underpinned by God's will and the primary purpose of social organization is religious salvation. Angels and demons have a role to play in determining the outcome of battles, foretelling the future, and much else. Moreover, ideologically formulated party politics in the modern Western sense was unknown among the regimes of the fourteenth-century Maghreb and the Mamluk Sultanate of Egypt and Syria. Having immersed oneself in all this strangeness, one may, if one wishes, contemplate one's own intellectual and social world with a fresher and perhaps more critical eye. The contrasts matter more than the comparisons.

Though there is no properly edited edition of the text of the *Muqaddima* in Arabic, in 1958 the Bollingen Foundation published *The Muqaddimah. An Introduction to History* in three volumes. A second edition of this translation was published by Princeton University Press in 1967 with corrections and an augmented bibliography. The translator, Professor Franz Rosenthal, an astonishingly erudite and productive scholar, carefully collated the surviving manuscripts of the *Muqaddima* in order to produce what amounts to a critical edition of the text. Over the years it has attracted much praise and some criticism and Rosenthal's approach to the problem of translating Ibn Khaldun will be discussed in more detail in chapters 5 and 10. (There is a similarly scholarly translation of the *Muqaddima*, as well as parts of the *'Ibar*, into French by Abdesselam Cheddadi, published in a handsome Pléiade edition.)[10]

In a later essay, Rosenthal implied that it is not good to be too young before writing about Ibn Khaldun.[11] The Middle Eastern historian Albert Hourani tried to deter his students from starting PhDs on Ibn Khaldun. I bought my copy of Rosenthal's translation in the 1960s and I have been living with it for a long time (but let me hasten to add that I have since supplemented that translation with an Arabic version).

Finally, here is what may be thought of as the literary equivalent of some housekeeping notes. I have used a simplified version of the standard way of transliterating Arabic. The forward facing apostrophe, when used for Arabic names and things, represents the letter *'ayn*, whereas the backward facing apostrophe represents a *hamza*. *'Ayn* represents a glottal scrape, whereas the *hamza'* represents an unvoiced glottal stop (so that in *rasa'il*, for example, the *i* is sounded directly after the *a*). The Arab sources use *hijri* dates, based on a lunar year and starting from the Prophet Muhammad's exodus from Mecca in 622 AD. Since hijri years do not correspond to Western ones, sometimes an event can only be registered as corresponding to two years in the Christian calendar. Western-style surnames were unknown in the medieval Arab world. *Abu* means "father of" and so does *Abi*. *Ibn* means "son of." *Banu* means "sons of." Maghreb is used to refer to the region currently comprising Morocco, Algeria, and Tunisia. Ifriqiyya is used to refer to the territory that is approximately occupied by

Tunisia today. From time to time I have used the words Morocco, Algeria, Tunisia, and Libya to conveniently identify regions, but, of course, those nations did not exist in the fourteenth century. Andalusia refers to that part of Spain that still remained under Muslim rule. Quotations from the Qur'an, if not reproduced from Rosenthal's translation of the *Muqaddima*, are taken from A. J. Arberry's *The Koran Interpreted*, 2 vols. (London, 1955). The chapters of the Qur'an are known as *Sura*s.

ACKNOWLEDGMENTS

I am most grateful to my agent, Juri Gabriel, and to Fred Appel at Princeton University Press for moving this book toward publication and I am also grateful for the comments on my text made by the Press's anonymous readers. Professor David Morgan and Mohamed Madani provided me with materials, which were otherwise difficult to access. Over the years I have learned much from conversations with Professor Hugh Kennedy. The library of London University's School of Oriental and African Studies has been a vital resource. Helen Irwin has worked hard to improve both the book and me.

CHRONOLOGY

1332 May 27 Ibn Khaldun is born.

1347 Merinid Abu'l Hasan occupies Tunis. Ibn Khaldun's teacher, the scholar al-Abili, is part of the intellectual entourage.

1348–49 The Black Death spreads throughout North Africa.

1353 Ibn Khaldun first meets the Merinid Abu 'Inan in Tlemcen.

1354 Ibn Khaldun is invited by Abu 'Inan to Fez.

1355 Ibn Khaldun is appointed secretary to Abu 'Inan.

1359 Ibn Khaldun is active in support of the succession of Merinid Abu Salim and is appointed *katib al-sirr* (head of the chancellery).

1359–62 Muhammad V, the Nasirid ruler of Granada, and his vizier Ibn al-Khatib are in exile in Morocco, where Ibn Khaldun first encounters them.

1361 Ibn Khaldun is made a kind of appeal judge, in charge of *mazalim* (the investigation of misdemeanors by officials). Later in the year Abu Salim is killed and Ibn Khaldun falls under a cloud.

1362 He is given permission to leave Morocco for Andalusia. In December he is received in Granada by Muhammad V.

1364 Ibn Khaldun is sent by Muhammad V on a successful mission to Pedro of Castille in Seville.

1365 Ibn Khaldun leaves Andalusia to become chief minister (*hajib*) of Abu 'Abdallah, the Hafsid amir of Bijaya (Bougie) in Algeria. He is dispatched to collect taxes from the Berbers in the mountains.

1366 After death of Abu 'Abdallah, Ibn Khaldun transfers to the service of the Hafsid ruler of Constantine, Abu al-'Abbas, who makes him *hajib*, but Ibn Khaldun soon falls out of favor. He takes refuge first with the Dawawida Arabs and then in Biskra.

1368 He is employed by the 'Abd al-Wadid ruler of Tlemcen, Abu Hammu, as intermediary with Riyah Arab tribes.

1370 Ibn Khaldun is captured by Merinid 'Abd al-'Aziz while trying to reach Granada.

1370–74 Ibn Khaldun is employed by the Merinid rulers as intermediary with the Riyah Arab tribes and subsequently kicks his heels as an attendant courtier in Merinid Fez.

1374 He flees to Granada.

1375 He is extradited. He is again employed by Abu Hammu to deal with Arab tribesmen. Then he takes refuge at Qal'at Banu Salama, a remote castle in western Algeria where he begins to write the *Muqaddima* and the *'Ibar*.

1377 In November the first draft of the *Muqaddima* is completed at Qal'at Banu Salama.

1378 Ibn Khaldun returns to Tunis and is reconciled with the Hafsid Abu al-'Abbas and made a confidante, but he is subjected to attacks by the chief qadi of Tunis, Ibn 'Arafa al-Warghani. The first version of the *Muqaddima* is dedicated to the Hafsid ruler.

1382 Ibn Khaldun secures permission to go on the *hajj*. He arrives in Alexandria.

1383 He settles in Cairo and secures the patronage of the Mamluk sultan al-Zahir Barquq.

1384 Ibn Khaldun is made professor of Maliki *fiqh* (jurisprudence) at the Qamhiyya *Madrasa* (college). Then in August he is appointed Maliki chief qadi in Egypt. The ship bringing his wife, daughters, and library sinks off the coast of Alexandria.

1385 He is dismissed as chief qadi.

1387 He is appointed to teach at the Zahiriyya *Madrasa*. He goes on the *hajj*.

1389 He is appointed to teach *hadith* at the Sarghitmishiyya *Madrasa*. He is also made head of the *Khanqa* (Sufi convent) of Baybars. Barquq is temporarily deposed by rebel emirs. Ibn Khaldun is one of those who agree to a *fatwa* against Barquq. On Barquq's return to power Ibn Khaldun is stripped of his professorship at the Zahiriyya *Madrasa* and his position at the *Khanqa* of Baybars.

1399 He is again appointed Maliki chief qadi. Barquq dies and is succeeded by his son, al-Nasir Faraj.

1400 Ibn Khaldun visits Damascus with Faraj. Later, after his return to Egypt, he is deposed from the qadiship. Timur invades Syria and Faraj leads an army out of Egypt to defend Damascus. Ibn Khaldun travels with him.

1401 In the first week of January Faraj decides to retreat back to Egypt. But Ibn Khaldun decides to stay and he has regular meetings with Timur. In March 1401 he returns to Cairo. He is appointed Maliki chief qadi.

1402 He is deposed from the qadiship. He is reappointed later in the year.

1403 He is deposed from the qadiship.

1405 He is appointed Maliki chief qadi, but deposed a few months later.

1406 He is reappointed Maliki chief qadi and dies in office on March 17.

Ibn Khaldun

♦♦♦

CHAPTER ONE

Ibn Khaldun among the Ruins

He lingered, poring on memorials
Of the world's youth, through the long burning day
Gazed on those speechless shapes, nor, when the moon
Filled the mysterious halls with fleeting shades
Suspended he that task, but ever gazed
And gazed, till meaning on his vacant mind
Flashed like strong inspiration, and he saw
The thrilling secrets of the birth of time.
— Shelley, "Alastor"

The tumult and the shouting dies;
The Captains and the Kings depart
. . . .
Lo, all our pomp of yesterday
Is one with Nineveh and Tyre!
Judge of the Nations, spare us yet,
Lest we forget—lest we forget!
— Rudyard Kipling, "Recessional"

Let us start with a story from *The Thousand and One Nights*, "The City of Brass." (It should be more correctly rendered as "copper," *nuhas*, a word whose triconsonantal root can be seen as presaging ill omen, since, among the related words, *nahasa* means "to make someone unhappy" and *manhus* means "ill-fated.") It is said that in the days of the Umayyad caliph 'Abd al-Malik ibn Marwan there was a discussion at his court about the copper jars within which centuries ago the jinn (genies) had been sealed by King Solomon. Whereupon the caliph ordered Musa ibn Nusayr, the governor of North Africa, to outfit an expedition to find one of those jars. After traveling for over a year in the trackless wastes, it became obvious that the expedition was lost. In their wanderings they came to the Black Castle, an abandoned palace that had once been the seat of King Kush of the tribe of 'Ad. Around his tomb they found many tablets bearing writings, which delivered stern messages about "the vicissitudes of life and the transitoriness of the world." For example:

> The people and their works lament the empire they have lost.
> The palace brings the last news of its lords, who all lie buried here.
> Death parted and destroyed them, throwing to the ground what they had gathered in.
> It is as though they halted here to rest, but then set off again in haste.[1]

After further adventures, including an encounter with a mighty jinni (genie), Musa ibn Nusayr's expedition reached the City of Brass. The great wall, which surrounded it, had no gate. Scattered on a neighboring hill they found tablets with more pious warnings for those who would be warned. Early attempts to scale the wall of the city failed, as each of the first ten men delegated to do so smiled on reaching the top of the wall before throwing himself down to his death. But then the spell was broken by a recitation from the Qur'an and so a deceitful and deadly mirage of the beckoning maidens was conjured away. On entering the city, the company made their way through a corpse-strewn labyrinth of streets until they reached the palace and entered a throne room. On the throne there sat a young woman, Queen Tadmur, who appeared to be alive, but on closer examination she turned out to be a corpse whose eyeballs had been filled with glittering quicksilver. Before her throne was a tablet informing them that the city was once ruled by Qush, son of Shaddad ibn 'Ad. It had been the center of a prosperous and happy empire, but suddenly famine had struck and all the wealth of the city could not save the people. Musa ibn Nusayr's company loaded up with lots of treasure and on their return journey they managed also to acquire a copper jar with a jinni sealed inside it. After they had delivered this jar to the caliph in Baghdad, Musa, having seen all that he had seen, decided to become a hermit.[2]

The City of Brass also features in the *Muqaddima*. It is one of the many ruined or abandoned places in that work. Ibn Khaldun, who grew up in the shadow of ruins, compared them to "faded writing in a book."[3] (This was one of the stock similes of the pre-Islamic poets.) North Africa has an exceptional number of magnificent ancient ruins: Cyrene, Apollonia, Leptis Magna, Carthage, Volubilis, El Jem, Sbeïtla, and many others. It was obvious to a fourteenth-century observer that the region had once been more prosperous and more heavily populated than it was now. "Formerly the whole region between the Sudan (the lands of the blacks in general) and the Mediterranean had been settled. This (fact) is attested by the relics of civilization there, such as monuments, architectural sculpture, and the visible remains of villages and hamlets."[4] Ibn Khaldun wrote repeatedly of North Africa's vanished glories. When he settled down to write the *Muqaddima* in the Castle of Banu Salama in western Algeria, the place to which he had retreated was in the vicinity of Roman ruins.

From earliest times laments over ruins had featured prominently in Arabic literature. The *Jahili* (pre-Islamic) poets of Arabia conventionally began their *qasida*s (odes) with an evocation of an abandoned desert campsite or a ruin and this would furnish the pretext for a lament over past loves and lost youth. In the centuries that followed, the imagery of the desert poets of pre-Islamic times continued to be employed by the urbane poets of 'Abbasid Baghdad and Basra—as in these verses by the ninth-century poet Abu Nuwas, in which, while he writes of the decay of the great city of Basra, it is really his lost youth that he is mourning:

Musalla is no more, desolate
the dunes which saw me once,
The square of Mirbad, of Labab,

And the great mosque which once combined
such gallantry and worship—
Withered and gone its courts and vast concourses.[5]

Basra's decline had begun with the sacking of the city by the rebel Zanj slaves in 871. In the next century it was sacked again by the Qarmatian heretics. Other Islamic cities were later to fall into ruin. Cordova, the capital of Muslim Spain, was sacked by Berber soldiers in 1013. Ibn Hazm, the eleventh-century author of *The Ring of the Dove*, a wonderful book on the etiquette of love, lamented the devastation of the city he had grown up in:

> I stood upon the ruins of our house, its traces wiped out, its signs erased, its familiar spots vanished. Decay had turned its cultivated bloom to sterile waste. In savagery after society, ugliness after beauty, wolves howled and devils played in the haunts of ghosts and dens of wild beasts that once had been luxurious and melodious. Men like swords, damsels like dolls, overflowing with riches beneath an ornamentation so palatial it reminded you of heaven, all were scattered with the change of time. Those elegant apartments, the plaything of destruction, were wilder now than the gaping mouths of lions, announcing the end of the world, revealing the fate of its inhabitants.[6]

Muslim North Africa's heyday had been under the Almohads in the twelfth and thirteenth centuries when this Berber dynasty created an empire that extended from the Atlantic to Libyan Tripoli and also included southern and central Spain. In the East, the decay of Baghdad, the capital of the once-mighty 'Abbasid Caliphate, took a slow course, but when the Andalusian traveler Ibn Jubayr visited it in 1184, he remarked that the place was "like statue of a ghost."[7] The sacking of the city by the Mongols in 1258 further contributed to the city's desolation.

RUINS DELIVERING MESSAGES

In fact, as in fiction, ruins were read as messages by pious and thoughtful Muslims. Nothing in this world lasts forever and the piling up of riches would not avail a man when death came for him. It was not by chance that Ibn Khaldun entitled his chronicle the *Kitab al-'Ibar*. '*Ibar* is the plural of '*ibra*, meaning "admonition," "warning," "example," or "advice." As in the Qur'an: "Surely in that is an example for men possessed of eyes" (Qur'an 3:13) and "In their story was a warning (*'ibra*) for those with understanding" (Qur'an 12:11) and "So take warning, you who have sight" (Qur'an 59:2). The Qur'an stressed the importance of historical understanding in the sense of taking lessons from the past. "So relate the story; haply they will reflect" (Qur'an 7:176). "Has there not come to you the tidings of those who were before you—the people of Noah, Ad, Thamood, and of those after them" (Qur'an 7:149). "How many generations We have destroyed after Noah!" (Qur'an 17:17).

As Muhsin Mahdi has written: "The Islamic community was urged to view past events, both reported and experienced, as 'indications' that should awaken its moral sense and enhance its ability to act according to the demands of God: to penetrate behind the apparently meaningless succession of events and discern the ever-present design of the Creator. *'Ibra* meant both negative admonition, and positive guidance and direction for future action."[8]

The Qur'an repeatedly refers to past peoples who failed to heed the messages of prophets who were warners. The Deluge destroyed most of Noah's generation. The people of 'Ad, who came after those drowned in the Deluge, are frequently mentioned in the Qur'an. They inhabited a sandy desert between Oman and the Hadramawt. The Prophet Hud was sent as a warner to them, but they did not heed his message and so were doomed. The people of 'Ad were succeeded by the race of Thamud and the Prophet Salih was sent to call them to repentance, but they slaughtered a she-camel that emerged from a rock, which was sent to them as a divine sign, and so too they were doomed. Pharaoh who refused to listen to Moses was another who incurred God's wrath and consequently he was drowned. 'Ad, Thamud, and the Amalekites were known as the "vanished Arabs." In the *'Ibar* Ibn Khaldun shows himself to be oddly credulous about these peoples and, for example, he reported without further comment that 'Ad, the ancestor of his race lived for 1,200 years and fathered 4,000 males and 1,000 females.[9]

'Ibra had many layers of meaning and there was also a later mystical sense. According to Jonathan Berkey, it was among other senses "a technical term in the Sufi vocabulary which indicated right guidance in matters concerning good and evil, the distinction between outward form and inward truth, and by extension how souls pass successfully from this world to paradise."[10]

In the opening of the *Muqaddima*, Ibn Khaldun presented his life and those of the peoples he has studied as existing in a book; "Our lives' final terms, the dates of which have been fixed for us in the book (of destiny), claim us."[11] History consists both of events and the writing down of those events. Indeed, it is almost as if the events take place in order to be written down in a book, for both the events and the reporting of them serve as *'ibar*—warnings or lessons. According to Ibn Khaldun, "the purpose of human beings is not only their worldly welfare. This entire world is trifling and futile. It ends in death and annihilation."[12] The *Muqaddima* has to be read with this in mind. But, though Ibn Khaldun meditated upon the ruins around him, he took moral messages from them and he did not approach them as an archaeologist. An archaeological approach to ruins lay centuries ahead. (Nor, for that matter, did Ibn Khaldun attempt to apply source-critical techniques to documents.)

'Ibra and related forms of the basic triconsonantal root in Arabic feature prominently in the *Nights* story of "The City of Brass." When the caliph 'Abd al-Malik heard about the brass jars in which the jinn were imprisoned by Solomon, he expresses a great desire to see such things, for they would be "an example to those who are instructed by such examples" (*'ibra li-man-i'tibar*). Then, when Musa ibn Nusayr's expeditionary party discuss advancing on the Black Castle, an aged shaikh exclaims, "Let us approach this castle—*huwa 'ibra li-man i'tibabara*—which is a warning for whoso would be warned." And on one of the tablets in the castle, the party reads "O you who arrive at this place, take warning (*i'tabir*) from what you see." Inside the Black Castle there "is the last report concerning chieftains who have been gathered in the dust. Death destroyed them and scattered them, and they lost in the dust that which they had gathered." "Sermons in stone" indeed.

The story of "The City of Brass" can be seen as a fantastical prefiguration of the theme that so preoccupied Ibn Khaldun—the ruins of North Africa and the lessons to be learned from the past generations who once dwelt in those now ruined castles and palaces. *Ubi sunt qui ante nos fuerunt?* ("Where are those who came before us?") was also a question that often introduced reflections on mortality and the transience of life in medieval Latin poetry. Ibn Khaldun intended his readers to take warning lessons from his history, lessons that would be conducive to Muslim salvation. He wrote of the evidence of former grandeur surviving in an era of chaos and desolation: "Formerly the whole region between the Sudan and the Mediterranean had been settled. This fact is attested by the relics of civilization there, such as monuments, architectural sculpture, and the visible remains of villages and hamlets."[13] He asked himself how such grandeur had given way to desolation. He believed that the desolate state of North Africa in his own time was in large part due to the devastating invasion of the region in the eleventh century by the Egyptian Arab tribal federations of the Banu Hilal and the Banu Sulaym (and we shall return to this topic in chapter 3). Then the question arose, was the passage from imperial grandeur to desolation inevitable?

THE BLACK DEATH AND DESOLATION

Besides featuring in *The Thousand and One Nights*, "The Story of the City of Brass" also features in *The One Hundred and One Nights*, a rival story collection that was compiled in North Africa and that, in its oldest recension, may predate *The Thousand and One Nights*. The story was known as early as the ninth century and, as noted, al-Mas'udi transmitted it in the tenth century. But the historian Jean-Claude Garcin argues, on the basis of numerous details in the story that feature in the version that has come down to us in the nineteenth-century printed editions of the *Nights*, that this particular version must have been put together no earlier than the fourteenth century. Garcin goes on to argue that the real subject of the story is not the quest for bottled jinn, but rather the desolation of the land and the death that came to so many innocent people. "The Story of the City of Brass" is then a fictional reflection on the Black Death that devastated the Middle East and North Africa in 1348 and perhaps also a commentary on the famines that struck Egypt some decades later. All men are mortal. There is no escaping death.[14] The coming of the Black Death provided the impetus for the retelling of this story—just as it had impelled Ibn Khaldun first to reflect on how the world had changed and then to write the *Muqaddima*.

To return to ruins, they also featured in Muslim literature as material evidence of bad government. In the course of his discussion of monarchical injustice in chapter 3 of the *Muqaddima*, Ibn Khaldun inserted the following fable: The Sassanian king Bahram ibn Bahram, on hearing the cry of an owl, asked the Mobedhan, the chief religious dignitary among the Persians, what the cry meant. The priest replied with a fable: when a male owl wanted to marry a female owl, she demanded twenty ruined villages, so that she could hoot in them. But the male replied that that would be no problem as long as King Bahram continued to rule in the way that he was doing, since the owl would be able to give her a thousand villages. Hearing this, the ashamed King resolved to manage the affairs of his kingdom better.[15]

After Ibn Khaldun had left Granada in 1365, Ibn al-Khatib, the cultivated vizier of the ruler of Granada, wrote to Ibn Khaldun eloquently (but very possibly insincerely) expressing his sadness at his departure and claiming that he now "sought remedy [for loneliness] in morning visits to abandoned ruins."[16] During his own earlier exile in the Maghrib Ibn al-Khatib had produced a melancholy travelogue about his movements around North Africa including many gloomy reflections on the transitoriness of life provoked by the contemplation of the ruins he saw there.[17] (The life and works of Ibn al-Khatib will be discussed in more detail in chapter 2.)

It is hardly possible to overestimate the devastating effects of the Black Death. Throughout his life Ibn Khaldun was to be stalked by tragedies and the first of these occurred in 1348 when the plague reached North Africa from Egypt. At the age of seventeen, Ibn Khaldun lost his parents as well as many of his teachers and friends to the plague. In the *Muqaddima*, he was to write as follows:

> Civilization both in the East and the West was visited by a destructive plague which devastated nations and caused populations to vanish. It swallowed up many of the good things of civilization and wiped them out. It overtook the dynasties at the time of their senility, when they had reached the limit of their duration. It lessened their power and curtailed their influence. It weakened their authority. Their situation approached the point of annihilation and dissolution. Civilization decreased with the decrease of mankind. Cities and buildings were laid waste, roads and way signs were obliterated, settlements and mansions became empty, dynasties and tribes grew weak. The entire inhabited world changed. The East, it seems was similarly visited though in accordance with and in proportion to [the East's more affluent] civilization. It was if the voice of existence in the world had called out for oblivion and restriction, and the world responded to its call. God inherits the earth and whoever is upon it.[18]

AL-MAS'UDI, THE HISTORIAN WHO HAS TO BE SURPASSED

The leading Arab historians of the fourteenth and fifteenth centuries, Ibn al-Khatib, Ibn Khaldun, and al-Maqrizi, all produced works of history that were saturated with melancholy and pessimism. People moved among abandoned houses and deserted villages. The contrast with, say, Whig historians, such as Macaulay in nineteenth-century England, is striking. The Arab historians had no belief in the progress of humanity. Instead they waited for God to declare the End of Time. Ibn Khaldun did not expect the world to get any better and he had no hopes for the future. Since the Black Death had changed everything, the new circumstances called for the writing of a new kind of history that would embody warnings from the past from which men must take heed. The kind of chronicle represented by the *Muruj al-dhahab* would become obsolete.

The *Muruj al-dhahab wa ma'adin al-jawhar* (Meadows of Gold and Mines of Jewels) was the literary masterpiece of Abu Hasan 'Ali ibn al-Husayn al-Mas'udi (896–956), a historian and geographer who wrote in 'Abbasid times. Al-Mas'udi traveled extensively in Iraq, Iran, India, Ceylon, Arabia, and elsewhere and he wrote copiously, drawing on his own observations and interviews, as well as on his remarkably wide reading. (It is not clear where this freelance scholar's income came from.) Al-Mas'udi was steeped in the writings of the ancient Greeks in a way that Ibn Khaldun never was. In his masterpiece, the *Muruj al-dhahab*, al-Mas'udi not only provided a chronicle of the Arabs, but he also covered the history of the six other great nations: Chaldaeans, Indians, Chinese, Greeks, Persians, and Egyptians. Unlike Ibn Khaldun, he was most curious about the non-Islamic world, including the lands of the *Franj* (that is, the Europeans). It is evident that Mas'udi thought of himself as working in the broad genre of *adab*—that is to say "culture," "refinement," or "belles-lettres." His book provided the sort of information that could inform a civilized conversation over dinner. The information he provided was diverse and, perhaps because of this, he described himself as a "woodcutter by night." In the *Fihrist*, the enormous catalog of Arabic literature compiled by the bookseller Ibn al-Nadim in the tenth century, al-Mas'udi's writing was placed in the section devoted to court companions, singers, and jesters. He was indeed a specialist in learned and entertaining digressions. Even so, the *Muruj* is more than just a work of entertainment, for al-Mas'udi was the first Arab historian to reflect seriously upon the underlying principles and purposes of history and Ibn Khaldun praised him for this.[19] In another later work, *Kitab al-tanbih wa-al-ishraf* (The Reminder and Summary Overview), al-Mas'udi refers to earlier works, now lost, in which he discussed the various types of government, the relationship between kingship and religion, and the causes of political and religious decline.[20] Though he boasted of having produced thirty-six books, there is curiously little trace of any of them, apart from the *Muruj* and the *Tanbih*.

It had been customary among Muslim historians to support their historical data by *isnad*s, chains of oral transmission that authenticated particular items of information. For example, "I heard on the authority of Abu Ishaq, who heard it from al-Sijistani, who was told by Ibn Waqidi that . . ." Al-Mas'udi, who did not think much of traditionists, dispensed with this formality and as a consequence was regarded with some disfavor by most Arab historians, though not by Ibn Khaldun, who also rarely bothered with *isnad*s.[21] Ibn Khaldun preferred to rely on his sense of the inherent probability of an alleged fact. He thought that there were certain ways in which things happen in human society and other ways in which they do not.

Ibn Khaldun's admiration for al-Mas'udi was immense and he called him "the imam of the historians"—that is, the leading historian. He admired al-Mas'udi's universalistic scope and readiness to tackle the history of non-Arabs and infidel cultures, as well as his emphasis on geography, climate, and race. Al-Mas'udi had also taken pains to organize his information systematically and to cross-reference it. Ibn Khaldun quoted him frequently.[22] It also seems likely that Ibn Khaldun's cult of the nomad was inspired by al-Mas'udi. The account given in the *Muruj al-dhahab* of Arab history begins with a presentation of the Arabs as essentially nomads and as such to be compared to the Kurds, Turks, Berbers, and others. Moreover, "the ancient Arabs (*al-qudama' min al-'arab*) chose desert life because they saw in urban settlement shame and shortcomings . . . the knowledgeable amongst them (*dhawu al-ma'rifa*) declared that the desert was more healthy and more conducive to a strong, salubrious life."[23]

But Ibn Khaldun's admiration was mixed with stern criticism, since al-Mas'udi had written to entertain, as well as to instruct, whereas Ibn Khaldun conceived of his sort of historiography as offering only instruction. It is for this reason that in the opening section of the *Muqaddima*, in which Ibn Khaldun set out the reasons why historians often get things wrong, he often took his examples from al-Mas'udi and this in turn explains why there is a discussion of the City of Brass in the *Muqaddima*.

This is what Ibn Khaldun wrote:

> Then there is also al-Mas'udi's story of the "Copper City." This is said to be a city built wholly of copper in [the] desert of Sijilmasah which Musa ibn Nusayr crossed on his raid against the Maghrib. The gates (of the Copper City) are said to be closed. When the person who climbs the walls of the city, in order to enter it, reaches the top, he claps his hand and throws himself down and never returns. All this is an absurd story. It belongs to the idle talk of storytellers. The desert of Sijilmasah has been crossed by travelers and guides. They have not come across any information about such a city. All the details mentioned about it are absurd.

And Ibn Khaldun went on to note that it was most improbable that enough copper could be amassed to build a whole city out of it.[24] But what Ibn Khaldun would not admit is that al-Mas'udi, who was a highly intelligent man, almost certainly did not believe in the story of the City of Brass himself and it is most unlikely that he expected his readers would believe it either, but he included the story in the hope that it would entertain them. So he placed it in a chapter devoted to the seas and the marvels of strange lands.[25] He was producing literature and accounts of mirabilia were an important part of medieval Arab literature.

WHERE AND WHAT WAS IRAM OF THE COLUMNS?

Another legendary abandoned place attracted the interest of the compilers of *The Thousand and One Nights*, as well as of al-Mas'udi and Ibn Khaldun. This was Iram of the Columns. The place is briefly and cryptically referred to in the Qur'an: "Did you not see what your Lord did with 'Ad—Iram, that of the pillars?" (Qur'an 89: 6–7). According to Qur'anic commentators, in pre-Islamic times Shaddad, son of 'Ad, created a garden in Yemen, which he blasphemously intended to rival Paradise and he called it Iram, but when he and his courtiers set out to admire the completed garden, it and they were destroyed by a terrible noise from heaven. An elaborate version of this exegesis appears in *The Thousand and One Nights* as "'Abd Allah ibn Qilaba and Iram City of the Columns."[26] In this story 'Abd Allah ibn Qilaba got lost in the desert when he went looking for two stray camels and then he stumbled across the wondrous city of Iram and "in it were lofty pavilions, all containing chambers made of gold and silver, studded with sapphires, coloured gems, chrysolite, and pearls, and the leaves of their doors were as beautiful as the fortress itself." The story of Iram of the Columns was subjected to ruthless scrutiny by Ibn Khaldun. He asked how it was that there were no credible reports of travelers in Yemen coming across this city. Also it seemed likely to him that *'imad* had been mistranslated and meant "tent poles" rather than "columns."[27]

The *Muruj al-dhahab* also related the story of the discovery of this deserted city by an Arab searching for his two lost camels on the authority of a certain Ka'b al-Ahbar. But al-Mas'udi also had his doubts: "Many learned men believe stories of this sort to be apocryphal lies invented by storytellers to gain favor with kings. It is these men who gave their contemporaries the idea of preserving these tales and repeating them in their turn." And al-Mas'udi went on to observe that such stories featured in various collections, including a Persian one, "which is known to the public as *The Thousand and One Nights*. It is the story of a king, his vizier, the vizier's daughter, and her slaves, Shirazad and Dinazad."[28]

Incidentally, the fantastical and damned Iram City of the Columns reappeared in some of the stories of the twentieth-century horror writer H. P. Lovecraft (who from childhood had been an enthusiast for the tales of *The Thousand and One Nights*). "Emaciated priests, displayed in ornate robes, cursed the upper air, and all who breathed it; and one terrible final scene showed a primitive-looking man, perhaps a pioneer of ancient Irem, the City of the Pillars, torn to pieces by members of the elder race. I remembered how the Arabs fear the nameless city, and was glad that beyond this place the grey walls and ceilings were bare."[29] The Arab who has ventured into the nameless city in quest of Satanic knowledge is driven mad by what he has seen. Again, in "The Call of Cthulhu" (first published in 1926), a mestizo sailor called Castro reveals what he knows about the ancient and gruesome rites of The Old Ones. "Of the cult, he said that he thought the centre lay amid the pathless deserts of Arabia, where Irem, the City of the Pillars, dreams hidden and untouched."[30]

Before tackling the story of "The City of Brass" in the preliminary remarks that are part of book 1 of the *Muqaddima*, Ibn Khaldun had this to say about another strange story: "Students often happen to accept and transmit absurd information that, in turn, is believed on their authority. Al-Mas'udi, for instance, reports such a story about Alexander. Sea monsters prevented Alexander from building Alexandria. He took a wooden container in which a glass box was inserted, and dived in it to the bottom of the sea. There he drew pictures of the devilish monsters he saw. He then had metal effigies of these animals made and set them up opposite the place where the building was going on. When the monsters came out and saw the effigies, they fled. Alexander was thus able to complete the building of Alexandria."[31]

Ibn Khaldun, quite reasonably, doubted this story on the grounds that a ruler would not dare take such a risk and indeed his subjects would not allow him to do so. Also the jinn are shape-shifters and are not confined to one specific form. Moreover, the cool air in the box would soon run out, so that the man inside would overheat. Although the story of Alexander and the sea monsters does not feature in the *Nights*, a variant, shorter version is given in "The Story of 'Arus al-'Ara'is and Her Deceit, as well as the Wonders of the Seas and Islands," which is one of the fantastic tales in a parallel story collection, the *Hikayat al-'ajiba wa'l-akhbar al-ghariba* (Tales of the Marvellous and News of the Strange).[32]

Ibn Khaldun was also hostile to what he judged to be al-Ma'su-di's fictions about the 'Abbasids. During the caliphate of Harun al-Rashid (786–809) the Barmecide clan of Persian administrators, headed by Ja'far, had seemed to be all-powerful in Baghdad, until in 803 Ja'far was suddenly arrested and executed and the rest of the Barmecide clan were imprisoned and their goods confiscated.[33] Ibn Khaldun dismissed the story found in the *Muruj al-dhahab* and other chronicles, according to which Harun, who was very fond of his sister al-'Abbasa, wanted her to attend his drinking parties and, in order to effect this, he married her to Ja'far stipulating that they must not sleep together. But al-'Abbasa tricked Ja'far into having sex with her when he was drunk and she became pregnant. When Harun found out he determined that Ja'far had to die.[34] In al-Mas'udi's chronicle the story provides the pretext for poems devoted to the transience of earthly glory, power, and wealth. The downfall of the Barmecides also features in some versions of *The Thousand and One Nights*.[35]

Ibn Khaldun ridiculed the notion that Harun al-Rashid regularly drank wine together with his cup companions.[36] Although Harun's wine-drinking and occasional drunkenness feature frequently in the *Nights*, all the historical evidence suggests that in reality he was a pious and strictly observant Muslim. On similar grounds, Ibn Khaldun had doubted the story given in the tenth-century anthologist Ibn 'Abd Rabbih's *'Iqd al-farid* (The Unique Necklace) of how Harun's son al-Ma'mun was wandering by night through the streets of Baghdad when he saw a basket being lowered by pulleys and cords from a high window. He clambered into the basket and was hauled up to a chamber in which he encountered a beautiful maiden, with whom he drank wine and had sex.[37] Ibn Khaldun rejected this story as being incompatible with what other sources tell us about al-Ma'mun's piety. Again, there is a similar story in *The Thousand and One Nights*, but there the adventure is attached to a contemporary of al-Ma'mun, the singer and poet, Ishaq al-Mosuli.[38]

WEIRD SCIENCE

To return to al-Mas'udi, Ibn Khaldun also attacked the earlier historian's contention that the first men created by God had perfect bodies and extraordinarily long life spans. "Thus in the beginning, the world had (people whose) lives had their full duration and whose bodies were perfect. Because of the deficiency of matter it steadily deteriorated to its present condition, and it will not stop deteriorating until the time of complete dissolution and the destruction of the world."[39] Ibn Khaldun rejected this as being a hypothesis that was unsupported by any convincing evidence. It is perhaps noteworthy that in criticizing al-Mas'udi, Ibn Khaldun relied on common sense and simple logic, rather than any very sophisticated philosophical methodology. But perhaps the *Muruj al-dhahab* did have to be attacked in order to create space for the *Muqaddima*.

The presence of such vast ruins as the Pyramids and the Persian Reception Hall of Khosraw raised the question of whether such gigantic constructions might not have been built by giants, as al-Mas'udi had argued. (This sort of fantasy was not confined to Islamic lore. For example, in the twelfth-century verse romance the *Roman de Brut*, a giant helped Merlin build Stonehenge, and the cyclopean masonry of the Ggantija Neolithic temples on the Mediterranean island of Gozo was long thought by antiquarians to have been the work of giants.) Ibn Khaldun mocked the view of those "who imagine that the ancients had bodies proportionate to (those monuments) and that their bodies, consequently, were much taller, wider, and heavier than (our bodies), so that there was the right proportion between (their bodies) and the physical strength from which such buildings resulted."[40] In particular, he attacked the widely held notion that the monuments popularly attributed to the ancient race of 'Ad were so enormous because the 'Adites were giants. The reality was that large monuments were the product of superior social organization and the skillful use of machinery.

Though Ibn Khaldun's readiness to employ logic and make generalizations based on logic and observation may make him seem rather modern, there were limits to his rationality. Some of his ideas about the way the world worked would be classified today as weird science. Not only that but many of his contemporaries would have found those ideas a bit strange too. For instance, in the course of discussing the supposed giants of antiquity, he wrote this: "One of the strangest of these stories is about Og, the son of Anak, one of the Canaanites against whom the children of Israel fought in Syria. According to these storytellers, he was so tall that he took fish out of the ocean and held them up to the sun to be cooked."[41] Earlier historians such as al-Tabari and al-Thalabi had testified to the giant stature of this king of Bashan, who was alleged to sleep only twice a year and who was so tall that the sea only reached up to his knees. Ibn Khaldun quite reasonably mocked the account of the giant, which had been produced by grossly ignorant storytellers, but then he dismissed the possibility that the giant held fish up to cook them by the heat of the sun in this fashion: "They believe that the sun is heat and that the heat of the sun is greatest close to it. They do not know that the heat of the sun is (its) light and that its light is stronger near the earth (than it is near the sun) because of the reflection of the rays from the surface of the earth when it is hit by the light. Therefore, the heat here is many times greater (than near the sun) . . . The sun itself is neither hot nor cold, but a simple uncomposed substance that gives light."[42] So he believed that the further the sun's rays traveled from the sun, the hotter they became. Ibn Khaldun believed that the sun was neither hot nor cold. It was just a luminous star. It is hard to guess where he got this notion.

In the course of a dismissive account of alchemy and the possibility of transforming base metal into gold, Ibn Khaldun nevertheless conceded that the spontaneous generation of scorpions, bees, and snakes did occur, since these things had actually been observed.[43] When he came to discuss the superiority of the crafts in Egypt to those practiced in the Maghreb, he said that he had heard that Egyptians had actually succeeded in teaching donkeys and other quadrupeds to speak.[44]

He was not more rational on the causes of the Black Death and other plagues. First, he suggested that it was a product of too much civilization and the consequent density of population, which gave rise to corruption of the air.[45] On the other hand, he also maintained that the presence of lots of people moving around in one place kept the air moving and prevented putrefaction.[46] Ibn al-Khatib, Ibn Khaldun's friend and rival, was sharper about the causes of plague, for he had deduced that it was spread by contagion. There were numerous other irrational elements in Ibn Khaldun's thinking. For example, when he discussed Alexander's submarine, he failed to realize that the emperor was more likely to die from suffocation than from overheating. Elsewhere in the *Muqaddima* he included a discussion of divine intervention as a deciding factor in certain battles.[47] As we shall see in future chapters, he also had some strange ideas about dieting and about sorcery.

RUINS, BAD GOVERNMENT, AND GOD'S JUDGMENT

As already noted, besides delivering messages about mortality, transience, and the vanity of riches, ruins served as indicators of bad government. But there is an apparent ambivalence that runs all the way through the *Muqaddima*. For most of the time, Ibn Khaldun argued that ruins are the product of natural causes or social developments—perhaps plagues, bad government, the extravagance and softness of townspeople, or the destructiveness of nomadic Arabs. "Time wears us out."[48] But at other times he feels obliged to state that human settlements are doomed by God's decree. "When God desires to destroy a village, we order those of its inhabitants who live in luxury to act wickedly. Thus, the word becomes true for it and we destroy it" (Qur'an 17:16). (The chronicler al-Maqrizi, who had been a student of Ibn Khaldun in Cairo, used the same citation in his *Ighathat al-umma bi-kashf al-ghumma*, a treatise on high prices and famines.)[49]

There are stories in *The Thousand and One Nights* that deliver messages about communities doomed by the decree of God—as for example the tomb inscription, the reading of which concludes the story of "'Abd Allah ibn Qilaba and Iram, City of the Columns":

> Be warned, you who have been deceived by length of life,
> I am Shaddad ibn 'Ad, lord of the strong castle,
> A ruler of power, might and great strength,
> All the world obeyed me, in fear of force and threats.
> Through the greatness of my power I held both east and west.
> We were summoned to the true way by a rightly guided man,
> But we did not obey and called out: "Is there no refuge?"
> Then came a cry out of the far horizon;
> We were cut down as though we were a harvest field.
> Shut in our graves, we wait for Judgement Day.[50]

So, as far as Ibn Khaldun is concerned, is it social developments or God's will that determines the doom of dynasties, cities, and villages? Both, for it seems that he conceived of God working through natural causes. God made the inhabitants of a certain place sinful in order that he might justly destroy that place. In the same manner, the eleventh-century scholar al-Ghazali had argued in *The Incoherence of Philosophers* that there is no link between cause and effect unless God wills it to be so.

As we shall see in chapter 4, according to Ibn Khaldun's thesis about the workings of *'asabiyya* (social solidarity), after a newly triumphant ruler and his tribal following have installed themselves in a city, in the course of three or four generations, an inevitable decay will set in, as the regime slowly comes to indulge in luxury and extravagance. Moreover, as the bonds created by tribal solidarity and nomadic austerity weaken, the ruler comes to rely on mercenaries and slave soldiers and, in order to pay for these troops, he starts to impose taxes that are not sanctioned by Islam. So it is that the fall of a dynasty is the product of social developments that are more or less inevitable and yet at the same time it will be the sinfulness and greed of the dynasty and its followers that justify the Divine decree determining the end of a people who have gone astray. So a single observed effect has been determined by two causes, when either alone would have been sufficient. (This sort of overdetermination will be familiar to readers of Freud's *The Interpretation of Dreams*.)

Ibn Khaldun's approach to social science is moralistic and throughout the *Muqaddima*, he like the Muslim theologians and philosophers who came before him, had problems in dealing with issues concerning predestination and causality. Indeed, he did not like thinking about causality at all. Perhaps theorizing about the divinely ordained nature of causality was too like probing the mind of God, something that might be close to blasphemy. He did not think that it was possible for ordinary mortals to understand the nature of causality and he wrote of the hypothetical philosopher who might seek to investigate this subject that "I can guarantee him that he will return unsuccessful. Therefore we were forbidden by the Lawgiver (Muhammad) to study causes."[51]

CHAPTER TWO

The Game of Thrones in Fourteenth-Century North Africa

North African politics, in the wake of the break-up of the Almohad Empire in the thirteenth century, was dominated by a prolonged and inconclusive struggle to reunite the territories formerly ruled by that dynasty. Although the Hafsid dynasty in Ifriqiyya (the eastern Maghreb corresponding approximately to modern Tunisia and part of eastern Algeria) regarded themselves as the true heirs of the Almohad caliphs, since they came from a dynasty of administrators who had served the Almohads, the Merinids in Morocco, who could raise larger tribal armies, came closer to reuniting the Maghreb. The Merinids relied chiefly on Berber tribesmen from eastern Morocco and western Algeria. But again and again the possession of Tlemcen in western Algeria by the 'Abd al-Wadid (or Ziyanid) dynasty presented an obstacle to Merinid ambitions. Control of Tlemcen was desirable because it sat on the transit route for the gold coming up from sub-Saharan Africa via Sijilmasa. From Tlemcen the route ran on to Oran from where the gold might be shipped on to Europe, Egypt, or Turkey. The unreliability of the tribal levies raised by the Merinids was a running problem for the dynasty. Moreover, what should have been a relatively simple three-cornered struggle was made more complicated by the fact that there were often rival claimants for the Merinid, Hafsid, and 'Abd al-Wadid thrones within the ruling families. An underlying problem for the Merinids and the other North African dynasties was that there was no rule of primogeniture. And across the Strait of Gibraltar on the edge of this struggle, the Nasrids of Granada also meddled in North African politics (and North Africans meddled in theirs).

TOPOGRAPHY

Ibn Khaldun lifted most of his information on topography from the *Nuzhat al-mushtaq fi ikhtiraq al-afaq* (Pleasure of Him Who Longs to Cross the Horizons), a geographical treatise compiled in the twelfth century by Muhammad al-Idrisi for Roger II of Sicily. Al-Idrisi had divided the world into seven climes and each clime into ten sections. The cold seventh clime and ferociously hot first clime did not support large populations.[1] The middle climes or zones were the most civilized and the important point for Ibn Khaldun was that the great North African cities and the centers of Berber power were in the third zone, as were most of the great Islamic centers in the East. According to the *Muqaddima*, "the sciences, the crafts, the buildings, the clothing, the foodstuffs, the fruits, even the animals, and everything that comes into being in the three middle zones are distinguished by their temperate (well-proportioned character). The human inhabitants of these zones are more temperate in their bodies, color, character qualities, and (general) conditions." The Byzantines, Persians, Israelites, Greeks, Indians, and Chinese flourished in these zones.[2] Idrisi, Ibn Khaldun, and most medieval Arab scholars took it for granted that the Earth was a sphere. Much of what Ibn Khaldun has taken wholesale from al-Idrisi and other Arab geographers is irrelevant to the historical concerns of *Muqaddima*. In this section of chapter 1, devoted to the temperate and intemperate zones, and in several other sections, the *Muqaddima* reads more like a comprehensive encyclopedia than a closely focused thesis about the underlying forces in history.

Despite Ibn Khaldun's skepticism regarding the City of Brass and Iram of the Columns, he accepted the reality of the monstrous races of Gog and Magog (Yajuj and Majuj), as well as reports of the geographical location of the dam that Alexander the Great had built to keep these creatures out.[3] Presumably he did so because their reality and apocalyptic menace was attested to in the Qur'an, in Sura 21 "The Prophets": 96–97:

There is a ban upon any city that We have destroyed:
They shall not return
Till when Gog and Magog are unloosed, and they slide down
    out of every slope,
And nigh has drawn the true promise, and behold, the eyes of
    the unbelievers staring: "Alas for us! We were heedless of
    this: nay, we were evil doers."

Ruby Island was another strange place. Rubies and deadly serpents abounded on that island, which was virtually inaccessible since it lay in the center of a ring of steep mountains. Nevertheless people in that region were able to call on divine inspiration in order to mine the rubies.[4]

Setting aside al-Idrisi's and Ibn Khaldun's schematic presentation of global geography, there are approximately 1,500 miles between Tunis and the Strait of Gibraltar. Taken as a whole, North Africa was somewhat more fertile in the fourteenth century than it is now. It has been estimated that in modern times the Sahara grows by hundreds of square miles every year. Overgrazing and the quest for firewood have contributed to the soil erosion.

The Maghreb and Ifriqiyya are part of the dry territory on the edge of the Mediterranean of which Fernand Braudel has written:

A poor land, without water: here there are few springs, streams, plants or trees. The sparse vegetation is graced with the name "pasture land." Wood is extremely scarce. So here in the arid zone begin the clay houses, the endless string of towns that from India to tropical Africa are "mud encampments": Stone buildings when they exist are masterpieces of an exceptional kind; built by a technique of piling stone on stone without any timber work . . . Here the problem was not, as in the Mediterranean, the building of ships and galleys, but everyday cooking, the humble campfire, lit between two stones. Everything was fuel for it: a few sprigs of brushwood, dry plants straw or esparto grass, the bark of palm trees, "the dung of camel, horse or ox which is dried in the sun."[5]

The Atlas Mountains run all the way from the Atlantic coastal strip to Ifriqiyya. Every winter the coastal regions and the mountains are watered by rain coming in from the Atlantic. The most important cities in Ifriqiyya (roughly equivalent to modern Tunisia) were Tunis and Qairouan. Ifriqiyya's coastal plain was and is fertile. Corn, wheat, and olives are cultivated on the northern strip, while barley was the chief crop in the drier southern and central regions. It is wet and cold from October to April. The medieval nomads mostly ranged over the steppe region to the south of the coastal mountains and north of the Sahara.

Constantine, Biskra, Bougie, and Tlemcen were the most important cities in the region that today forms Algeria. The Tell region comprises Algeria's coastal strip and mountainous hinterland. The most fertile land is to be found on the western coastal plain. Elsewhere steep slopes militate against large-scale farming. The Atlas Mountains descend slightly to the High Plateaux, a region in which the herding of sheep and goats predominated. The High Plateaux then descends to the Sahara.

Fez and Marrakesh on the fertile Atlantic plains, together with Sijilmasa to the south, were Morocco's chief towns in the fourteenth century. The Rif designates a highland region on the northern coast with some fertile valleys. In the fourteenth century it was still quite heavily forested. Settled agriculture was mostly carried out to the north and west of Morocco's mountain ranges. If one proceeds from north to south from the Rif, one comes successively to the Middle Atlas, the High Atlas, and the Anti-Atlas. The High Atlas rises like a wall from the plain. Its southern and eastern slopes get a lot of rain and streams run down their gorges. Terrace agriculture was and is practiced on the slopes. Toward the end of spring, people in lowland villages took their flocks up to pasture on the slopes of the High Atlas. The highest northern slopes are forested, but steppe vegetation predominates on the southern slopes and melting snow provides pasture and some cultivable land. The High Atlas was traditionally a territory of dissidence and it was difficult for the Merinids in Fez to exercise any control over the mountainous regions and, much later, the French colonialists used to refer to them dismissively as "*le Maroc inutile*." The Sahara beyond the Atlas ranges was the territory of the Sanhaja Berbers. Broadly speaking the Sanhaja roamed the deserts, the Masmuda Berbers dominated the mountains, and the Zanata

Berbers were found in the plains. The Zanata tribesmen provided lightly armed cavalry not only to the North African regimes but also to Nasrid Granada.

IBN KHALDUN'S EARLY CAREER IN NORTH AFRICA

Ibn Khaldun moved from city to city and ruler to ruler and served in a variety of administrative and scribal capacities. In the *Muqaddima* he dilated on the qualities that a senior scribe should possess: he should have a good literary style; he should come from the upper classes, and have a wide general knowledge. "He will have to concern himself with the principal branches of scholarship, because such things may come up in the gatherings and audiences of the ruler." Finally, the secretary should have good manners.[6] At times Ibn Khaldun seemed on the verge of becoming the power behind a throne, but at other times he ended up in prison or in flight. He was a kind of bureaucratic condottiere and he operated in dangerous waters in which death was commonly a penalty for political failure.

Wali al-Din 'Abd al-Rahman ibn Khaldun was born in 1332 in Hafsid Tunis. As will be seen from what follows in this chapter, Ibn Khaldun's career as an administrator, diplomat, courtier, and teacher, prior to his departure to Egypt, was a bemusingly complicated one, as he held a bemusing variety of posts at various courts.[7] His aristocratic ancestors, who boasted that they could trace their origins back to the tribe of Kinda in the pre-Islamic Hadramawt, had allegedly settled in Seville during the early Islamic conquest, but fled from there prior to the *Reconquista* and the city's occupation by the forces of Castille in 1248. The Banu Khaldun then settled in Ifriqiyya. (Throughout the thirteenth, fourteenth, and fifteenth centuries the rulers of Tunis, Fez, and especially Tlemcen welcomed exiles from Andalusia and gave positions at court to those refugees who had administrative experience or a scholarly background.) Ibn Khaldun took great pride in his lineage and he identified himself with Andalusi culture. His was a dynasty of scholars and administrators and his father was a scholar and a *faqih* (an expert on jurisprudence).

Although the Almohad Empire in North Africa and Andalusia came to an end in 1269 and that empire was divided among the successor states of the Hafsids, 'Abd al-Wadids, and Merinids, the ghostly presence of the Almohads can be detected in the way politics was conducted in Tunis, Tlemcen, and Fez. Many of the governing elite, in Hafsid Tunis, particularly the military aristocracy, were of Almohad descent. This old elite had taken care to preserve Almohad institutions and entitulature. But in the fourteenth century Andalusian refugees and their descendants were becoming increasingly influential at court and competed with them for office. Tunis was the center of Andalusian culture in North Africa. Anselm Adorno, a pilgrim who visited Tunis in 1470, described the place as strongly fortified and populous with many large houses made from white marble and built around courtyards. There was a flourishing suburb outside the eastern gate of the city, which was inhabited by Genoese, Venetian, Pisan, Florentine, and Catalan merchants. The ruler at that time had eight or nine thousand Bedouin recruited as cavalry, but, though they were camped near Tunis, they were never allowed to pass the night within the city walls. The ruler needed these Arabs to defend him from other Arab tribes.[8] Although Ibn Khaldun greatly admired Ibn Tumart who had declared himself the Mahdi and established an Almohad Empire in the Maghreb and al-Andalus, Ibn Khaldun was hostile to the Hafsid's nostalgic cult of the Almohads and, more generally, he looked back on Almohad rule with some hostility and he seems to have preferred the Merinids who had replaced them in the western Maghreb.

From the late thirteenth century Hafsid rulers posed as caliphs. Nevertheless, Hafsid Tunis was militarily weak and it was a cultural backwater compared with Fez in Morocco. Under the rule of the Merinid Abu'l-Hasan 'Ali (1331–48), Fez had become the capital of the most powerful realm in North Africa. A year after the death of the Hafsid ruler Abu Yahya in 1346, Abu'l-Hasan occupied Tunis and brought with him a retinue of courtiers and scholars to support him. Abu'l-Hasan, who was an exceptionally strict Muslim, had studied the Qur'an with Ibn Marzuq (on whom more below). The ruler was also a noted calligrapher and he spent much of his spare time copying the Qur'an and used his beautifully calligraphed Qur'ans as diplomatic gifts. He composed poetry and he showed favor to Sufis and intellectuals.[9] More generally, it was a striking feature of the age that North African rulers took care to present themselves as being waited on and served by distinguished scholars. The ostentatious display of a body of learned men at court could be seen as one of the insignia of royalty, almost in the same category as the royal parasol, the right to be named as ruler during the Friday prayer and the right to mint coins. But it was a form of conspicuous display that was peculiar to the Maghreb and Andalusia, for, although the Mamluk Sultans of Egypt and Syria patronized scholars, they almost never gave them important political posts, nor did the sultans' prestige depend significantly on the patronage they provided to intellectuals.

At first the young Ibn Khaldun was educated by his father and family friends, but later he benefited from the arrival of Abu'l-Hasan's Moroccan scholars in Tunis. In particular he took lessons with Muhammad ibn Ibrahim al-Abili. Al-Abili was a well-known mathematician and a master of rational sciences (al-'ulum al-'aqli-yya). He had been born in Tlemcen and as a child he became possessed by a passion for mathematics. After a false start as a soldier in Muslim Spain, he traveled to the eastern Arab lands to study with the great scholars there, but while in the east he had some kind of a mental breakdown. On his return to the Maghreb, he studied fiqh (religious jurisprudence) and kalam (theology). Later he studied the rational sciences and became an enthusiast for and expert on the writings of the twelfth-century theologian and Qur'anic exegete Fakhr al-Din al-Razi. Eventually al-Abili joined Abu'l-Hasan's court and council. While in Tunis he lodged with Ibn Khaldun's father and he started to teach the son fiqh, kalam, and the philosophic and mathematical disciplines and this continued for three years.[10]

Nothing that al-Abili wrote has survived, but there are quite a few references to him in the Ta'rif, in which Ibn Khaldun introduced him as "the eminent master of the religious sciences." Al-Abili taught him logic, as well as the philosophical and mathematical disciplines.[11] Also in the Muqaddima, Ibn Khaldun repeatedly acknowledged him as his master.[12] In addition to Ibn Khaldun, al-Abili also tutored the much older Ibn 'Arafa, another figure who was to become one of the leading intellectuals in the western Islamic world. Al-Abili refused to teach at *madrasa*s (religious teaching colleges), probably because their syllabus was tightly controlled by the ruling regime.[13] He was also opposed to the proliferation of textbooks and abridgements and Ibn Khaldun was to follow him in this. It was more important to travel in order to sit at the feet of many different teachers.

Though it is clear that Ibn Khaldun's education benefited from the arrival of the sophisticated people from the West, the Merinid court's occupation of Tunis was only temporary, as Abu'l-Hasan's rule was not popular and his tenure of Ifriqiyya precarious. In particular, the Bedouin Arabs of the Banu Sulaym confederacy in the hinterland, angry at his attempt to abolish their right to collect taxes from settled communities, rose up against him. Abu'l-Hasan was deserted by his levy of Zanata tribesmen that he had recruited from the region of Tlemen and he was defeated in a battle near Qairouan in 1348. In the meantime the Black Death had arrived in Tunis. It killed many of Abu'l-Hasan's retinue and army, before he and what was left of his following fled the plague-ridden region and retreated in the direction of Fez. As already noted, the plague killed Ibn Khaldun's parents, as well as friends and teachers. In the *Muqaddima* Ibn Khaldun quoted a Tunisian poet on the subject:

In Tunis, both in the morning and the evening—
And the morning belongs to God as does the evening—
There is fear and hunger and death,
Stirred up by tumult and pestilence[14]

Eventually the plague died down, leaving Tunis even more of a one-horse town than it had been before.

After Abu'l-Hasan's defeat at Qairouan in 1348, his son Abu 'Inan Faris declared that Abu'l-Hasan had died and, then, when his father reappeared, Abu 'Inan defeated him in battle and forced him to sign a document that announced his abdication. Abu'l-Hasan died a little later, presumably murdered. As happened so often on the occasion of a royal accession, Abu 'Inan went on to conduct a further purge of his relatives. He had two cousins killed and sent two brothers into exile. (Granada was traditionally the place of exile for ousted Merinid princes and politicians.) Then, once he was firmly established in Fez, Abu 'Inan thought to follow in his father's footsteps and he set about planning a renewed campaign in the east.

In 1350 the most powerful man in Tunis was the *hajib*, Ibn Tafraghin, who was also the senior shaykh of the Almohad council. *Hajib* literally means "doorkeeper," but the office was more important than the name suggests. He ran the palace, assured the ruler's security, and controlled access to him. In the fourteenth-century, his authority and range of competence was similar to that of a grand vizier. Ibn Tafraghin had put the young Hafsid prince Abu Ishaq on the throne to reign as his puppet in Tunis. That same year Ibn Khaldun found his first job when he was employed by Ibn Tafraghin as *sahib al-'alama* (master of the sultan's seal). In formal terms this made the holder responsible for writing the sultan's elaborate signature at the end of official documents—a calligraphic chore. But in North Africa the term *sahib al-'alama* was often used to refer to the head of the chancellery, a man who, in addition to overseeing the drafting of all important documents, usually had diplomatic responsibilities as well. The *sahib al-'alama* ranked third in the hierarchy of officialdom below the grand vizier and the *hajib*.[15] So Ibn Khaldun's first ever appointment was a senior one. But he was only a big fish in a small pond, since the writ of Ibn Tafraghin and his puppet ruler hardly extended much beyond the semi-rural suburbs of Tunis and Ibn Khaldun seems to have nourished grander ambitions.

Moreover, Ibn Tafraghin and his Hafsid prince faced challenges from rival members of the Hafsid clan who were based in Constantine and Bougie and consequently the region was in turmoil. The Merinid prince Abu 'Inan Faris profited from this and in 1352 Hafsid Bougie was taken by a Merinid army. At this point Ibn Khaldun deserted the Hafsids and joined al-Batha ibn Abi 'Amr, the Merinid *hajib* who had been appointed to occupy and govern Bougie (or Bijaya in what today is eastern Algeria).

Ibn Khaldun stayed in Bougie until in 1354 he was summoned to the imperial city of Fez by Abu 'Inan and for the next few years he unenthusiastically doubled as a courtier and as one of the sultan's secretaries.[16] But at least he found libraries and intellectual stimulation in the Merinid capital. Abu 'Inan was, like his father, a scholarly figure, who liked to preside over intellectual debates, and Fez, like Tunis, had become a place of refuge, for scholars and courtiers from Andalusia and Merinid culture owed a great deal to these immigrants.

The Qarawiyyin Mosque in Fez, founded in 859 and expanded several times subsequently, was the biggest mosque in North Africa. It was not only a Friday mosque (one of the mosques at which all Muslim men are enjoined to assemble for the Friday noon prayer), but also the main academic institution in the city, as it was where Qur'anic studies, *Shari'a* law, geography, medicine, astrology, and arithmetic were taught and students were even given a regular monetary allowance. Ibn Khaldun studied there and its large library, which has survived to the present day, contains an autograph copy of his *Muqaddima* and *'Ibar* donated by Ibn Khaldun after he had settled in Cairo. He stipulated that the manuscript could be borrowed for up to two months by reliable people on payment of a deposit. From the late thirteenth century onwards, the wide-ranging teaching provided by this mosque and other smaller mosques was supplemented by the establishment of *madrasa*s, or religious teaching colleges. The *madrasa* was a Sunni institution that had appeared first in the eastern Islamic lands and one of its original functions had been to combat Shi'ism. In Morocco the teaching that was conducted in Arabic in the *madrasa*s fostered the use of that language in religion and government at the expense of Berber. The *madrasa*s of Fez lured scholars from all over Morocco to come and study there. In Fez many of these, most notably the Bou 'Inaniya *Madrasa*, founded in 1355 by Abu 'Inan, were established in the vicinity of the Qarawiyyin Mosque. Abu 'Inan had favored *madrasa*s, seeing in them an instrument for strengthening state control of the religion and scholarship, since all the *madrasa*s were under Merinid control. But *madrasa*s taught a narrow syllabus that was largely confined to religious studies and

Ibn Khaldun does not seem to have ever studied at a *madrasa*, or to have had much regard for them.

Although Ibn Khaldun studied intensively in Fez and it was perhaps the chief place where he received his intellectual formation, it seems that he thought that service as one of the court secretaries was beneath his dignity and so he joined an anti-Merinid plot to restore a Hafsid prince, Abu 'Abd Allah, to Bougie. But the plot was discovered and in 1357 he was consigned to prison, where he was to spend twenty-one months. That same year Abu 'Inan attempted to reoccupy Tunis in part of a broader campaign to reunite North Africa. But he was deserted by the Dawawida Arabs who formed a large part of his army and who were reluctant to campaign for so long, far from their customary camping grounds, and he then had to retreat back to Fez. In the following year Abu 'Inan, whose failure to consult with his counselors had made him unpopular, fell ill and one of his viziers, al-Hasan Ibn 'Umar al-Fududi, seized the opportunity to strangle him. His murder marked the beginning of the decline of the Merinids and from then on the throne was repeatedly contested by rival Merinid princes and their sponsors.

After Abu 'Inan's murder, al-Fududi, having placed al-Sa'id, the infant son of Abu 'Inan, on the throne, sought to rule as regent. The vizier also sanctioned the release of Ibn Khaldun from prison. But Ibn Khaldun showed no gratitude to the man who had released him and instead offered his support to another Merinid prince, Abu Salim, a brother of the late sultan, and Ibn Khaldun went out into the hinterland to recruit Banu Merin Berber tribesmen to Abu Salim's cause.

At the same time that Ibn Khaldun was talking to the tribesmen in the hinterland, Shams al-Din Abu 'Abd Allah ibn Marzuq was working for the cause of Abu Salim within the walls of Fez.[17] Although the two scholar-politicians were temporarily on the same side, Ibn Marzuq was to become one of Ibn Khaldun's bêtes noirs. Born in 1310 or 1311 in Tlemcen, Ibn Marzuq was older than Ibn Khaldun and in his day much better known. As a young man he had studied in Mecca, Medina, and Cairo. In 1333 he joined Abu'l-Hasan's court, but from 1347 onwards he took service with the 'Abd al-Wadids of Tlemcen and later the Nasrids of Granada, before eventually returning to the Merinid court in Fez, where he served as Abu'l-Hasan's secretary, diplomat, and court preacher. In 1371, while at the Hafsid court, he composed a panegyric in praise of the Merinid Abu'l-Hasan's reign, the *Musnad al-sahih al-hasan fi ma'thir mawlana Abi al-Hasan* (The Sound Flawless Tradition Regarding the Noble Attributes of Our Lord Abi'l-Hasan).[18] The aim of this chronicle was to attract the patronage of the Merinid 'Abd al-'Aziz (r. 1366–72). Ibn Marzuq's chronicle placed great stress on how important he himself had been to 'Abd al-'Aziz's father, Abu'l-Hasan. Apart from eulogizing the exemplary rule of Abu'l-Hasan, the chronicle ranged so widely that it came close to being an encyclopedia (in that respect resembling the *Muqaddima*), but Ibn Marzuq provided material details about costume, cuisine, and folk customs, the kind of things that tended to be neglected in Ibn Khaldun's writings. Ibn Marzuq was the teacher of the future Andalusian viziers, Ibn al-Khatib and Ibn Zamrak. Apart from the chronicle, Ibn Marzuq wrote widely and eloquently on other subjects, he traveled a lot, and held high office in Fez and Tlemcen. North African politics being the dangerous business it was, he was dismissed from office and imprisoned several times.

Besides the support of Ibn Marzuq and Ibn Khaldun, Abu Salim was assisted by troops from Christian Castille. On taking power, Abu Salim (r. 1359–61) appointed Ibn Marzuq grand vizier and made Ibn Khaldun *katib al-sirr* (literally "scribe of the secret": in Fez, "deputy head of the chancellery").[19] It is likely that Ibn Khaldun had hoped to be given the vizierate. Even so, Ibn Marzuq, who struggled to monopolize authority under the sultan, disliked the favor shown to Ibn Khaldun and further tension arose when Ibn Khaldun was given authority over *mazalim*, that is, responsibility for investigating and punishing abuses committed by officials that were not covered by Shari'a law.[20]

THE GLORY OF THE AGE, IBN AL-KHATIB

It was while Ibn Khaldun held high office in Merinid Fez that he first encountered another of the great intellectual scholar-politicians of the age. Lisan al-Din Muhammad ibn al-Khatib (1313–74), who had studied with Ibn Marzuq, had gone on to serve Muhammad V, the Nasrid ruler of Granada, as his vizier from the commencement of his reign in 1354. The sixteen-year-old prince was for some years effectively Ibn al-Khatib's disciple. When, in 1359, Muhammad was deposed in a coup and his younger brother Isma'il installed in his place, Ibn al-Khatib followed Muhammad into exile in Fez. Since Muhammad, guided by Ibn al-Khatib, had pursued a consistently pro-Merinid policy, they were welcomed in Fez. There Ibn al-Khatib and Ibn Khaldun met and became friends. The administrative aristocrat Ibn al-Khatib was in his lifetime more famous, more powerful, and more productive than Ibn Khaldun, and for centuries his fame would outshine that of his younger contemporary. He was perhaps the single most influential person in Ibn Khaldun's life. In the Ta'rif, Ibn al-Khatib was described as "one of the miracles of God in the areas of poetry, prose, knowledge and culture." Lisan al-Din, "Tongue of the Religion," was an honorific bestowed on the man as a tribute to his eloquence. He was also referred to as "the man with two lives," because he suffered from chronic insomnia, and he would use the wakeful night hours to continue with his writing. He produced more than sixty books in a variety of genres.

Ibn al-Khatib believed in history as a source of good examples and claimed that, if it were not for history, virtue would die with its possessors. He wrote history in the flowery style that was so admired at the time and his chronicles were peppered with poetry. Unlike Ibn Khaldun, who was preoccupied with the general laws that underlay historical processes, Ibn al-Khatib preferred to focus on dramatic incidents and individual personalities and motivations. He wrote a history of Granada and he started but left unfinished what had been a chronicle of the reigns of rulers who had been minors when they came to their thrones but the book expanded into a universal history, the A'mal al-a'lam (Deeds of the Great). He argued that all dynasties were in the long run doomed by corruption, greed, and ambition. History was a vicious cycle of usurpations and depositions. It is curious to note that, in all he wrote about Ibn Khaldun, Ibn al-Khatib never refers to him as a historian (and, equally strange, Ibn Khaldun never refers to Ibn al-Khatib's chronicles in his account of the man).

As already noted, like Ibn Khaldun, Ibn al-Khatib was gloomily aware of ruins, and the moral and political messages that they seemed to carry. A couple of lines from H. F. Lyte's Victorian hymn could serve to describe his position: "Change and decay in all around I see; / O Thou, who changes not, abide with me." A gloomy and arrogant aristocrat, Ibn al-Khatib regarded the masses with disgust. In addition to the histories, Ibn al-Khatib wrote three great travelogues, of which *The Shaking of the Bag* covers his exile in Morocco and return to Granada, and concludes with a famous account of the extravagant celebration held in the Alhambra in December 1362 to mark the Prophet's birthday.

Ibn al-Khatib was also a devout Sufi and after he had arrived in Fez, he did not linger long there, but removed himself from political intrigue for several years by retreating to Salé on the Moroccan coast where he spent his time of exile in mystical studies and meditation. Later in 1367 he compiled the *Rawdat al-ta'rif bi'-hubb al-sharif* (Garden of Instruction in Noble Love), a poetic anthology that served to illustrate divine truths. Sufism was the path of love and love moved the stars and made the universe go round. In his discussion of the poetic form of the *zajal* (on which see chapter 9), Ibn Khaldun cited with approval these lines from a Sufi poem by Ibn al-Khatib:

> Between sunrise and sunset, love poems of various kinds were
> composed.
> Gone are the mortals who were created and not been before.
> There remains God who never ceases.[21]

Ibn al-Khatib drew a lot on the writings of Ibn al-'Arabi and Ibn Sab'in, two thirteenth-century Andalusian Sufis whose orthodoxy had been widely questioned and thus was dangerous.[22] Indeed it was one of the things that eventually contributed to his violent death.

In 1362 Muhammad V was restored to his throne and Ibn al-Khatib returned with him to Granada. Meanwhile politics in Fez continued to be turbulent. Ibn Marzuq's determination to keep all power in his hands had alienated those under him and then in 1361 a vizier, 'Amar ibn 'Abdallah, led a revolt against Abu Salim, who disappeared and was presumably murdered. Ibn Marzuq was thrown into prison.[23] When eventually he was released, he made his way to Tunis where the all-powerful Vizier Ibn Tafraghin welcomed him, but soon things got difficult for him there too and in 1372 Ibn Marzuq abandoned North African politics and fled to Egypt, where he spent his last years in scholarly pursuits, dying in 1379. His turbulent career as an administrator and scholar has many parallels with that of Ibn Khaldun.

IBN KHALDUN IN SPAIN

As for Ibn Khaldun, he was allowed to leave Fez by 'Amar ibn 'Abdallah on the condition that he did not move to Tlemcen, where he might have offered dangerous support to its 'Abd al-Wadid ruler. So in 1363 Ibn Khaldun set off for Granada where he could expect to be warmly received by its ruler and vizier. Muhammad V did indeed favor him and gave him a number of important tasks.[24] Most notably in 1364 he was sent on a diplomatic mission to Seville where he entered into negotiations with Pedro the Cruel, the King of Castile. (In visiting Seville, Ibn Khaldun was visiting the home of his ancestors.) The mission was successful and Pedro offered him a place at court and the return of his family lands, if only he would convert to Christianity. Ibn Khaldun refused and returned to Granada. But it was precisely his successes in Andalusia that put him in peril, as the hitherto well-disposed Ibn al-Khatib seemed to have become suspicious that Ibn Khaldun wanted to replace him as vizier and eminence grise. It has been suggested that Ibn Khaldun had dreamed of making Muhammad V into a philosopher-king with himself acting as Aristotle to Muhammad's Alexander.[25] But as we shall see in a later chapter, there are grounds for doubting this.

BACK TO NORTH AFRICA

Judging it better not to face Ibn al-Khatib's outright enmity, Ibn Khaldun left Andalusia in 1365 and went back to reengage in the dangerous game of North African politics. The Hafsid prince Abu

'Abd Allah Muhammad, with whom Ibn Khaldun had previously conspired during the reign of Abu 'Inan, had recently succeeded in reinstalling himself as ruler of Bougie and he made Ibn Khaldun his *hajib* and *khatib* of the court's mosque.[26] This was perhaps the peak of Ibn Khaldun's political career.

At about the same time Ibn Khaldun's younger brother, Yahya, who was also a historian of note, was appointed vizier.[27] Once again the older Ibn Khaldun was involved in dealing with tribesmen, as he was made responsible for collecting taxes from the Berbers of the highlands. In 1366 Abu 'Abd Allah was defeated and killed in battle by the Hafsid ruler of Constantine, Abu'l-Abbas. Although Abu'l-'Abbas offered to keep Ibn Khaldun in office, he refused and shortly thereafter left Bougie. His brother went to serve the 'Abd al-Wadid sultan Abu Hammu II (1359–89), the ruler of Tlemcen, who made Yahya his *katib al-sirr*.

Meanwhile the older Ibn Khaldun made a half-hearted attempt to retire from politics and pursue scholarship in Biskra (an oasis town in the south-eastern part of what today is Algeria, which was then under the nominal rule of the Hafsids, though semi-independent). "I was in fact cured of the temptation of office. Furthermore I had for too long neglected scholarly matters. I therefore ceased to involve myself in the affairs of kings and devoted all my energies to reading and teaching."[28] He corresponded extensively with Ibn al-Khatib. It was also in Biskra that he became interested in the prophetic device known as *za'iraja* (on which more later). While in Biskra he was under the protection of the town's local petty Arab dynasty, the Banu Muzni, who were allies of the powerful tribe of Dawawida Arabs. The Dawawida collected taxes from the settlements of the Zab region around Biskra in the name of the Hafsids and revenue they collected was treated by the Dawawida as pay for their military service.[29]

But he soon found himself drawn into political intrigues again. First he tried to broker an alliance between Hafsid Tunis and Abu Hammu of Tlemcen and sought to rally Arab and Berber tribal leaders for this. Then he switched to backing the Merinid ruler of Fez. Though he was at first welcomed in Fez, he was later arrested, then released and finally allowed to return to Granada in 1375.

But there too he was not welcome, as he was perceived to be a partisan for Ibn al-Khatib, who had fallen out of favor with Muhammad V and gone into exile in Morocco in 1371. Ibn Khaldun was obliged to return to North Africa where he briefly settled in Tlemcen.

By then his friend Ibn al-Khatib had been killed. Though Ibn al-Khatib had at first been welcomed in Fez, his enemies, the new vizier in Granada Ibn Zamrak, allied with Ali al-Nubahi, the chief qadi of Granada, put pressure on the Merinid ruler 'Abd al-'Aziz to have Ibn al-Khatib tried for heresy and executed. The trial for the linked heresies of monism and incarnationism was inconclusive, but in 1375 he was strangled at night in his prison cell. In the *Muqaddima* Ibn Khaldun described his death as that of "a martyr."[30]

Ibn Khaldun wrote a long poem about Ibn al-Khatib's death, which ends as follows:

> So, tell the enemies; "Yes, Ibn al-Khatib is gone,
> But is there anyone who will not be gone one day?"
> And tell those of you who rejoice at this news:
> "Only he who thinks he will never die
> Can rejoice on a day like this!"[31]

There was nothing "New Age" about fourteenth-century Sufism and it was possible for a Sufi to become a powerful politician and a murderer. All the same, Ibn Zamrak, who had pressed for Ibn al-Khatib's imprisonment and sent the thugs to kill him, was a man of considerable culture. He had studied Sufism with Ibn Marzuq and many of Ibn Zamrak's verses are found on the walls of the Alhambra. Ibn Zamrak, who had orchestrated the murder of Ibn al-Khatib, would in turn be murdered sometime after 1393.

In 1378, Ibn Khaldun's younger brother Yahya met a similar unhappy fate. An enthusiast for belles lettres and poetry, he was more of a literary figure than his elder brother and he was famous for his elegantly written history of 'Abd al-Wadid Tlemcen, the *Bughyat al-ruwwad fi dhikr al-muluk min Bani 'Abd al-Wad* (The Object of Visitors' Desire with Respect to Knowledge of the 'Abd al-Wadid Kings). But he was also a politician, had served a number of rulers, and, like so many politicians in that age, had been in prison several times. He ended up in Tlemcen, where the 'Abd al-Wadid ruler Abu Hammu II, who was fond of scholars and poets and had himself written a treatise on political ethics, made him *katib al-sirr*. But in 1379 the son of Abu Hammu had Yahya murdered, for reasons that are unknown. By then his brother had left politics and was devoting himself to writing the great book on the underlying principles of North African history.

As can be seen from the above, the narrative of that history is a twisted and violent tale of contested thrones, betrayals, exiles, imprisonments, and murders. As Patricia Crone observed: "In practice, government was more often than not both weak and oppressive: weak in the sense that it could not get much done, oppressive in the sense that rulers would freely sacrifice the lives and property of their subjects in order to stay in power and keep some semblance of order. It was normal for members of the elite, scholars included, to spend time in jail; most high-ranking governors and generals died violent deaths; and torture, assassination, and extortion were matters of routine."[32] And yet curiously little of this nightmarish turbulence featured in the *Muqaddima*.

Ibn Khaldun moved from Bougie to Fez, to Granada, then Bougie, Fez again, Granada again, Tlemcen, Tunis, and Cairo. The historian who was to write so much about nomads was himself a nomad. The striking prominence of scholars in politics in medieval North Africa has already been remarked upon—Ibn Marzuq, Ibn al-Khatib, Ibn Zamrak, Ibn Khaldun, and his younger brother. It is hard to think of parallels elsewhere in world history. The elder Ibn Khaldun's intrigues had been successful only in the sense that, at the end of them all, he was still alive. As the British politician Enoch Powell observed, "All political lives, unless they are cut off in midstream at a happy juncture, end in failure, because that is the nature of politics and of human affairs."[33] Muhsin Mahdi and Patricia Crone (on both of whom see chapter 10) have suggested that Ibn Khaldun wrote the *Muqaddima* in order to understand why he was a political failure and there may be something in this. In that respect, he may be compared to Machiavelli and to Edward Hyde (later Lord Clarendon), both of whom had played an active role in politics and who then wrote histories when their careers were in eclipse. In chapter 6 of the *Muqaddima* Ibn Khaldun devoted a couple of pages to explaining why scholars were unfamiliar with politics and he argued that their penchant for abstract thought and generalizations, as well as their searching for analogies, detached them from the detailed realities of political situations.[34]

During these last years of Ibn Khaldun's engagement in politics and warfare in the Maghreb, before he withdrew to write the *Muqaddima* and the *'Ibar* in Qal'at Banu Salama, he had been increasingly employed by the rulers of Fez, Tunis, and Tlemcen as a tribal negotiator and recruiter of nomad armies. It is time to examine Ibn Khaldun's ideas about the role of the nomads in history.

CHAPTER THREE

The Nomads, Their Virtues, and Their Place in History

Dost thou think, because thou art virtuous, there shall be no more cakes and ale?
—Shakespeare, *Twelfth Night*

And now, what's going to happen to us without barbarians?
They were, those people, a kind of solution.
—Cavafy, "Waiting for the Barbarians"

The sociologist Max Weber defined a state as follows: "A human community that successfully claims a monopoly of the legitimate use of physical force within a given territory."[1] There were no states in Weber's sense in fourteenth-century North Africa. The Arab and Berber tribes were far too powerful and they both created ruling dynasties and destroyed them. Examination of this cycle of creation and destruction is, as we shall see, at the heart of the *Muqaddima*.

In 1375 Abu Hammu, the 'Abd al-Wadid ruler of Tlemcen, sent Ibn Khaldun on a mission to the Dawawida Arabs, but, perhaps taking warning from the fate of Ibn al-Khatib, Ibn Khaldun decided to retire for a while from politics in order to write the *Muqaddima* and the *'Ibar*. An earlier happier phase in Ibn al-Khatib's career may also have inspired Ibn Khaldun's retirement. When in 1359 Ibn al-Khatib followed Muhammad V of Granada into exile, he had first gone to Fez (where he had met Ibn Khaldun). But thereafter, as already noted, he retreated to Salé on the Atlantic coast and there, having sought and obtained the protection of the shaykh of the Hintata tribe, Amir ibn Muhammad ibn Ali in the High Atlas, Ibn al-Khatib had devoted himself to mystical studies and devotions, until he was called back to a political career in Granada.

Like Ibn al-Khatib, Ibn Khaldun sought the protection of a powerful tribe in the hinterland and, for reasons that are mysterious, the Awlad ʿArif, the leading clan of the Suwayd Arab confederacy in western Algeria and the subjects of the Merinid ruler, welcomed Ibn Khaldun with open arms and lent him a castle, Qalʿat Banu Salama, where he could live with his family and work remote from distractions. He was forty-five years old. His austere workplace has been described as a "troglodytic Berber village cut into the scarp of the high plains of western Algeria where they fall away in great steps towards the desert in the south. The Qalʿat, or ʿfortress,ʼ where he wrote, no longer exists and today there is only a village of drystone buildings. The Qalʿat was named after the maraboutic family which presided over it."[2] (The term "marabout" was originally used to designate a holy warrior stationed in a *ribat* or garrison, but later it was used to describe hermits who had withdrawn from civilization to find sanctity in the wilderness.) Ibn Khaldun's eyrie was perched on a cliff that was difficult to access. From it he could look down on a fertile plain where cereal crops were grown.[3] In the Qalʿat Banu Salama, far from libraries and intellectual companionship, this Arab Prospero was to write for the next four years before returning to Tunis where he could check his facts in the city's libraries and where he would be tempted to meddle in politics once more.

In the meantime, his withdrawal from politics could be compared to the Sufi practice of *khalwa*, a temporary withdrawal from society in order to meditate, though Ibn Khaldun's meditations were focused specifically on how God worked in the world through social processes. He wrote in the *Taʿrif* of how he wrote the theoretical introduction to his history: "I completed its introduction in that remarkable manner to which I was inspired by that retreat, with words and ideas pouring into my head like cream into a churn, until the finished product was ready."[4] It may be that watching the ʿArif tribe managing their affairs and tending their flocks provided a stimulating alternative to reading more books. Certainly, tribesmen and their part in bringing about the rise and fall of successive North African regimes have a central role in his vision of history. Though he started with a study of the Berber and Arab tribes of North Africa, subsequently the *Muqaddima* and the *'Ibar* expanded into a comprehensive account of civilization and social organization. It was an ambitious undertaking. "It should be known that the discussion of this topic is something new, extraordinary, and highly useful. Penetrating research has shown the way to it."[5] He had no doubts about the merits of his work and its originality: "When our discussion in the section on royal authority and dynasties has been studied and due critical attention given to it, it will be found to constitute an exhaustive, very clear, fully substantiated interpretation and detailed exposition of these sentences. We became aware of these things with God's help and without the instruction of Aristotle or the teaching of the Mobedhan [a Zoroastrian priest]."[6]

Although Ibn Khaldun was the scholarly product of an urban culture, he had acquired a lot of experience of life in the hinterland and had become a specialist in negotiating with the Berber and Arab tribesmen in the semi-deserts and highlands beyond the cities. Because of the turbulent and kaleidoscopically changing tribal politics of the time, it would be both tedious and confusing to list all those negotiations, but, briefly, the various Merinid and Hafsid rulers had sent Ibn Khaldun out on missions to raise either taxes or armies from the Arab and Berber tribesmen. Though the core of the Merinid and Hafsid armies was usually composed of members of the extended ruling clan, as well as of mamluks (slave soldiers) and mercenaries, for any major campaign the bulk of the army would have to be provided by semi-nomadic tribesmen. In this period the Dawawida Arab tribal cavalry, who pastured their camel herds on the plains of Bougie and Constantine, provided the largest and most important military force and they sold their services to the highest bidder. Obviously the Dawawida had no interest in seeing North Africa united under a single strong ruler and consequently they kept switching sides. Not only was Ibn Khaldun repeatedly responsible for negotiating with tribesmen and bribing them to fight, but he sometimes also led them into battle. On one occasion, when Abu Hammu sent him out with a small force to rally the Dawawida for yet another campaign, he found himself attacked by another body of Arabs that included his future hosts, the Awlad 'Arif. So when he wrote about the nomads he did not do so as an armchair theoretician. It was tough, dangerous work. As Allen Fromherz has noted: "Not many philosophers have been obliged to eat their own horse."[7]

The tribesmen that Ibn Khaldun was most familiar with were not fully nomadic. Pure nomadism was hardly known in that area of the Maghreb lying north of the Sahara. Unlike the camel rearers of Arabia's Empty Quarter, Ibn Khaldun's Berbers and Arabs did not range widely and unpredictably over a desert in a quest for grazing that was determined by the rare incidence of rain. Rather they were transhumants who followed a regular path from winter to summer grazing grounds. In Morocco, for example, tribes moved up into the highlands of High Atlas or the Aures for summer pasturage. In the winter they moved down into the southern desert and semi-desert. Transhumance could be up and down a slope, or it could take the form of a long-distance migration. Ibn Khaldun wrote of the Zanata Berbers practicing transhumance.[8] Despite their wildness, Ibn Khaldun admired them and in his writings he set out to praise them, in the same way that earlier the Sanhaja had been praised by those who wrote under the Almoravids.

Transhumant nomads might also engage in settled agriculture during the autumn and winter. Many, perhaps most, of the tribes herded sheep. The famous breed of Merino sheep is probably so-called because they were first bred in Merinid Morocco. The reluctance of the transhumant tribesmen to spend long periods of time away from their familiar grazing grounds and their plantations sabotaged quite a few ambitious military campaigns planned by generals based in the towns. Since the tribesmen needed to sell or barter their wool, meat, and hides in order to purchase weapons, grain, and other things, there was a symbiotic relationship between the tribesmen and urban centers. Ibn Khaldun thought that those in the countryside were more dependent on the towns than vice versa. Besides making a living from their livestock and selling their services as mercenaries, the tribesmen were also accustomed to levy taxes on settled communities. These taxes were not sanctioned by the Qur'an and, motivated by piety or by greed, the Merinid sultans made repeated attempts to abolish them, but, as has been noted, they were not successful.

HOW HEALTHY ARE THE NOMADS?

In the fifth prefatory discussion of book 1 of the *Muqaddima*, Ibn Khaldun noted that nomadic Arabs and Berbers were rarely able to produce their own grain and that, though they had little money, they usually had to purchase grain and he continued as follows: "They obtain no more than the bare necessities, and sometimes less, and in no case enough for a comfortable or abundant life. . . . In spite of this, the desert people who lack grain and seasonings are found to be healthier in body and better in character than the hill people who have plenty of everything. Their complexions are clearer, their bodies cleaner, their figures more perfect and better."[9] And he went on to explain that eating too much food caused excessive moisture to circulate in the body, which creates "putrid humors, pallor, obesity, ugliness and stupidity." (Note that, though Ibn Khaldun often uses *badawi* in the sense of dweller in the countryside, from his description of the *badawi* diet, he must here be using *badawi* in the more specific sense of desert people.)

Bruce Chatwin (1940–89) was another enthusiast for nomadic tribes and their healthy way of living. The eclectically, eruditely camp novelist and travel writer was obsessed with nomads. *The Songlines*, based on his traveling around Australia with Salman Rushdie and Chatwin's affair with the camel expert Robyn Davidson, is a novel that combines fragments of autobiography with an exploration of Aborigine mythology.

Within the *The Songlines* is a chrestomathy devoted to the theme of traveling, and the *Muqaddima* is quoted in it: "The Desert People are closer to being good than settled peoples because they are closer to the First State and are more removed from all evil habits that have infected the hearts of settlers." He glossed the "desert people" as being "the Bedouin such as those he once recruited, as mercenaries from the heart of the Sahara, in the days of his warlike youth." And Chatwin added, "Years later, when he had gazed into the slanting eyes of Tamerlane and witnessed the piles of skulls and smouldering cities, he too, like the Old Testament prophets, felt the fearful anxiety of civilisation, and looked back with longing to life in the tents." Then Chatwin went on to suggest that Ibn Khaldun regarded the desert as "a reservoir of civilisation." The nomads were "more abstemious, freer, braver, healthier, less bloated, less craven, less liable to submit to rotten laws, and altogether easier to cure."[10]

All the same, it has to be said that Ibn Khaldun's observations on the healthiness of the Bedouin diet have not been widely replicated. "Dysentery of the Arabian coast sort used to fall like a hammer blow, and crush its victim for a few hours: after which the extreme effects passed off, but it left men curiously tired, and subject for weeks to sudden breaks of nerve," according to T. E. Lawrence.[11] H.R.P. Dickson, who was a British political agent in the Gulf in the 1920s and '30s, delivered this verdict: "There is a great deal of sickness and disease among the Badawin, mostly traceable to lack of nourishment and poor water . . . and the span of life is normally short."[12] Wilfred Thesiger, who spent time in Arabia's Empty Quarter, reported that the "Bedu suffer much from headaches and stomach trouble." Also their teeth were mostly "nothing but blackened shells."[13] The American anthropologist Donald P. Cole, who did fieldwork in Saudi Arabia, had this to report: "Doctors we interviewed in the field unanimously expressed the opinion that the Bedouin suffer from malnutrition and anaemia and often have eye diseases."[14]

Somewhat eccentrically, Ibn Khaldun denied that hunger could cause death and he added that he had observed someone who had eaten nothing for forty days. Moreover his teachers had encountered two holy women in Andalusia who had eaten nothing for years. Others he knew lived on nothing but goat's milk.[15] According to *The SAS Survival Guide*, an adult can survive three weeks without food (though only three days without water).[16] Ibn Khaldun also believed that excessive moisture in the brain caused stupidity.

'ASABIYYA

The most famous and perhaps the central thesis of the *Muqaddima* is that, in the harsh conditions of desert life, tribal groups of necessity develop a special kind of group solidarity which Ibn Khaldun called *'asabiyya*. The word appears over five hundred times in the *Muqaddima*. The root verb *'asaba* means "he twisted [a thing]" and *'usbah* means "a party of men who league together to defend one another." *'Asabiyya* was defined in medieval Arabic dictionaries as "a strong attachment, which holds several persons closely united by the same interest or the same opinion." (There is an old joke that every Arabic verbal root has a camel-related verb or noun derived from it. It is not much of a joke; *'usub*, derived from the same root as *asabiyya*, means "a she-camel that will not yield her milk copiously unless her thigh be bound with a cord.") It may be that Ibn Khaldun envisaged *'asabiyya* as evoking the way in which the mutually dependent lives of desert-dwelling tribesmen were so tightly intertwined. On the other hand, the reference may have been to the colored turbans or headbands worn as a sign of tribal or party allegiance: *ta'assaba* means "he bound a turban or fillet round his head."

The former explanation seems more likely and in *Arabian Sands* the explorer Wilfred Thesiger described the interdependence of the nomads of the Arabian Peninsula's Empty Quarter:

> The society in which the Bedu live is tribal. Everyone belongs to a tribe and all members of the same tribe are in some degree kinsmen, since they are descended from a common ancestor. The closer the relationship the stronger is the loyalty which a man feels for his fellow tribesmen, and this loyalty overrides personal feelings, except in extreme cases. In time of need a man instinctively supports his fellow tribesmen, just as they in like case support him. There is no security in the desert for an individual outside the framework of his tribe. This makes it possible for tribal law, which is based on consent, to work among the most individualistic race in the world, since in the last resort a man who refuses to accept a tribal decision can be ostracised.[17]

Thesiger also wrote that "the Arabs are a race which produces its best only under conditions of extreme hardship and deteriorates progressively as living conditions become easier."[18]

Ibn Khaldun has been described by some modern scholars as an ethnographer. Perhaps he was, but only in a somewhat restricted sense. Whereas Thesiger was interested not only in bonds of solidarity within a nomadic tribe, but also in their stock-rearing techniques, social rituals, diet, mode of dress, ways of saddling and loading camels, and so on, these sort of details did not interest Ibn Khaldun and, if the sources did not tell us otherwise, one might have guessed that he had never spent a single day of his life in a nomadic encampment. Only *'asabiyya* was of real interest here. As he presented it, *'asabiyya* seems to have a life of its own as it inevitably seeks power for its constituents. There is nothing static about this "group solidarity," for the word *'asabiyya* seems also to carry the connotation of dynamism and élan vital. *'Asabiyya* drives a tribe in the direction of power. "It is . . . evident that royal authority is the goal of group feeling."[19] *Asabiyya* is one of God's tools and through it His divine plan for mankind is worked out.[20]

According to the *Muqaddima*, the leader who controlled an *'asabiyya* group of sufficient strength and importance might succeed in founding a dynasty and in winning *mulk* (kingship) for himself and his family. (The tribesmen did not all have to be kinsmen, for clients could also be bonded within the tribe.) Ibn Khaldun argued that group solidarity, together with the tribesmen's hardihood and courage gave the tribes who possessed it a military advantage—an advantage that was further reinforced if religion acted as an additional agent of cohesion. He went so far as to argue that "Arabs can obtain royal authority only by making use of some religious coloring, such as prophecy or sainthood, or some great religious event in general."[21] So it was that the wild and sometimes fanatically religious tribesmen were able to defeat and conquer empires and cities and go on to create new regimes.

But within a few generations, perhaps three, maybe four, these conquering tribesmen lost their *'asabiyya* and became civilized. They succumbed to luxury, extravagance, and leisure. Soft urban life led to degeneracy. The ruler, who could no longer rely on fierce tribal warriors for his defense, had to raise extortionate taxes in order to pay for other sorts of soldiers and this in turn would lead to further problems. The ruler became vulnerable when his government was seen as corrupt and extravagant; his rule was finally doomed when it was seen as impious. His regime would fall to an assault by the next wave of puritanical tribesmen from the desert. So his city was occupied by new warriors, fresh from the desert, and the cycle continued. As the anthropologist Ernest Gellner summarized this eternal cycle: "Characteristically the tribe is both an alternative to the state and also its image, its limitation and the seed of a new state."[22] The senility of dynasties is irrevocable. "Dynasties have a natural lifespan like individuals."[23]

Ibn Khaldun even called on the Old Testament in support of his vision of decay over the generations: "In the Torah, there is the following passage: 'God, your Lord is powerful and jealous, visiting the sins of the fathers upon the children unto the third and fourth generations.' This shows that four generations in one lineage are the limit of ancestral prestige."[24] (But it is not clear that this passage does offer support to the central thesis of the *Muqaddima*.)

It is curious to compare Ibn Khaldun with Edward Gibbon who in his *History of the Decline and Fall of the Roman Empire* (1776–88) presented that decline and fall as being due to barbarism and religion.

By contrast, Ibn Khaldun presented barbarism and religion as the sources of empire, for, as we have seen, he believed that empires were regularly renewed by barbarian incursions and he believed that religion was a desirable supplement to 'asabiyya for tribal conquerors who aimed to conquer an old regime and set up a new one. Religion could and should serve as the cement of empires and the duty of the rulers of those empires should be to maintain the religious law, the observance of which would lead to salvation in the afterlife. The first Arab tribal conquerors could never have established a great empire without the additional unifying bond of the new religion. (But it should be noted that religion played no part in inspiring the Mongol or Chagatai Turkish tribal conquerors, nor had it had a role in the establishment of the Merinid regime.) Ibn Khaldun argued that puritan reform movements rarely lasted more than a hundred years or at most one hundred and twenty years. Gibbon had worried whether Augustan Europe would share the fate of the Roman Empire. Ibn Khaldun knew that the great Age of the Arabs was over.

Ibn Khaldun's theoretical historical model seems to work quite well for the early Islamic Arab conquests under Muhammad and the Rightful Caliphs, as well as for much of the history of North Africa in the Middle Ages. It can be applied to the rise in the eleventh century of the Almoravids, who were Sanhaja Berber tribesmen and whose militantly Maliki Sunni warriors were initially garrisoned in *ribat*s (hence al-Murabitun, or Almoravid), and it may apply also to their eventual decline in the twelfth century. The model also seems to fit the rise in the twelfth century of the Mahdist Almohads at the head of the Masmuda Berbers and their fall in the thirteenth century.

Whether Ibn Khaldun's cyclical model, four-generations-and-you-are-out, works for other times and other places is questionable and in fact he does not seem to have intended his cyclical theory to be universally applicable. He made an exception of the more urbanized and heavily settled Muslim territories in the eastern Islamic lands and in Andalusia. In the *'Ibar* he also noted that the Mamluk regime in Egypt and Syria constituted a special case (and that will be discussed in chapter 5). But even within North Africa, the model does not seem to have universal applicability. Not only was the warlike *'asabiyya* of the Zanata Berber Merinids not given additional force by any specifically religious ideology or purpose, but their dynasty (1217–1465) was to last much longer than four generations and the same turned out to be true of the Hafsids and the 'Abd al-Wadids.

'Asabiyya is divinely ordained as it is one of God's tools.[25] But there was no need for it in the lifetime of the Prophet and in the years that immediately followed, for this was a time of divine pronouncements, angels, and miracles, in which normal socio-political laws were irrelevant.[26] Ibn Khaldun was unusual in his enthusiasm for tribal *'asabiyya*. Many people today would see tribalism as the curse of the Middle East. Certainly the concept of *'asabiyya* and its historical implications play a leading role in the arguments presented in the *Muqaddima*, but even so its importance has been overstressed

in some modern readings of the book. There is more to the *Muqaddima* than a cyclical theory of history based on a skewed reading of the fortunes of selected Arab and Berber tribes in the Maghreb.

THE OLD TIMES WERE BEST

In the broader context of the encyclopedic *Muqaddima*, what seems to underpin Ibn Khaldun's pessimistic cyclical theory is a historical mythology that was widely shared by the early Arab chroniclers, concerning the Arab warriors who took part in the conquests of the first century of Islam. In anecdote after anecdote those warriors were portrayed as austere, brutish, rude, and fearless. They had no knowledge of or interest in cushions, silks, fine food, or kingly pretensions. Earlier, the *Jahili* poets of pre-Islamic Arabia had celebrated the austerity and danger of life in the desert and this attitude had carried over into the Islamic era.

Ibn Khaldun looked back with yearning to the days of the *Rashidun*, the first four Rightly Guided Caliphs: "The world and its luxuries were more alien to them than to any other nation, on account of their religion, which inspired asceticism where the good things of life were concerned, and on account of the desert outlook and habitat and the rude severe life to which they were accustomed." He commended the diet of the Arabian tribe of Mudar who used to eat camel hair ground with stones mixed with blood and then cooked. Despite the amount of booty accumulated during the earliest Arab conquests, "they kept to their rude way of life. 'Umar used to patch his sole garment with pieces of leather. 'Ali used to say 'Gold and silver! Go lure others, not me!' Abu Musa refrained from eating chicken, because chickens were very rare among the Arabs of that time and not generally known to them. Sieves were non-existent among the Arabs, and they ate wheat kernels with the bran."[27]

These somewhat-ascetic cameos came from "the golden age of the Arabs" and they were part of a historico-literary trope in which chroniclers summoned tales of improbable austerity and then explicitly or implicitly went on to compare those accounts with the decadence of the writers' own times. Tall buildings, jeweled daggers, ornamental fruit trees, and luxury foods all boded ill. It was, I think, this kind of moralizing, more than a newly invented sociology, which inspired Ibn Khaldun's engine of history. "The entire world is trifling and futile. It leads to death and annihilation."[28]

As Patricia Crone has observed, poverty was seen in the medieval Islamic world as the guardian of virtue: "In patriarchal Medina, we are assured, things were right because society was small, simple and poor. Government was minimal, wholly just, and without any kind of oppression or violence, except of course against evildoers. There were no palaces, wide courts, crowns, thrones . . . no jails or doorkeepers, no taxes, confiscations or forced labour, and no differences between elite and commoners: everybody lived much like everyone else."[29] Alas, luxury proved to be corrosive and the booty accumulated as a result of the Muslim victories over the Persians and the Byzantines contributed largely to the ruin of this primitivist utopia.

The view that the long-term enjoyment of material comfort brings about the ruin of economies and empires still has currency today. In *Biohistory: Decline and Fall of the West* (2015), Jim Penman argues that successful cultures are all ultimately doomed because prosperity and comfort alter people's temperaments and make them incapable of preserving or perpetuating themselves. The West is doomed to follow the fate of the Roman and Greek Empires and Penman quoted Vico on the fatal sequence: "The nature of peoples is first crude, then severe, then benign, then delicate, finally dissolute." (For more on Vico, see chapter 4.) Penman quotes Tacitus: "Prosperity is the measure or touchstone of virtue, for it is less difficult to bear misfortune than to remain uncorrupted by pleasure."[30] According to Penman, elites are particularly vulnerable because they live in high-density cities and their vigor is undermined by affluence. Like Ibn Khaldun, Penman thinks that harsh living conditions favor tribal warriors. But unlike Ibn Khaldun or Vico, Penman has identified such things as changes in child-rearing patterns, declining levels of anxiety, and the loosening of controls over women as the most important solvent factors behind the collapse of civilizations.

"Bedouins are closer to being good than sedentary people are."[31] By contrast, sedentary people were too concerned with pleasure and luxuries and they became contaminated by greed and excess, so that "sedentary life constitutes the last stage of civilization and the point where it begins to decay. It also constitutes the last stage of evil and of remoteness from goodness."[32] There was a Qur'anic and traditional background to this sort of prejudice. Qur'an 17:16: "When we desire to destroy a village, we order those of its inhabitants who live in luxury to act wickedly within. Thus the word becomes true for it, and we destroy it."[33] There was also a well-attested saying of the Prophet: "The Final Hour will not come until people compete with one another in the height of their buildings."

Generalizing somewhat, Ibn Khaldun presented life in the cities as being easier than in the countryside. But the idea that the inhabitants of North African towns in the fourteenth century for the most part led lives of luxury and ease seems sweeping and somewhat implausible. It is unlikely that water-sellers, tanners, bathhouse stokers, and chicken farmers felt themselves to be succumbing to the evil effects of luxurious living. On the other hand, Ibn Khaldun was unfamiliar with prosperous rural communities, such as might have been found in fourteenth-century Italy or fifteenth-century Norfolk and Suffolk. Furthermore, the distinction between rural and urban life was not as hard-edged as one might have imagined. In North Africa and in Italy it was quite common for farmers to ride out from the town in the mornings to the fields and orchards that they were cultivating and then ride back to town in the evening.

WHO IS A BEDOUIN? WHO IS AN ARAB?

A major problem in reading the *Muqaddima* is that Ibn Khaldun's use of language was somewhat slippery. This is particularly the case with the terms that are customarily rendered in English as "Bedouin" and "Arab." *Badawi* can be translated as "Bedouin" or "nomad," *badawa* as "desert life" or "desert attitude," and *badw* as "desert." But Rosenthal has argued that Ibn Khaldun's Bedouin did not have to be nomadic; they just had to live at some distance from a town. So non-nomadic peasants who lived in the countryside could be considered to be *badawi*s and *'umran badawi* refers to the culture of the countryside and not just that of the desert. *Badawi* can be applied to everyone outside the city, including bee-keepers and breeders of silk worms. Early on in the *Muqaddima*, Ibn Khaldun made it clear that there was no hard and fast distinction between the nomadic Bedouin of the desert and the mostly sedentary agricultural folk. "Those who live by agriculture or animal husbandry cannot avoid the call of the desert, because it alone offers wide fields, acres, pastures for animals, and other things that the settled areas do not offer."[34] Also, when he returned to the subject of agriculture, he had this to say: "This craft has existed especially in the desert, since, as we have stated before, it is prior to and older than sedentary life. Thus it became a Bedouin craft which is not known or practised by sedentary people, because all their conditions are secondary to those of desert life and their crafts, thus, secondary and subsequent to (Bedouin) crafts."[35] Ibn Khaldun also noted that the desert-dwelling Bedouin were economically dependent on the towns for buying and selling.

Similarly, when Ibn Khaldun used the word "Arab," its sense depended on context. The first meaning was straightforwardly ethnic and referred to all those who were racially Arab. Ibn Khaldun was, as already noted, proud of his Arab lineage, whose origins he traced back to the Hadramawt in the southwest corner of the Arabian Peninsula. But he often used the word pejoratively to refer to those Arabs who were nomadic invaders. They had "a savage nature" and were "people who plunder and cause damage." "Places that succumb to the Arabs are quickly ruined."[36] Yemen, Iraq, and Syria had all been ruined by the Arabs.[37] Evidently, there is an ambivalence here. He deplored the savagery and destructiveness of the nomadic Arab invaders and yet at the same time he praised their courage, austerity, and their loyalty to one another.

THE LEGEND OF THE BANU HILAL

The ruinous fate suffered by Yemen, Iraq, and Syria allegedly befell North Africa in the eleventh century when the Arab tribes of the Banu Hilal and the Banu Sulaym were sent from Egypt by an Egyptian vizier to invade Ifriqiyya. Ibn Khaldun described how these Arab nomads, like "a swarm of locusts" (*jarad muntashir*), brought devastation to its plains and depopulated areas that once were densely settled. (The reference to locusts has a Qur'anic resonance, since in Sura 7, locusts were one of the plagues inflicted by God on Pharaoh's godless people.) Ruins testified to the havoc brought about by these Arabs. Strong government became impossible.[38] Pastoralism replaced settled agriculture in many areas. (He also thought that it was this invasion that spread a version of colloquial Arabic among the Berbers.) He was an enthusiastic admirer of the popular epic, the *Sira of the Banu Hilal*, devoted to the legendary exploits of the tribal confederacy of the Banu Hilal and their fight against the Berbers.[39]

In recent decades Ibn Khaldun's version of the Hilali apocalypse in North Africa has been challenged. There are indications that the Zirid dynasty was already in decline and pastoralism may have gained ground as the cities' trade and demand for agricultural products was declining. It is not true that an Egyptian vizier sent the Hilali Arabs to attack Zirid Tunis in the mid-eleventh century. There was no invasion of North Africa comparable to "a swarm of locusts." Initially the Arabs came by invitation and served the local dynasties as mercenaries. The Zirid sultan in Tunis al-Mu'izz recruited the Banu Hilal to fight against rebellious Berbers in the hinterland. The Hilali migration into underpopulated North Africa was probably a slow business lasting some fifty years.[40] As we shall see in chapter 10, Ibn Khaldun's use of the word "Arab" in a pejorative sense was to play a large part in French colonialist discourse in the nineteenth and twentieth centuries.

BERBERS

Berbers are the indigenous inhabitants of North Africa. Berber communities are found across the region from the Atlantic coast to the Egyptian oasis of Siwa, but most Berbers were and are found in what is now Morocco. The term "Berber," derived from the Latin "*barbari*," meant "outsider" and was imposed on those inhabitants by the Romans. Berber is not, like Arabic, part of the Semitic family. The Berber language is Hamitic and is broken up into a number of mutually incomprehensible dialects. A written form of Berber existed, but it was difficult to use and therefore the Berbers mostly composed their written histories and legends in Arabic. Though the Berbers put up a lot of resistance to the Arab conquest of North Africa in the seventh and eighth centuries, by the fourteenth century they had become Islamized and many Berbers spoke Arabic, especially in the cities. Politically the Berbers were in the ascendant by then and the main ruling dynasties were all of Berber descent (though the medieval Berbers did not think of themselves as one people). There were three broad tribal confederacies, Sanhaja, Zanata, and Masmuda, and three corresponding dialects. Berber identity was based on tribal affiliation, whether real or fictitious.

In the 'Ibar Ibn Khaldun described the Zanata as one of the most ancient peoples of the Maghreb, before going on to remark how Arabized they were in their costumes, their rearing of camels and horses, their practice of winter and summer pasturage, their raiding, and their resistance to authority. Though quite widely dispersed, they were mostly to be found in the central Maghreb.[41] The Merinids of Fez and 'Abd al-Wadids of Tlemcen belonged to two closely related Zanata clans. (But, though the Merinid rulers were Berbers, they tended to favor Arabs when making official appointments.) The Hafsids came from the Masmuda confederacy. The Masmuda tribes were to be found in the highlands of the far west of the Maghreb. Much of the territory they occupied was suitable for agriculture and arboriculture.[42] The Dawawida, the Arab tribe that played such a prominent part in events during Ibn Khaldun's time in North Africa, occupied the plains in the region of Bougie and Constantine.[43] There was a broad tendency for nomadic Arab tribes to occupy the lowlands in the Maghreb and for the Berbers to be settled in the highlands. But this was not absolute and, for example, there were numerous camel-rearing Berbers in the desert and transhumant Arabs in the highlands, while many Arab tribes who were of nomadic origin had become settled peasants.

Despite Ibn Khaldun's claim to an Arab lineage and his multifarious dealings with the Arabs of the Maghreb, his *Kitab al-'Ibar* seems to have been originally planned to be a history of the Berbers but then it was expanded to cover the Arab tribes and dynasties of North Africa. Later yet the achievements of other races and dynasties were added. *'Ibar*, which was initially intended to explain the underlying dynamics of Berber history, worked backwards from current Berber dynasties to earlier ones.

Ibn Khaldun's history was full of praise for the Berbers. *Mafakhir al-Barbar* (boasts of the Berbers) was already an established literary genre in Arabic. A chapter of the *'Ibar* was devoted to the "Virtues and noble qualities of the Berbers who have risen to the highest ranks of power, political authority and kingship." The Berbers were "a powerful, formidable, brave and numerous people; a true people like so many others this world has seen—like the Arabs, the Persians, the Greeks, and the Romans." They were a race whose past achievements, particularly military ones, entitled them to be ranked with the other great races of the world. They had been famed for such moral qualities as honesty, hospitality, charity, and strength in adversity. But in Ibn Khaldun's own time wealth and decadence had brought them low.[44] In the *'Ibar* Ibn Khaldun revealed himself to be specifically a partisan for the Zanata Berbers, the tribe to which the Merinids belonged.

GENEALOGY

Genealogy (*'ilm al-nasab*) was one of Ibn Khaldun's most consistent preoccupations.[45] The science was believed to have had its origins among the Bedouin of the Arabian Peninsula. For Ibn Khaldun, expertise in genealogy was a specialty of the nomadic Arabs, while townspeople and sedentary folk had much less need for expertise in lineages. Urban solidarity tended to be based on affinal relations—that is relationships through marriage. He was aware that some genealogies were invented traditions and that lineages might be fabricated for political purposes. Ancestors were retrospectively discovered who might be useful for cementing alliances or invoking protection. Lineages, real or invented, served to reinforce 'asabiyya. One rather simple method Ibn Khaldun used to check the genuineness of a proposed lineage was to count the number of generations it took to reach the purported founding father of a line of descent. If there were fewer than three ancestors per hundred years in that line of descent, then it was probably an invented lineage.

Ibn Khaldun's awareness of the potential fraudulence of so many ancestral origins led him to doubt all sorts of alleged historical events. It was common throughout the Muslim world for communities to seek to enhance their status by claiming that their ancestors came from the Arabian Peninsula. Thus the Sanhaja and Kutama Berbers claimed descent from Yemeni troops left behind after their ruler Ifriqish had invaded North Africa in pre-Islamic times. Ibn Khaldun found the whole story ridiculous.[46] The mythical Yemeni conquest of North Africa was said to have reached its limit when the Yemeni army reached the impassable Sand River, but Ibn Khaldun wondered how it was that, in more recent times, no traveler had reported coming across this river of flowing sand.[47] Even so he was prepared to allow that the Sanhaja Berbers might have had Yemeni origin, having migrated from there when the Sheba Dam burst.

On the other hand, he thought that some Berbers might have had a Palestinian origin, as they might be Canaanite or Amalekite descendants of defeated remnants of Goliath's army. In the 'Ibar he stated that the Zanata Berbers descended from Canaan (a biblical toponym, which Ibn Khaldun took to be a person, whom he identified as Shem, the son of Noah) and he rejected the view of contemporary Zanata genealogists that they descended from Goliath, who was alleged to be an Amalekite.[48] There were various legends about the Arabian or Old Testament origins of the various Berber tribes and Ibn Khaldun was not entirely successful in sorting through them, though he did reject some claims to Palestinian or Yemeni origins. It should be noted that Ibn Khaldun did not make a hard-edged distinction between Arab and Berber and he also believed that some Arab tribes were Berber in origin. He contradicted himself on the genealogies of the Lamtuna and Sanhaja families.[49] In short he was thoroughly confused about the origins and ethnic identity of the Berbers and, of course, the medieval Berbers were too. They do not seem to have thought of themselves as a single race.

Romantically fictional lineages abounded and, for example, the Dawawida Arabs claimed descent from the Barmecides, the clan of Persian administrators, who had served the 'Abbasid caliph Harun al-Rashid, while the Banu Fadl, the paramount Bedouin clan in Mamluk Syria, traced their lineage back to a sister of Harun.[50]

Though he was well aware of the doubtful status of many genealogies, Ibn Khaldun took a more relaxed attitude regarding certain claims. For example, he was an admirer of the achievements of the Almohad dynasty and especially of their founder Ibn Tumart who had claimed to be the Mahdi and to be descended from Muhammad. With regard to that alleged descent, Ibn Khaldun wrote those who doubted Ibn Tumart's claim had no proof and went on: "Were it established that he himself claimed such descent, his claim could not be disproved, because people are to be believed regarding the descent they claim for themselves."[51]

The piece of historical deconstruction that earned Ibn Khaldun his greatest notoriety was his defense of the claim of the Shi'i Fatimid caliphs, who had ruled in Egypt from 969 until 1171, to be descended from Fatima, the daughter of Muhammad and wife of the Prophet's cousin, 'Ali. Inevitably this Fatimid lineage had been denied and disparaged by historians working under the patronage of the Sunni 'Abbasid caliphs in Iraq. "They base themselves in this respect on stories that were made up in favour of the weak 'Abbasid caliphs by people who wanted to ingratiate themselves with them through accusations against their active opponents and who (therefore) liked to say all kinds of bad things about their enemies."[52] Had there been doubts about the lineage of the Fatimids, they would not have succeeded in gathering support among the Berbers in North Africa. Ibn Khaldun's admiration for Fatimid achievements is clear and his defense of the Fatimid pedigree led to (unjust) accusations that he was a crypto-Shi'ite. He admired their success, but not their Shi'i doctrines.

As Ibn Khaldun recognized, genealogies were constructed to fit social needs. They were usually designed to incorporate separate groups within a single tribal confederacy, rather than to exclude groups from that confederacy. Tribal genealogies were works of fiction that were being continuously redrafted in order to fit the needs of the moment. Incidentally, Ibn Khaldun's own genealogy may have been fabricated at some earlier date in Muslim Spain, for the *un* ending was commonly added to the names of Christian converts to Islam in Andalusia.[53] Moreover, Robert Serjeant, the great expert on the history of South Arabia, noted that he had found no references at all to the Banu Khaldun in that region.[54]

What led Ibn Khaldun, an Arab who was a specialist in negotiating with Arab tribesmen, to set out to write a history that was initially intended to celebrate the ancestry and achievements of the Berbers? Although he immensely admired al-Mas'udi's ambitious history of the world, al-Mas'udi was not particularly well informed about the Maghreb and this may have encouraged Ibn Khaldun to begin by filling this gap. But possibly also it was in the expectation of presenting the finished work to the Berber ruler of Fez, or maybe to the Berber ruler of Tunis or the Berber ruler of Tlemcen, and thereby securing greater scholarly recognition and with it political promotion. This was standard practice and, for example, it has been noted that Ibn Marzuq composed the *Musnad*, his chronicle of the reign of the Merinid Abu'l-Hasan, in order to attract the patronage of a later Merinid sultan. Similarly, Ibn Khaldun's brother Yahya, while in the service of the 'Abd al-Wadid ruler of Tlemcen, wrote a history of the 'Abd al-Wadids.

WISDOM LITERATURE AND THE *MUQADDIMA*

It should be noted that the *Muqaddima* does not restrict itself to strictly historical issues. In parts, it rather reads as if it should be classed among those works that are known as "mirrors for princes" (in Arabic *nasihat al-muluk* and in Persian *andarz*). In the *Muqaddima*'s preliminary remarks, Ibn Khaldun acknowledges a debt to the wise sayings and improving anecdotes ascribed to such historical or legendary pre-Islamic Persians as the Zoroastrian priest Mobedhan and the Sassanian ruler Anurshirwan, as well as to the later mirrors produced by Ibn al-Muqaffa' and al-Turtushi. Chapter 3 is devoted to "dynasties, royal authority, the caliphate, government ranks, and all that goes with these things." Ibn Khaldun included in this chapter the complete text of a letter written in 821 by Tahir ibn al-Husayn, a general in the service of the 'Abbasid caliph al-Ma'mun, to his son instructing him on how rulers and governors should conduct their affairs.[55] This letter has been described by a modern scholar as follows: "It is a sophisticated theoretical exposition of the ethos of rulership and the qualities of the perfect ruler, tightly constructed and unadorned by historical examples or anecdotes, and emphasises the ruler's dependence on God and on Islamic religion as the mainspring of all his doings."[56]

Ibn Khaldun also drew heavily on a compendium entitled *Sirr al-asrar* (Secret of Secrets), which was believed to be a letter composed by Aristotle for the guidance of Alexander the Great, though in fact the imposture may have been put together as late as the tenth century. (One of Alexander's greatest merits in the eyes of medieval scholars was that he had listened to scholarly advice.) Ibn Khaldun misidentified the *Sirr al-asrar* as being Aristotle's *Politics*.[57] According to the *Sirr al-asrar*, Aristotle gained his wisdom from the Persians and Indians. Though the core of the *Sirr al-asrar* offered guidance on how a king should conduct his affairs, the encyclopedic scope of the work ran much more widely than that and covered topics in physiognomy, astrology, alchemy, magic, and medicine. This work, translated as *Secretum Secretorum* was as popular in Christendom as it was in the Islamic world. Since it was supposed to be by Aristotle, Ibn Khaldun took it very seriously, but, as he observed, the discussion of politics got mixed in with a lot of other things. He cited its sententious extended metaphor: "The world is a garden, the fence of which is the dynasty. The dynasty is an authority through which life is given to proper behaviour. Proper behaviour is a policy directed by the ruler. The soldiers are helpers who are maintained by money. Money is sustenance brought together by the subjects. The subjects are servants who are protected by justice. Justice is something familiar, and through it the world persists. The world is a garden."[58] Three such virtuous circles feature in the *Muqaddima*, variously attributed to Aristotle, Bahram, and Anushirwan. This extended political metaphor, known as the Circle of Justice, made a great impression on the Turks, when, centuries later, they came to read Ibn Khaldun. Of course, the real version of Aristotle's *Politics* centered round the ideal city, but, as far as Ibn Khaldun was concerned, there was little or nothing ideal about cities. Neither Tunis nor Fez seemed likely to become the sort of city that philosophers had dreamed of.

Elsewhere in the *Muqaddima*, Ibn Khaldun, who was obsessed with predicting the future, quoted pseudo-Aristotle on *hisab al-nim* (predictions based on the numerical value of letters).[59] Pseudo-Aristotle was also an authority on the use of banners and trumpets to frighten the enemy in battle.[60] Besides citing pseudo-Aristotle on political and ethical matters, Ibn Khaldun also drew on *andarz* materials, much of which featured the wise sayings and deeds of the pre-Islamic Persian emperors. It is possible (though unlikely) that he dreamt of reading the *Muqaddima* and the *'Ibar* to a young ruler and of further commenting on the texts in order to guide him, thereby reenacting the role of Aristotle with Alexander. He may have imagined himself mentoring a future philosopher-king of the Maghreb, but, if so, he was to be disappointed. After finishing the first draft of his great work, he left Qal'at Banu Salama and returned to Tunis and there he was to dedicate the first draft of the book to Abu'l-Abbas, the city's Hafsid Berber ruler.

THE 'IBAR

The *Kitab al-'ibar wa diwan al-mubtada wa'l-khabar* (The Book of Warning and Collection of New Things and Historical Information) is very long and in its standard Arabic edition it runs to more than three thousand pages. It is a history of tribes and of the dynasties produced by some of the tribes, rather than a year-by-year chronicle. (By contrast, historians writing in fourteenth-century North Africa, Egypt, and Syria tended to proceed year by year and to include lists of official appointments, as well as obituaries of the politically powerful and the pious.) As Ibn Khaldun worked on the *'Ibar*, he extended its scope to include not just Berber dynasties, but also Arab dynasties in the East, as well as in the West, and the Seljuq Turks, Mongols, Mamluks, Persians, Jews, and Franks. Nevertheless the history lacks the universalist scope of al-Mas'udi's *Muruj al-Dhahab*, since the *'Ibar*'s treatment of the history of the Franks, Turks, and other races is perfunctory. Ibn Khaldun only gave substantial coverage to regions where Arabic was spoken. Yet the days of the Arab were over, since the Turks had taken over from the Arabs in the east and the Berbers had taken over from them in the west.

Though Ibn Khaldun was a bold and original theorizer in the *Muqaddima*, when he actually came to write the history, of which the *Muqaddima* was supposed to serve as the prelude, it was pretty conventional stuff. As D. M. Dunlop put it, the *Kitab al-'Ibar* "is in general what one might expect from an eighth/fourteenth century compiler," and Dunlop went on to remark, "Most of the faults for which he blamed his predecessors are conspicuous in his own *History*. Nor could it be otherwise, since for the most part he contented himself with abridging them."[61] Talbi's article on Ibn Khaldun in the *Encyclopedia of Islam* similarly noted that the content of the *'Ibar* does not live up to the theoretical promise of the *Muqaddima*, but added: "This is obvious, but it could not have been otherwise. No one man could write alone a universal history according to the demands of the *Muqaddima*."[62]

Robert Brunschvig noted that Ibn Khaldun made a number of mistakes regarding the early history of the Almohads.[63] Donald Little, who made a close comparative study of Ibn Khaldun's account of Mamluk history in the 1290s, concluded that "In spite of the great expectations raised by Ibn Khaldun in his *Muqaddima* for a new approach in Muslim historiography, his own chronicle, *Kitab al-Ibar* fails to fulfil his standards, and we find him plodding in the same path worn by his predecessors" and Little later added, "his version has no claim whatsoever to distinction and is unimportant as a source for the period."[64]

Though this is true, the *'Ibar* does contain some information about the later Bahri Mamluk period that is not found in other sources. For example, Ibn Khaldun reports the mamluks as using cannons in Cairo and Alexandria in 1367 and 1369. (David Ayalon in *Gunpowder and Firearms in the Mamluk Kingdom: A Challenge to a Medieval Society* (1956) had argued that the mamluks only started to make use of artillery toward the end of the fifteenth century.)[65] More obviously both the *'Ibar* and the *Ta'rif* are important sources for the later history of Egypt and Syria in the Circassian Mamluk period from 1382, for which Ibn Khaldun was able to draw upon information provided to him by the sultans al-Zahir Barquq and al-Nasir Faraj, as well as by senior emirs who were protagonists in the power struggles of the period. (On this, see chapter 5.) Moreover, it has been widely agreed that the sections of the *'Ibar* that deal with the Berbers and Arabs in the Maghreb do provide useful facts and insights that are not found in other chronicles and that part of the *'Ibar* is systematically laid out. First, the territory is described, then a supposed genealogy is set out, and finally the constituent tribes deriving from a common ancestor are discussed one by one.

More generally, Ibn Khaldun was weak on chronology. For much of the time he had so few books on hand as he wrote that he had to rely on his amazing, yet still imperfect, memory. If he had intended the events chronicled in the *'Ibar* to illustrate the ideas found in the *Muqaddima*, then he should have provided the chronicle with more markers to indicate that this was what he was doing. One possibility (and it is only a possibility) is that he first wrote the draft of those chapters of the *'Ibar* that dealt with North African dynasties and only then turned to writing the *Muqaddima*. So the *Muqaddima* might be viewed as being a vastly extended series of afterthoughts that had come to Ibn Khaldun while he had been working on the narrative histories of the various Berber and Arab dynasties. But, having then produced this profound overview of the underlying processes in those dynastic histories, he was never able to reconfigure his narrative history in such a way that it could fully illustrate the propositions advanced in the *Muqaddima*.

The *'Ibar* downplayed the role of personalities and individual actions and it made little use of anecdotes. Broad causes lay behind big events. Fairly bald summaries of those events may have been intended to demonstrate the workings of historical laws, though usually this was implicit and, though the focus may have been on the management of power and, more specifically, the operation of 'asabiyya, the reader has to work hard in order to find in the 'Ibar the workings of the general laws of history as they had been set out in the Muqaddima.

Since Ibn Khaldun was a contemporary of the French chronicler Jean Froissart (1337–c. 1404), it may be instructive to compare and contrast their approaches to the writing of history. Froissart gained much of his information from interviewing the protagonists in the great events of his lifetime and he started writing his Chroniques, a record of aristocratic chivalry and warfare in the 1360s. Its standard edition runs to fifteen volumes. It opens with the following sentence (in Lord Berners's famous translation into English, done in the early sixteenth century): "To the intent that the honourable and noble adventures of feats of arms, done and achieved by the wars of France and England, should notably be enregistered and put in perpetual memory, whereby the prewe and hardy may have ensample to encourage them in their well-doing, I, sir John Froissart, will treat and record an history of great louage and praise."[66]

The Hundred Years' War between England and France dominated the narrative and Froissart delighted in providing all the details of the battles, skirmishes, and sieges. Though he set out to celebrate chivalry, courtesy, and bravery, many of the events that he recorded reveal barbarism, treachery, and cruelty—notably the massacre carried out by the Black Prince after the capture of Limoges in 1370. Froissart loved flourish and display. The famous Dutch historian Jan Huizinga commented on Froissart's eye for colorful details, as in his description "of vessels at sea with their pavilions and streamers, with their rich decoration of many-coloured blazons, sparkling in the sunshine; or the play of reflected sunlight on the points of the lances, the gay colours of the pennons and banners, of a troop of cavaliers on the march."[67] But Ibn Khaldun did not paint word pictures and his narrative is almost uniformly colorless. Froissart relied heavily on dialogue to carry his stories along: Ibn Khaldun did not.

Froissart gave no thought to the underlying causes of the events he chronicled. He simply celebrated courage, ambition, honor, and fidelity, without reflection on their deeper meaning. By contrast, Ibn Khaldun's readiness to analyze, theorize, and produce generalizations based on the evidence gives his writing the perhaps delusive appearance of modernity. Froissart praised the courage and courtesy of noble warriors, whereas Ibn Khaldun had little praise for anything except conformity to the religious law. Heroism had little part to play in his history. Finally, Ibn Khaldun thought that the Black Death had changed everything, whereas Froissart barely mentions it.

Though Ibn Khaldun is famous today as a philosopher of history and as a writer of history, he does not seem to have regarded history as a separate discipline and so the study and writing of history was not included in his discussion of the sciences in chapter 6 of the *Muqaddima*.

CHAPTER FOUR

Underpinning the Methodology of the *Muqaddima*

PHILOSOPHY, THEOLOGY, AND JURISPRUDENCE

The *Muqaddima* is full of ideas about the nature of history and social developments. What were those ideas based on? In Rosenthal's translation of the opening page of the foreword to the *Muqaddima*, we read the following:

> The inner meaning of history . . . involves speculation and an attempt to get at the truth, subtle explanation of the causes and origins of existing things, and deep knowledge of the how and why of events. (History,) therefore, is firmly rooted in philosophy. It deserves to be accounted a branch of (philosophy).[1]

Here it seems that Ibn Khaldun is announcing without any ambiguity that he is a philosopher and that the *Muqaddima* should be considered a work of philosophy. But things are not what they seem. The normal Arabic word for "philosophy" was and is *falasifa* and a "philosopher" is a *faylasuf*. Plato was a *faylasuf* and so were Aristotle, Avicenna, Averroes, and al-Farabi. But the word that Rosenthal has translated as "philosophy" in the passage quoted above is *hikma*, and *hikma* has a subtly different range of meaning. It can be translated as "wisdom," or "what prevents one from ignorant behaviour." *Hikma* described those sciences that did not derive from the Qur'an and *hadith*. It was also used to describe a body of literature that offered aphorisms, wise counsel, and improving examples taken from the lives of kings, sages, and (yes) philosophers.

Sura 31 of the Qur'an, which bears the title "Luqman," is devoted to the legendary sage of that name, who was credited with many wise sayings, proverbs, and, later, fables. "Indeed, we gave Luqman wisdom (*hikma*)." There is also a saying attributed to the Prophet: "In poetry there is wisdom (*hikma*)." A *hakim* is one who possesses wisdom. The *Muqaddima* often quotes the wise sayings of *hakim*s, among them a Zoroastrian priest who he calls Mobedhan, the Sassanian ruler Anurshirwan, the Sassanian vizier Buzurjmihr, and the pseudo-Aristotle of the *Sirr al-asrar*.[2]

Some short anecdotes embodying *hikma* wisdom appear as makeweights in *The Thousand and One Nights*. In "Anurshirwan and the Peasant Girl," after Anurshirwan has received generous hospitality from a girl in a village, he decides to tax that village more heavily, but changes his mind when the wise girl says, "I have heard men of intelligence saying that when a ruler's good intentions towards his people change, their blessings vanish and their advantages diminish."[3] In the story, "Alexander the Great and the Poor King," Alexander passes through a village that is so poor that its inhabitants own nothing at all and they eat grass. Here Alexander is subjected to a series of homilies by its king on mortality, vanity, greed, and injustice. Alexander, impressed, offers the king half his empire, but he replies "Never! Never!" Alexander wants to know why. "Because all mankind are your enemies, thanks to the wealth and the kingdom that you have been given . . . whereas for me they are all true friends because I am content with my poverty. I have no kingdom, there is nothing that I want or seek in the world. I have no ambition here and set store by nothing except contentment." Alexander embraced the king and went on his way.[4] The story that follows, "King Anurshirwan the Just," delivers the message that it is the duty of the ruler to care for the prosperity of his subjects.[5] Plainly there was a strong moralizing content in *hikma* literature.

Hikma overlaps with *nasiha*, advice literature that was, nominally at least, addressed to kings. The belletrist Ibn al-Muqaffaʻ (eighth century) adapted and added to a group of Indian fables. His Arabic version of the fable collection, entitled *Kalila wa Dimna*, used animal stories to provide sage political advice. His *Risala al-sahaba* (Letter on the Companions [of the Caliph]) was addressed to the ʻAbbasid caliph al-Mansur and offered advice on how to govern well. Ibn Khaldun noted that Ibn al-Muqaffaʿ had sought to address many of the same problems that the *Muqaddima* sought to tackle, but without offering any proofs: "He merely mentioned them in passing in the (flowing) prose style and eloquent verbiage of the rhetorician."[6] Ibn Khaldun then passed on to mention the *Kitab Siraj al-muluk* (The Book of the Light of the Kings) by Abu Bakr al-Turtushi (1059–c.1130), a work in the same genre and one which also set out to tackle some of the same problems that the *Muqaddima* dealt with, but which relied on quoting the sayings of numerous ancient sages in an unsystematic and unanalytic fashion.[7] Ibn Khaldun quoted one particular example of *nasiha* literature at length in its entirety, "as the best treatment of politics that I have found." This was the *Risala* (letter) of a ninth-century general, Tahir ibn al-Husayn, which was addressed to his son, who was about to take up a provincial governorship. It gave advice on how he should comport himself in secular and religious affairs.[8] The *Risala*, which is sternly moralizing and full of banalities that would not be out of place in the mouth of Polonius, sits a little oddly in the *Muqaddima*. There could a religious dimension to advice. According to a *hadith*: "To give advice (*nasiha*) is religion (*din*)." Of course, Ibn Khaldun's own ideas about history and statesmanship were religiously based and moralistic, but they were more subtly woven into arguments that are dispassionately phrased and more profound in their aims.

IBN KHALDUN'S DISTANCE FROM PHILOSOPHY

Although Ibn Khaldun might look to us like a philosopher, he did not think of himself as one. In his preliminary remarks in the *Muqaddima*, he boasted of the thoroughness and depth of his study of royal authority and dynasties, before announcing, "We became aware of these things with God's help and without the instruction of Aristotle or the teaching of the Môbedhân."[9] Later he declared, "It should be known the opinion the philosophers hold is wrong in all its aspects."[10] During his lifetime no one called him a philosopher. Philosophy did not flourish in the fourteenth-century Maghreb, since the Merinid rulers and the clerics that they patronized did not favor it and it was not on the syllabus of the *madrasa*s. Exceptionally al-Abili taught Ibn Khaldun and others the rational sciences, but we do not have much idea of what that amounted to. One text that Ibn Khaldun did study with al-Abili was the *Muwatta'*, the legal compendium of Malik ibn Anas. If al-Abili did indeed teach philosophy to Ibn Khaldun, then it is likely that Averroes would have featured prominently in his teaching. According to Ibn al-Khatib, Ibn Khaldun later abridged several books by Averroes, as well as the *Muhassal fi usul al-din* (Compendium on the Principles of Theology) of the twelfth-century theologian Fakhr al-Din al-Razi.[11] But these were youthful essays of which Ibn Khaldun was not proud and he did not mention them in the autobiographical *Ta'rif*. Moreover, by the time he came to compose the *Muqaddima*, he was ready to denounce the practice of producing abridgements of other people's books.[12] So presumably he had repented of these early essays.

In the twelfth century, Averroes, as he was known in medieval Europe (though his real name in Arabic was Ibn Rushd), was the most famous and controversial philosopher in the Islamic world. He was born in Cordova in 1126 and died in Marrakesh in 1198. He produced extensive commentaries on Aristotle's works. He advocated the use of reason to validate the Islamic religion. He had an elitist view of religion and believed that only philosophers were capable of fully grasping its meaning, while the masses had to be satisfied with stories, metaphors, and simplifications.

But Averroes, the last of the great medieval Arab philosophers, was fighting a rearguard defense of philosophy that was under attack from theologians, and, though translations of his works were to be much read in the universities of Christian Europe, he had little influence on later generations of thinkers in the Muslim world. Though Averroes had attempted a thorough refutation of *The Incoherence of the Philosophers* by the eleventh-century religious scholar al-Ghazali, the latter's anti-philosophic arguments remained more influential and it seems clear that Ibn Khaldun preferred al-Ghazali to Averroes. "He who wants to arm himself against the philosophers in the field of dogmatic beliefs should turn to the works of al-Ghazali."[13]

While noting Averroes's fame, Ibn Khaldun hardly mentioned him by name, except to disagree with him on peripheral issues. For example, he was critical of Averroes's view that the equator was in a symmetrical position between cultivable regions, because no allowance had been made for the fact that the southern part of the hemisphere was mostly water.[14] For Averroes, following the Greek philosophers, the city embodied the highest form of political life and those whose families had lived longest in the city enjoyed the most prestige. This was obviously very different from Ibn Khaldun's way of thinking and he explicitly rejected it: "I should like to know how long residence in a town can help anyone (to gain prestige) if he does not belong to a group that makes him feared." Averroes grew up in a time and a place (Andalusia) where he had little experience of *'asabiyya*.[15] His version of political philosophy was, as it were, confined within city walls, whereas Ibn Khaldun's theories comprehended life in the deserts and mountains.

In "The Refutation of Philosophers," which is part of chapter 6 of the *Muqaddima*, Ibn Khaldun wrote of philosophers "poring over the *Kitab al-Shifa'*, the *Isharat*, the *Najah* (of Avicenna), and over Averroes's abridgement of 'The Text' (*Organon*) and other works of Aristotle. They wear out the pages of these works. They firmly ground themselves in the arguments they contain, and they desire to find in them that portion of happiness they believe that they contain. They do not realise that in this way they only add to the obstacles on the road to happiness."[16]

Nevertheless, there may have been an unacknowledged debt to Averroes's *Exposition of the Republic*. Having no access to Aristotle's *Politics*, Averroes had produced an extended commentary on an abridged Arabic version of Plato's *Republic*. In that commentary he had stressed the ruler's duty to educate his people and had also had argued for the Shari'a as superior to other forms of law not only because it was divinely inspired, but also because it made happiness possible within the state. Moreover, the idea that luxury was a solvent of virtue could be found in Plato's *Republic* and in Averroes's reading of the translation of that work.

After Averroes's death, his writings were not much read in the Arab lands and Ibn Khaldun was one of the few intellectuals to make any use at all of them. But mostly what Ibn Khaldun took from Averroes, or at least shared with him, was not a philosophic doctrine, but a mood—pessimism. Averroes believed that good government of a city would in the long run be doomed by the lust of the important men for power and money and thus degenerate into tyranny. The perfect Islamic regime had not lasted longer than the time of the Prophet and first four Rightful Caliphs. The *fitna*, the struggle that broke out between 'Ali and Mu'awiya in 656, was the watershed.[17] Ibn Khaldun noted that since Mu'awiya, the founder of the Umayyad dynasty of caliphs, was fat, he was the first caliph who was allowed to sit on a throne.[18] Nevertheless he was a great admirer of Mu'awiya, in part, perhaps because this caliph relied on *'asabiyya* to take power and he thought that Mu'awiya should have been ranked with the first four Rightful Caliphs. But under the later Umayyads, the caliphate, brought low by the pursuit of wealth and then of pleasure, degenerated into a tyranny. Then there was a revival of good government under the 'Abbasids. "Not one of those people (the early 'Abbasids) had anything to do with effeminate prodigality or luxury in matters of clothing, jewelry, or the kind of food they took. They still retained the tough desert attitude and the simple state of Islam."[19] But eventually the same process of decay occurred. According to Ibn Khaldun, though the early Ummayad caliphs and the early 'Abbasid caliphs provided a reasonable amount of justice and security, later luxury and indolence took their toll, and the caliphs were caliphs only in name, for their rule had become merely kingship (*mulk*).

CYCLICAL THEORIES OF HISTORY
AND THEIR UNDERLYING PESSIMISM

Intellectual pessimism was a characteristic of the age. We have already noted Ibn al-Khatib's gloomy vision of history and later we shall remark on the similarly downbeat view of history expounded by the Egyptian historian al-Maqrizi. The Qur'an had declared that every regime was ultimately doomed: "To every nation a term; when their term comes they shall not put it back by a single hour nor put it forward" (Qur'an 7:34).

Perhaps also a pessimistic view of the fate of dynasties was implicit in Arabic political vocabulary. *Dawla* means "dynasty." As Bernard Lewis has noted: "The basic meaning of the root *d-w-l*, which also occurs in other Semitic languages, is 'to turn' or to 'alternate'—as for example in the Qur'anic verses 'These [happy and unhappy] days, we cause them to alternate (*nudawiluha*) among men.'" It also had the sense of "turn" as in a turn in rule or office and hence when the 'Abbasid caliphs replaced the Umayyads, it was described as their turn, or *dawla*, and hence by extension *dawla* came also to mean dynasty. But it seems implicit in the word that the turn will be of limited duration and then it will be the turn of another dynasty. Lewis suggests that "It is possible that cyclical theories of politics, derived from Greek or Persian sources, may have contributed to this use of the word *dawla*."[20]

Ibn Khaldun discussed the calculations of the ninth-century astrologer and polymath al-Kindi regarding the predestined end of the 'Abbasid dynasty. (Allegedly al-Kindi had predicted that its fall and the destruction of Baghdad would take place in the thirteenth century.) Though Ibn Khaldun refers to the relevant treatise as *al-Jafr*, he had not actually seen it, and he may have been thinking of al-Kindi's *Risala fi mulk al-'Arab*, a treatise that predicted the end of the caliphate and was one of the first treatises to use *dawla* in the sense of dynasty. The authors of a tenth-century encyclopedia, the *Rasa'il Ikhwan al-Safa'* (Letters of the Brethren of Purity), argued that *dawla* passed from dynasty to dynasty or nation to nation every 240 years.[21]

Pessimism tends to be a characteristic of cyclical theories of history.

In Ibn Khaldun's case, the pessimism may have been confirmed by what he perceived to be the successive failures of various dynasties to impose unity over the Maghreb, as well as from the murders of his brother and of his esteemed friend Ibn al-Khatib and, perhaps also, from his memories of the Black Death. Moreover, he saw that the glory days of the Arabs were over and the Berbers and

Turks were taking over. Ruins and abandoned settlements were all around him. Who in the fourteenth-century Arab world could have found grounds for thinking that the world was getting better?

The late Patricia Crone, a historian of Islam, has drawn attention to the parallel between Ibn Khaldun's cyclical theory of history and that of Confucian thinkers. In both Ibn Khaldun and the Chinese versions, the fall of settled dynasties was inevitably brought about by tribal conquerors. But the Chinese evaluation of the process was very different from that of Ibn Khaldun and really rather glum: "Tribal conquest belonged at the rock bottom of the cycle, and of tribal decay the Chinese had no real notion: being barbarians, the tribesmen possessed no virtue that could be corrupted. That barbarians could not govern China as such was taken as axiomatic . . . the transition from tribal to settled rule could not fail to be a transition to better, stronger and more enduring government." Ibn Khaldun by contrast viewed things from the tribesmen's point of view and regarded tribal conquest as the high point of the cycle and settled civilization was effeminate.[22]

Polybius (c. 203–c. 120 BC), a Greek chronicler of the decline of Greece and of Rome's rise to power, sketched out a cyclical historical sequence in which monarchy was followed by aristocracy, and then by democracy, before a monarchy could be established again, and so the cycle recommenced. More generally, those Greeks and Romans who thought about history, such as Hesiod, Sallust, and Tacitus, were encouraged by organic metaphors to posit the inevitability of the decline of states and civilizations. The age of gold would give way to the age of silver, then bronze, and ultimately to the age of iron. Vico was steeped in the reading of these and other classic authors.

La scienza nuova, by the Neapolitan priest Giambattista Vico (1668–1744), was published in three versions between 1725 and 1744. Like Ibn Khaldun, Vico has been described as a man born out of his time, "neither more nor less than the nineteenth century in embryo" as the philosopher Benedetto Croce put it. Vico believed that it was possible to discover the general laws underlying historical processes. Like Ibn Khaldun, Vico drew on his study of law to inform his theories about history. Like Ibn Khaldun, Vico's study of history had a religious impetus. Like Ibn Khaldun, Vico had an exalted view of history, for his "new science" was history, a science that dealt with the real world and that, because history was made by men, was perfectly knowable by men. It was a truth beyond all question that since the world of civil society has certainly been made by men, "its principles are therefore to be found within the modifications of our own mind." Societies are like individuals, for they are born, mature, decay, and die. But as one society perished another arose in its place. *Ricorsi* (recurrence) inevitably followed *corsi* (sequence). There were three phases: superstitious, heroic, and human—corresponding to theocracy, aristocracy, and democracy. Vico identified seven civilizations: Hebrews, Chaldaeans, Scythians, Phoenicians, Egyptians, Greeks, and Romans. He had a dark view of history as being driven by ferocity, ambition, and avarice. Nations advance from barbarism to make conquests, but then as they become settled and secure, they are weakened and fall victim to a new generation of barbarians. Luxury had an important role in the decay of empires. In an early essay, *On the Sumptuous Feasts of the Romans*, Vico argued that Rome, in conquering Asia, had been conquered by Asian luxury and, in the same way, the Spanish Empire in Vico's own time was being corrupted by the wealth it had acquired in the Americas. But Vico's insights were almost entirely ignored by his contemporaries.[23]

Cyclical theories of history embody prophecies, since they are as much about the future as they are about the past. One of the best known of theories of cyclical history was produced by Oswald Spengler under the title *Der Untergang des Abendlands* (The Decline of the West).[24] This two-volume work was produced in the wake of the catastrophic German and Austrian defeat in the First World War. In it Spengler predicted a doom-laden future for Faustian Europe. With all the confidence of an autodidact, he predicted that the triumph of European materialism would in turn engender violence, but the concomitant violence would rejuvenate Europe. He worked with a seasonal metaphor, according to which all civilizations progress from spring to winter, as well as with the organic metaphor of birth, maturity, and death. He identified eight civilizations that had been subject to the law of rise and decline.

Like Ibn Khaldun, Spengler was somewhat hostile to the urban culture and presented the phenomenon of the "world city" with its population of rootless parasites as constituting the last phase of a civilization. Spengler's ideas strongly influenced Arnold Toynbee and Toynbee's claim to have been also influenced by Ibn Khaldun will be discussed in a later chapter.

Another late and unrelated parallel to Ibn Khaldun's model of decline and fall over three generations can be found in a novel by Thomas Mann, *Buddenbrooks, Verfall einer Familie* (Buddenbrooks, The Decline of a Family), first published in German in 1901. This book traced the history of a family in North Germany over four generations in the nineteenth century. The robust and jovial Consul Johann presides over a prosperous and respected family business, but in the generations that follow both the business and the family decline. Finally Hanno, a sickly intellectual, withdraws from life and dies of typhoid. Decadence, disease, and death have brought the once-mighty Buddenbrooks clan low. Mann's novel was greatly influenced by his reading of the philosopher Schopenhauer's *The World as Will and Representation* (1818). Bertrand Russell has described that book's pessimistic doctrine as follows: "Will has no fixed end, which if achieved would bring contentment. Although death must conquer in the end, we pursue our futile purposes 'as we blow out a soap bubble as long and as large as possible, although we know perfectly well that it will burst.' There is no such thing as happiness, for an unfulfilled wish causes pain and attainment brings only satiety."[25] Schopenhauer judged that it was pointless to seek to reform political institutions or society since their failings merely reflected the dreadful failings of human nature. Man is the source of the evils that befall him. (Incidentally Mann was to compare reading Spengler to reading Schopenhauer for the first time.)

Buddenbrooks traced the rise and decline of a dynasty. In his novel *Malhamat al-harafish* (1977, translated as *The Harafish* in 1993) the Nobel-Prize-winning Egyptian novelist Naguib Mahfouz presented a somewhat similar narrative, as he followed the rise and decline of al-Nagi dynasty in a slummy part of Cairo. *Malhamat* literally means "slaughterings," but the term is also applied to a genre of apocalyptic prophetic literature. The *harafish* are the common people of the alley and Ashur al-Nagi, a very strong, energetic, and puritanical man, establishes an ascendancy over them as their gang-lord. His son and grandson, though they are somewhat less impressive, manage to maintain that overlordship for a while, but then in the latter part of the reign of the grandson there is a terrible deterioration: "He no longer looked the part of a clan chief: he was bloated and indolent, addicted to stimulants and luxury. His stomach swelled out in front, his buttocks drooped behind, and he ate so much that he would fall asleep as he sat in his accustomed place in the café."[26] Mahfouz's fine novel (for it is one of his best) continues as a fantastical chronicle of the cyclical rise and decline of clan fortunes. Surely Mahfouz must have read Ibn Khaldun?

All civilizations are mortal. In 1919 the poet and essayist Paul Valéry produced a gloomy vision of the future:

> We had long heard tell of whole worlds that had vanished, of empires sunk without trace, gone down with all their men and all their machines into the unexplorable depths of the centuries, with their gods and their laws, their academies and their sciences pure and applied, their grammars and their dictionaries, their Classics, their Romantics, and their Symbolists, their critics and the critics of their critics . . . We were aware that the visible earth is made of ashes, and that ashes signify something. Through the obscure depths of history we could make out the phantoms of great ships laden with riches and intellect; we could not count them. But the disasters that had sent them down were, after all, none of our affair.[27]

Ibn Khaldun took a similarly bleak view of society and politics and set out no program of reform. He did not even bother to discuss the utopian program of the perfect city (state) (*al-madina al-fadila*) as set out by the philosopher al-Farabi (c. 872–950). (Incidentally it is striking how very little influence works on political philosophy by thinkers such as al-Farabi and Averroes had on the actual practice of politics in the Islamic lands.) Ibn Khaldun conceded that the study of formal logic had some use, but philosophers went too far in deploying it in the realm of faith. Intellect should not be employed to determine divine matters. Reason was like a scale, good for weighing gold, but useless for weighing mountains. Since man's mind is finite, it cannot understand the universe, which is infinite. One should not use reason in speculations about the oneness of God, the world of the unseen, the nature of prophecy, divine attributes, or other similarly holy and difficult matters.[28]

IBN KHALDUN VERSUS ARISTOTLE

Mainstream philosophy in the medieval Islamic lands consisted of variations on a Neoplatonic version of Aristotelianism. Ibn Khaldun's hostility to Neoplatonist philosophers was somewhat similar to his rejection of the over-reaching claims of the logicians, as he argued that they were attempting to take speculation beyond what could be empirically known. But he also suggested that their ideas were damaging to religion and therefore to society. As we shall see, this was also the background to his denunciations of alchemy, divination, and treasure hunting. But, though speculative philosophy was "pernicious," logic was separately discussed and cautiously approved, though there were grounds for unease when logic clashed with theological truths. He seems to have been well versed in logic (*mantiq*) and his impressively systematic exposition of it does indeed seem to draw on Aristotle's *Organon*, albeit at one or more removes.[29]

Metaphysics was also separately discussed, squeezed in between agriculture and the sciences of sorcery and talismans.[30] Though metaphysicians considered that theirs was a noble calling, Ibn Khaldun believed that he had no difficulty in refuting this. As in his discussion of philosophy, he cited al-Ghazali in his support. Speculative theology could be justified because that was based on revelation and divine truth, but speculative philosophy lacked any such sound basis.

The Arabic word *faylasuf* derived from the Greek and Ibn Khaldun identified Aristotle as the leading representative of the philosophers.[31] But, as we have already noted with reference to the *Sirr al-asrar*, Ibn Khaldun was not so very well acquainted with the genuine writings of Aristotle. Not only did he believe that the *Sirr al-asrar* was by Aristotle, he also believed that the Neoplatonic *Theologia* was by him too. The *Theologia* was actually a resumé of parts of the third-century *Enneads* by Plotinus, dealing with psychology, metaphysics, logic, and epistemology. It should also be borne in mind that it was common practice among medieval Arab scholars to quote fragments of Aristotle's writings, or of what they supposed to be by Aristotle, in order to establish their intellectual credentials. Even if Ibn Khaldun had had better access to the works of Aristotle, it is questionable whether he would have found much in them to interest him, for one of the striking features of Aristotle's writings is his lack of interest in history.[32]

Philosophy was an alien import into Islamic culture. It was to be classed with astrology and alchemy as one of the *'ulum al-awa'il*, one of the sciences of the ancients, and as such to be regarded with suspicion. While study of the subject might sharpen the mind, it was still dangerous. "The student should beware of its pernicious aspects as much as he can. Whoever studies it should do so (only) after he is saturated with the religious law and has studied the interpretation of the Qur'an and jurisprudence."[33] The use of logic could and should be deployed in theology, but that was all: "The books and methods of the ancients are avoided, as if they had never been, although they are full of useful results and useful aspects of logic as we have stated."[34]

Although philosophy was closely associated with the ancient Greeks, Ibn Khaldun did not believe that the philosophical tradition originated with them. Rather, like most Arab and Persian scholars, he believed that the Greeks had appropriated Persian Zoroastrian philosophy as well as other branches of knowledge: "Among the Persians [in antiquity], the intellectual sciences played a large and important role, since the Persian dynasties were powerful and ruled without interruption. The intellectual sciences are said to have come to the Greeks from the Persians (at the time) when Alexander killed Darius and gained control of the Achmaenid empire. At that time, he appropriated the books and sciences of the Persians."[35] When the Arabs conquered Persia they discovered many books and papers dealing with the Persian sciences, but the caliph 'Umar allegedly ordered them to be destroyed since the Arabs had received better guidance from God.[36] The *Sirr al-asrar* presented Aristotle as having gained his wisdom from Persia and India. Allegedly, only the Greek versions of the Persian sciences had survived and that was because the caliph al-Ma'mun was so fond of commissioning translations from the Greek. "The knowledge that has not come down to us is larger than the knowledge that has."[37]

Before moving on to theology, it remains to be observed that, of course, in a loose modern sense Ibn Khaldun was obviously a philosopher, "a lover of wisdom," as *The Chambers Dictionary* has it. He thought deeply about big questions and he tried to tackle things logically. But that was not enough to make him a philosopher in the fourteenth-century Maghreb. Even so, what made him almost unique among medieval historians was his capacity to reason abstractly and to generalize about social and historical phenomena.

THEOLOGY AND ITS LIMITS

Turning now to theology, Ibn Khaldun defined theology (*kalam*) as the science "that involves arguing with logical proofs in defence of the articles of faith and refuting innovators who deviate in their dogmas from the early Muslims and Muslim orthodoxy."[38] He described the religious scholar Abu Hamid Muhammad al-Ghazali (1058–1111) as "the first of the moderns." Ibn Khaldun, who was an Ash'arite, also described al-Ghazali as an Ash'arite—that is to say, a scholar who followed the tenth-century theologian Abu a'l-Hasan al-Ash'ari in using rational argumentation in favor of Islamic orthodoxy.[39] Al-Ghazali, who favored the Aristotelian syllogism, ushered in a more relaxed acceptance of the deployment of logic, which he made use of in his refutation of the contentions of the philosophers. But he did so with caution "like a skilled snake handler who must extract poison for useful purposes." He was also a defender of Sufism and he demonstrated how mysticism could be reconciled with orthodox Islam. But despite his use of reasoning in confirming certain theological positions, he held that not all articles of faith could be established by reason. Moreover, the study of theology could be dangerous and was not for everyone.

According to Ash'arite doctrine, God's omnipotence meant that "everything good and evil is willed by God. He creates the acts of men by creating in men the power to do each act." That is to say that God's will not only determines what men do but He also wills that the men should will what they do. This was known as the doctrine of *kasb* (literally "acquisition"). Men's actions are "creations of God." As has been noted in chapter 2, al-Ghazali maintained that there is no link between cause and effect unless God wills it to be so. Thus, for example, al-Ghazali held that cotton would not burn just because it has been set on fire. Rather, al-Ghazali said that the cotton caught fire because God made it do so, because in God's universe the only law is what God wills. What we call cause and effect are nothing more than God's habit.[40] Al-Ash'ari and al-Ghazali after him were occasionalists who taught that things only appear to have continuous existences over time because at every instant God wills their continued existence.

Ibn Khaldun seems to have agreed with al-Ghazali's stress on God's omnipotence, though he does not seem entirely consistent on the matter, and at one point he despaired of ever fully understanding the nature of causation: "A man who stops at the causes is frustrated. He is rightly (said to be) an unbeliever. If he ventures to swim in the ocean of speculation and of research into (causes), (seeking) each one of the causes that cause them and the influence they exercise. I can guarantee him that he will return unsuccessful. Therefore we were forbidden by the Lawgiver (Muhammad) to study causes. We were commanded to recognise the absolute oneness of God."[41]

After al-Ghazali, the Persian Fakhr al-Din al-Razi (1149–1209) was the leading theologian in this same Sufi and Ash'arite tradition. He wrote on an encyclopedic range of subjects. In particular, he produced a vast treatise on occult sciences, *Al-Sirr al-maktum* (The Hidden Secret), which Ibn Khaldun mentioned, but was unable to get hold of. As already noted, the young Ibn Khaldun abridged al-Razi's *Muhassal* (which was itself a précis of the ideas of earlier scholars, philosophers, and theologians) and he later made copious use of his writings in the *Muqaddima*, referring to him as "Ibn al-Khatib" or "the Imam al-Khatib" (who is nevertheless not to be confused with Ibn Khaldun's contemporary and friend, the Andalusian vizier and author Ibn al-Khatib). Ibn Khaldun particularly admired al-Razi's treatise on speculative theology, the *Kitab al-Mahsul*.[42] Like al-Ghazali, al-Razi used dialectic to refute the philosophers. "Those who want to inject a refutation of the philosophers into their dogmatic beliefs must use the books of al-Ghazali and the imam Ibn al-Khatib."[43]

Ibn Khaldun taught that men's souls are shaped by what they do, by their mastery of various skills and the acquisition of particular habits. The souls of kings, shopkeepers, and carpenters are shaped by their habitual activities. Prayer is or should be a habitual activity and regular praying conduces a person's soul to obedience and submission to God. A person is made by what he or she does (though it should be noted that here and elsewhere he paid little or no attention to women.) Worship and good deeds purify the soul.[44]

Ibn Khaldun was not entirely hostile to speculative theology, but he thought that it was really only useful for the refutation of heresy and unacceptable innovations and that neither of these things was much of a problem in the Maghreb in the fourteenth century. "Heretics and innovators have been destroyed."[45]

THE PRIMACY OF MALIKI LAW

The most important subject taught in North African mosques and *madrasa*s, second only to Qur'anic studies, was Maliki jurisprudence. Fez was the chief center for the teaching of the Maliki *madhhab*. A *madhhab* (literally "way followed" or "doctrine") is a school of *fiqh*, or Islamic jurisprudence. Four great *madhhab*s, differing in various points of belief and practice, have coexisted in Sunni Islam. Shafi'ism was favored by most Arabs in the eastern lands, though the stricter, more literalist Hanbalism also had numerous adherents. Turks, including the Turco-Circassian military elite in Egypt and Syria, were mostly Hanafis. Malikism was the dominant *madhhab* throughout the Maghreb and Andalusia, while there were significant colonies of Malikis in Egypt and elsewhere. The Maliki *madhhab's* name derived from its founder, Malik ibn Anas (d. 796). In his treatise, the *Muwatta'* (The Well-Trodden Path), Malik, a practicing judge, had summarized and systematized the views and practices of the jurists of eighth-century Medina, the holy city that was then the home of religious scholarship. He held that those jurists had most faithfully preserved the practice and opinions of the Prophet, since Medina had been for some years the hometown of the Prophet and his Companions. The *Muwatta'* contained some 1,700 *hadith*s (sayings and deeds attributed to the Prophet and his Companions). In the *Ta'rif* Ibn Khaldun included the text of his inaugural lecture at the Sarghitmishiyya *Madrasa* in 1389, which was on the *Muwatta'*. In this lecture (which is quite dull) Ibn Khaldun was careful to establish his authority to teach the *Muwatta'* by tracing a chain of teachers from his immediate masters all the way back to Malik. As he put it in the *Muqaddima*, Malik "was of the opinion that by virtue of their religion and traditionalism, the Medinese always necessarily followed each immediately preceding generation of Medinese, in respect of what they cared to do or not to do."[46] Malik was hostile to theological speculation and Ibn Khaldun tended to follow him in this. In medieval North Africa and Andalusia Malik was honored as a kind of saint.

Malikis tended to be conservative in their doctrines and practices, though in the centuries that followed the death of Malik they increasingly allowed *istislah* (having regard for public interest) to shape their interpretations of the Shari'a. Public interest comprehended the protection of life, the mind, religion, private property, and offspring. Public interest might sometimes be determined by *ijma'a* (a consensus of opinion, but more specifically the consensus of early Islamic legal experts). Malikis had a moralistic view of the law and they stressed the importance of good intentions in validating actions. Malikis also esteemed *taqlid* (belief based on authority). *Furu'* (applied *fiqh* or applied ethics, literally "branches") was important. But *furu'* in Malikism also has the sense of codified special rulings. Since Malikis were Ash'aris, they believed in the deployment of rational arguments in defense of Sunni orthodoxy.

Ibn Khaldun was a jurisconsult of the North African Maliki school of religious law. In Tunis in the years 1378–82 he lectured on Maliki law and later in Egypt he several times occupied the post of chief Maliki qadi. There he also lectured on Maliki law and on *hadith*s. In the preliminary remarks to book one of the *Muqaddima*, Ibn Khaldun announced that his methodology owed something to the principles of jurisprudential reasoning, since "the laws pay attention to the things that belong to civilization."[47] According to Ibn Khaldun, "It should be known that the science of the principles of jurisprudence is one of the greatest, most important, and most useful disciplines of the religious law."[48] The basic principles of jurisprudence (*fiqh*) drew upon the Qur'an, the *Sunna* (sayings and doings of the Prophet), *ijma'* (consensus), and *qiyas* (reasoning by analogy). Knowledge about the relative reliability of transmitters of information, and the use of personal prudential elaboration and analogy (*qiyas*), was reapplied by Ibn Khaldun to assess the truth or falsehood of reported historical events (though he tended to reject long chains of transmitters (*isnad*s). So his *'usul al-ta'rikh* (principles of history) was modeled on *'usul al-fiqh* (principles of Muslim jurisprudence), since a reapplication of *'usul al-fiqh*, as the basis for deducing law from revelation and establishing the sources of law, could provide a methodology that could be used to reject erroneous statements about historical events. Independent judgment no longer had any role in Islam, if it ever had, and adherents to a particular *madhhab* simply had to obey what was handed down by tradition.

Having been educated within the Maliki *madhhab*, he was steeped in the *Muwatta'*.[49] But, more than that, he approved of Malikism, because he thought that it was the *madhhab* that was closest to the simplicity of the Arabian desert dwellers, whereas the other *madhhab*s had evolved in the cities of Iraq and Syria and, as already noted, he idealized desert simplicity and was generally hostile to urban sophistication. His was a strict version of Islam. He held that Christians and Jews had three options; they could convert to Islam, they could submit to Islamic rule and pay a special tax, the *jizya*, or they would be killed. He was proud of the institution of jihad, for it was an indication that Islam was the universalist religion and all people had to submit to it. Adultery was abominable as it led to the confusion of genealogies. The penalty for homosexuality was stoning. More generally, he advocated austerity. He was against rich food. "Food is the origin of all illness."[50] He also denounced hunting, music, and fine clothes, and he took it for granted that men had complete authority over women.

As the great Arabist Hamilton Gibb observed, "Ibn Khaldun was not only a Muslim, but as almost every page of the *Muqaddima* bears witness, a Muslim jurist and theologian, of the strict Maliki school. For him religion was far and away the most important thing in life . . . the *Sharia* the only true guide."[51] It is hard to contest Gibb's summing up of Ibn Khaldun's political theory in the *Muqaddima*:

> The careful reader will note how he drives home the lesson, over and over again, that the course of history is what it is because of the infraction of the *Sharia* by the sin of pride, the sin of luxury, the sin of greed. Even in economic life it is only when the ordinances of the *Sharia* are observed that prosperity follows. Since mankind will not follow the *Sharia* it is condemned to an empty and unending cycle of rise and fall, conditioned by the "natural" and inevitable consequences of the predominance of its animal instincts. In this sense Ibn Khaldun may be a "pessimist" or "determinist," but his pessimism has a moral and religious, not a sociological basis.[52]

Ideally the state should not only provide good government but also provide the environment that enforced the Shari'a, which in turn led to salvation. But it does not seem that Ibn Khaldun thought that full restoration of Shari'a rule might be possible. Although he was capable of envisaging a politics that was not based on prophets and holy books, he believed that laws that were based on revealed religion served society better. (But his devotion to the law sits oddly with his admiration for the wild Zanata Berbers who refused to submit to it.) Finally, although Ibn Khaldun included Sufism and dream interpretation among the religious sciences, these will be discussed in subsequent chapters, as will eschatology.

CHAPTER FIVE

Ibn Khaldun's Sojourn among the Mamluks in Egypt

As I approached the shore, I felt like an Eastern bridegroom, about to lift up the veil of his bride and to see, for the first time, the features which were to charm, or disappoint, or disgust him. I was not visiting Egypt merely as a traveller, to examine its pyramids and temples and grottoes, and, after satisfying my curiosity, to quit it for other scenes and other pleasures: but I was about to throw myself entirely among strangers.

—Edward William Lane, early draft of *Description of Egypt*

After Ibn Khaldun's four-year-long retreat in Qal'at Banu Salama, he put down his pen in 1378, returned to Tunis and made his peace with the Hafsid Abu'l-'Abbas (who had formerly ruled in Bougie and Constantine). This was Ibn Khaldun's first visit to the city since he had left it as a young man in 1352. There were libraries in Tunis and doubtless he filled in some of the gaps in his history. He seems to have avoided politics and confined himself to teaching. But his pedagogical career in Tunis did not prosper because of local animosities. For reasons that are mysterious, despite his low profile, he attracted the fierce hostility of the leading Maliki scholar and jurist of the age, Ibn 'Arafa al-Warghani (1316–1401). Ibn 'Arafa was a Berber in origin and a former student of a great Maliki scholar, al-Sharif al-Tilimsani. After serving as imam and *khatib* (preacher) at the Nasirid court in Granada, Ibn 'Arafa had become chief qadi in Tunis and imam of the Great Mosque. Thanks in large part to his writings, in which he sought to reconcile legal principles and custom, Maliki *mufti*s (jurisconsults) and their *fatwa*s exercised an unprecedented amount of authority under the Hafsid regime.[1]

Like Ibn Khaldun, the austere Ibn ʻArafa was critical of the materialism of the age, but, unlike Ibn Khaldun, he had a huge number of disciples. Though Ibn Khaldun in the *Taʻrif* claimed that Ibn ʻArafa was jealous of him because students were deserting Ibn ʻArafa to attend his lectures, this seems quite unlikely. Ibn Khaldun is our only source for their quarrel, as Ibn ʼArafa wrote nothing about it and never even deigned to mention Ibn Khaldun in his prolific writings. But in 1382 Ibn ʻArafa allegedly spearheaded the campaign that led to Ibn Khaldun being forced to leave Tunis. Ibn Khaldun sought the Hafsid ruler's permission to go on the *hajj*. This was a pious stratagem that was often used by politicians and scholars as a way of gracefully retiring from a fraught environment. In the *Muqaddima* he had noted how difficult it was for anyone who had been in official service to escape from it and how the ruler would seek to prevent him from traveling to other lands.[2] Earlier, when the scholar Ibn Marzuq fell out of political favor he had sought permission to go on the *hajj*, but then went on to retire in Cairo. Like Ibn Marzuq, Ibn Khaldun did not go on the *hajj* straight away, but instead proceeded to Mamluk Cairo. His family was not at first allowed to follow him and probably they were being detained in Tunis as political hostages.

ARRIVAL IN EGYPT

He arrived in Egypt in December 1382 and made his way to Cairo, where he was to spend most of the next quarter of a century. He had moved from an intellectual backwater to what was then the cultural capital of the Islamic world. In *The Thousand and One Nights* the father and uncles of a Jewish physician who is one of the protagonists of the Hunchback cycle of stories extol the wonders of Cairo:

> "Travellers claim that on the face of the earth there is no city more beautiful than Cairo by the Nile." When I heard this, I felt a longing to see Cairo and my father said: "Whoever has not seen Cairo has not seen the world. Its soil is gold; its river is a wonder; its women

are houris; its houses are palaces; its climate mild; its scent surpasses that of frankincense, which it puts to shame. There is nothing surprising about this, as Cairo is the whole world" . . . . My father went on "Were you to see its gardens in the evening in the slanting shadows, you would see a wonder and be filled with delight."[3]

Ibn Khaldun was similarly impressed. In the *Tar'if* he wrote that

he who has not seen Cairo does not know the grandeur of Islam. It is the metropolis of the world, garden of the universe, assemblage of the nations, the ant-hill of the human species, the portico of Islam, the throne of royalty, a city embellished with palaces and arcades, decorated with dervish monasteries and with schools, and lighted by the moons and stars of erudition. The city extends along the shores of the Nile—the river of Paradise—the waters of heaven, whose flow satisfies the thirst of men, providing them with abundance and wealth . . . He who has not seen Cairo cannot know the extent of the power and glory of Islam.[4]

No other city—not Tunis, not Fez, not Granada—had evoked such a eulogy from him.

In the *Muqaddima* he had also written that "many of the poor in the Maghreb want to move to Egypt . . . because they hear that the prosperity in Egypt is greater than anywhere else."[5] Cairo had a particular attraction for scholars, since the great number of *madrasas* and *khanqas* (Sufi colleges) in Cairo furnished many opportunities for scholarly patronage. These religious establishments were funded by *waqf*s, unalienable endowments, often estates in mortmain entailed in such a manner that their proceeds would accrue to members of the donor's family and their descendants. Ibn Khaldun explained that the profusion of *waqf*s in the Mamluk Sultanate was due to the fear of emirs that after their disgrace or death the sultan would seek to confiscate their wealth and leave their heirs penniless. "The Turkish emirs under the Turkish dynasty were afraid that their ruler might proceed against the descendants that they would leave behind, in as much as they were his slaves or clients, and because chicanery and confiscation are always to be feared from royal authority. Therefore they built a great many colleges, hermitages and monasteries, and endowed them with mortmain endowments that yielded income. They saw to it that their children would participate in these endowments, either as administrators or by having some share in them."[6] As a consequence, learning thrived and scholars came from Iraq, Iran, and the Maghreb in the hope of finding teaching or administrative posts in Egypt and Ibn Khaldun was, of course, an example of this phenomenon.

Mamluks, slave soldiers, usually formed part of the armies of the fourteenth-century North African regimes, but they did not dominate politics and warfare in that region, whereas mamluks, mostly of Kipchak Turkish or Circassian origin, had governed Egypt and Syria since the mid-thirteenth century and the sultans came from their ranks. Ibn Khaldun was as enthusiastic about the mamluk institution as he was about Cairo, since he saw it as a way for a regime artificially to reinforce its 'asabiyya by repeatedly importing vigorous warriors from remote tribal regions. In the Ta'rif he remarked how the thirteenth-century Ayyubid sultan of Egypt and Syria, al-Salih Ayyub had wished to add to the 'isaba (solidarity) of his dynasty by purchasing mamluks. And in the 'Ibar Ibn Khaldun described the Mamluks as a gift of God for the salvation of Islam. After the decline of the 'Abbasid caliphate and its suppression by the Mongols, it

> was by the grace of God, glory be to Him, that He came to the rescue of the true faith, by reviving its last breath and restoring in Egypt the unity of the Muslims, guarding His Order and defending His ramparts. This He did by sending to them (the Muslims), out of this Turkish people and out of its mighty and numerous tribes, guardian emirs and devoted defenders who are imported as slaves from the lands of heathendom to the land of Islam. This status of slavery is indeed a blessing . . . from Divine Providence. They embrace Islam with the determination of true believers, while retaining their nomadic virtues which are undefiled by vile nature, unmixed with the filth of lustful pleasures, unmarred by the habits of civilization, with their youthful strength unshattered by the excess of luxury. The rulers have them paraded and bid against one another to pay the highest prices for them. The purpose of their purchase is not to enslave them but to intensify their zeal and solidarity and strengthen their prowess.[7]

In *Slaves on Horses* Patricia Crone commented, "The passage brilliantly describes the *mamluks* as institutionalized tribal conquerors."[8] Ibn Khaldun had taken the theme of the providential nature of Mamluk institution as "a gift of God" to deliver Islam from its enemies from an earlier Mamluk chronicle by Baybars al-Mansuri, since it fitted in so well with his ideas about tribal *'isaba*.

Ibn Khaldun's fame had gone before him, in part because his friend Ibn al-Khatib had previously sent a copy of his history of Granada to Egypt, a book in which Ibn Khaldun was praised.[9] Soon after his arrival in Egypt he attracted the favorable attention of the Circassian Mamluk sultan Barquq's *amir majlis* 'Ala al-Din Altunbugha al-Jubani al-Yalbughawi. As *amir majlis*, Altunbugha was one of the most powerful emirs in Egypt. According to the chronicler Ibn Taghribirdi, Altunbugha was well educated and intelligent.[10] He was for several years Ibn Khaldun's most enthusiastic patron. It was he who recommended Ibn Khaldun to Barquq, who had usurped the throne earlier in 1382, and Barquq then appointed Ibn Khaldun to a professorship at the Qamhiyya *Madrassa*. Ibn Khaldun's inaugural lecture at the *Madrassa* was a distinguished affair, for his reputation had preceded him, and the lecture was attended not only by Altunbugha, but also by Yunus the *dawadar*, the four chief *qadis*, and sundry other notables. Ibn Khaldun took care to include a panegyric to Barquq in his lecture.

In Egypt there were four chief qadis or judges. Most Egyptian Muslims followed the Shafi'i rite and brought their lawsuits before Shafi'i judges, and the Shafi'i chief qadi was the senior judge in Egypt. But, as previously noted, the Mamluk elite mostly followed the Hanafi rite and a minority of Arabs followed the rigorous Hanbali rite. The Malikis in Egypt were mostly immigrants from North Africa or Andalusia. (In Marrakesh, Tunis, and Granada the Maliki chief qadi was the most senior judge.) Ibn Khaldun was briefly appointed to the post of Maliki chief qadi in 1384–85. Doubtless his appointment to this post without having first served as qadi in one of the lower courts caused some resentment among the Egyptians.[11] He had tried to refuse this post as he had little legal experience. Though he was to occupy the qadiship four more times, his tenure was always brief, as his rigor and incorruptibility attracted as much blame as praise. He also taught at the famous al-Azhar Mosque, where he mostly lectured on *hadith* and Maliki *fiqh*, and especially the *Muwatta'* of Malik. The lecture was particularly preoccupied with problems relating to the reliability of chains of transmission of *hadith*s.[12] In 1387 Barquq made him director of the new Zahiriyya *Khanqa*, a Sufi foundation that took its name from Barquq's regnal title al-Zahir. Then, after Ibn Khaldun's return from the *hajj* in 1387, Barquq appointed Ibn Khaldun to be shaykh of the Baybarsiyya *Khanqa*. This was the grandest of Cairo's Sufi institutions and the post was a lucrative one. Since Baybars al-Jashankir (r. 1309–10), the founder of this *Khanqa*, had stipulated that its shaykh had to be chosen from one of the Sufis in the *Khanqa* and not appointed from outside, Ibn Khaldun was first made a Sufi of the *Khanqa* before being appointed its shaykh a day later.[13]

Barquq liked to have scholars about him and Ibn Taghribirdi recorded that he would rise to greet them when they were brought into his presence.[14] Besides occupying teaching posts and sometimes serving as Maliki chief qadi, Ibn Khaldun also served the sultan as an adviser on North African and Andalusian affairs and drafted some of the correspondence with its rulers. Incidentally, it is surprising, even shocking, that in the *Ta'rif*, when discussing correspondence with Granada, Ibn Khaldun referred to Ibn Zamrak, the man who supervised the strangling of Ibn al-Khatib and who replaced him as vizier in Granada, as his "friend."[15]

It was probably at Barquq's request that in 1384 Abu'l-Hasan al-Mustansir, the ruler of Tunis, had allowed Ibn Khaldun's family to follow him to Egypt. But Ibn Khaldun's life continued to be dogged by tragedy, as his wife, five daughters, and his library were lost in a shipwreck off the coast of Alexandria. (His two sons arrived separately later.) By convention, medieval Arab "autobiographies" kept family matters private and we only learn that Ibn Khaldun had a wife and five daughters when he briefly recorded their deaths.

CIRCASSIAN MAMLUK TURBULENCE

Barquq was a benevolent patron, but his tenure of the sultanate was from the first precarious and it depended on the consent of other senior emirs. Throughout most of the fourteenth century, Egypt and Syria had been ruled by descendants of the great Kipchak Mamluk sultan Qalawun (even if that rule was nominal in several cases). The child sultan Hajji II whom Barquq had deposed in 1382 was the last of Qalawun's descendants to reign, even if only nominally. As for Barquq, his claim to the sultanate hardly seemed to be based on anything more substantial than his skill at street fighting and intrigue. There was persistent feuding between Circassian and Turkish mamluks. In the opening years of his rule he had already faced a series of minor rebellions. Then in 1389 he faced a major revolt led by the emir Yalbugha al-Nasiri who was joined by the emir Mintash, governor of Malatya (on the borders of Anatolia). The coalition presented themselves as Qalawunid loyalists and they denounced Barquq's favoritism toward mamluks of Circassian origin.

According to the *Muqaddima*: "it is easy to establish a dynasty in lands that are free from group feeling. Government there will be a tranquil affair, because seditions and rebellions are few, and the dynasty there does not need much group feeling (*'asabiyya*). This is the case in contemporary Egypt and Syria. They are [now] free from tribes and group feelings; indeed one would never suspect that Syria had once been a mine of them, as we have [just] stated. Royal authority in Egypt is most peaceful and firmly rooted, because Egypt has few . . . tribal groups."[16] It is surprising that Ibn Khaldun never saw fit to revise this passage, since his description of Mamluk Egypt and Syria as untroubled by tribes and group feelings was nonsense and was belied by the leading role played by Arab, Turkoman, and Kurdish tribes in the civil war that broke out in 1389.[17]

The rebel emirs Yalbugha and Mintash were backed by other senior emirs and by the Banu Fadl, the paramount Bedouin tribe in Syria. In Cairo they also received significant support from the *zu'ar* (organized gangs of beggars and criminals). Barquq was swiftly overthrown and imprisoned in Kerak in what is now southern Jordan. The child Hajji II was reinstalled by the coalition of senior emirs as sultan. Mintash and his allies then summoned the caliph (a figurehead in Mamluk Egypt with only notional spiritual authority), the four chief qadis, and Ibn Khaldun, (because of his status as director of the Baybarsiyya *Khanqa*). It was then demanded that they sign a *fatwa* document denying the legitimacy of Barquq's rule. Only the Maliki chief qadi Shams al-Din Muhammad al-Rakraki (a leading enemy of Ibn Khaldun) refused and he was thereupon savagely beaten. Ibn Khaldun, despite all he owed to Barquq, signed the document. It is, of course, not something that he lingered over in the *Ta'rif*.

But Barquq soon escaped from prison and advanced on Egypt with an army composed of Bedouin from the region of Kerak. Mintash fled to Syria and Hajji II was once again deposed in 1390. After Barquq's triumphant return to Cairo, there was still hard fighting in Syria.

Mintash continued to be backed by some senior emirs and by the Banu Fadl. Nuayr, the head of the Banu Fadl clan, was a major player in Mamluk politics and warfare during the turbulent reign of Barquq. On the other hand, the Turkoman tribes and the semi-nomadic tribesmen of Palestine and Lebanon mostly supported Barquq. In Upper Egypt the Bedouin had also supported Mintash and, because of this, Barquq had brought in the Arabized Berber tribe of the Hawara and from the 1390s onwards until the end of the Mamluk Sultanate in the early sixteenth century the Hawara seem to have been the dominant power in Upper Egypt. Barquq had two more years hard fighting before Mintash was killed in Syria and even after that there were two more years before other rebel emirs were defeated.[18]

Ibn Khaldun's history writing is focused on the doings of the Mamluk elite. Not only did he neglect the role of tribesmen in politics and warfare in Egypt and Syria, but also he took little or no account of the other disasters that befell the sultanate. The *Muqaddima*, the *'Ibar*, and the *Ta'rif* do not mention the plagues of 1388 and 1389 or the Egyptian famines of 1394–96 and 1403–4. The famine of 1403–4 was accompanied by plague. According to Ibn Khaldun's pupil, al-Maqrizi, "the situation became critical; conditions became perilous, disaster was widespread and calamity universal, to the degree that more than one-half of the population of land [of Egypt] died of hunger and cold."[19] The sufferings of lesser folk did not engage Ibn Khaldun's attention. His Pollyanna-ish presentation of the Mamluk Sultanate in *Muqaddima* was perhaps intended to please the sultan and the emirs as he quested for more patronage. Ibn Khaldun was always more interested in winners than in losers. Of losers, he had this to say: "The vanquished always want to imitate the victor in his distinctive marks, his dress, his occupation, and all his other conditions and customs, and just as the vanquished seek to imitate the victorious, so also the subjects of a ruler tend to take him as a model to be followed."[20]

Given Ibn Khaldun's complaisance regarding the *fatwa* against Barquq, it is not surprising that, when the sultan regained Cairo, Ibn Khaldun was removed from his post as director of the Baybarsiyya *Khanqa* (though in his memoir he preferred to blame this on the intrigues of a hostile Mamluk emir). When the chronicler Ibn Taghribirdi came to sum up Barquq's reign, he stressed the sultan's respect for the pious and scholarly, before adding that "it is true that during his second reign he became bitter against the men of law . . . because they had approved the legality of waging war against him and seeking his death; but despite the intensity of his anger he did not cease to pay them honor."[21]

REVISING THE *MUQADDIMA* IN EGYPT

Ibn Khaldun, out of office, wrote a fawning letter to Altunbugha, hoping that he might intercede for him, but Altunbugha, after being briefly imprisoned by Barquq, had been restored to high rank and sent to govern Syria where he was to die in 1390 in the fight against Mintash's forces. So Ibn Khaldun was out of office until 1399, when he was reappointed Maliki chief qadi. He seems to have done some teaching and he continued to research and add to the *Muqaddima* and the *'Ibar*. Although the core of the *Muqaddima* had been written in Qal'at Banu Salama, a great deal was added in Egypt. In the opening pages of the later recension of the *Muqaddima*, he noted how, once he had arrived in Egypt, he was able to fill the gaps in his knowledge about the Persian and Turkish dynasties.[22] It was in Egypt that he not only expanded the scope of the *'Ibar* into a universal history, but also updated the story of the Berbers up to the 1390s. Some additional revisions to the *Muqaddima* may have been prompted by his students' interest in *hadith*s and *fiqh*. He also added a great deal on occult and supernatural matters (on which see chapter 7). The final Egyptian text of the *Muqaddima* is half as long again as the one he had presented to the ruler of Tunis and the *'Ibar* may have been expanded even more. The *Muqaddima* was still being revised as late as 1404, the year before Ibn Khaldun's death.

As already noted, Ibn Khaldun's account of the early Bahri Mamluk period derives from other earlier chronicles and is of little or no interest. But for the decades immediately before his arrival in Egypt and those that followed he was occasionally able to draw on information provided by the sultan and senior emirs. Altunbugha al-Jubani was an important oral source on mamluk infighting. So it is at times an insider's history, though he also borrowed and abridged some of the Egyptian chronicler Ibn al-Furat's *Ta'rikh al-duwal wa al-muluk* (The History of Dynasties and Kings).[23] Ibn Khaldun's account of Egyptian history is not cast in the form of annals; it is short on dates and that is a more general feature of the *'Ibar*. He was more interested in the political maneuvering of the military than in the logging of the military and religious appointments that are such a feature of chronicles produced by contemporary Egyptian and Syrian historians. From Egypt he sent an early copy of the *'Ibar* to the Merinid sultan Abu Faris. Did he think that he might one day return to Fez?

OFFICE HOLDING IN EGYPT AND THE MAGHREB

In chapter 3 of the *Muqaddima*, Ibn Khaldun tried to present an overview of office-holding under the various Muslim dynasties. But here he encountered considerable difficulties, since not only did the status and authority of a particular post vary from regime to regime, but also the powers attached to a post tended to increase or decrease over time. Thus, for example, in North Africa the grand vizier was so powerful that he was effectively the double of the ruler and he was usually commander-in-chief of the army, whereas in Egypt the vizier, who had been the chief adviser of the Ayyubid sultans of the late twelfth and early thirteenth centuries (but without any military role), had subsequently lost most of his authority under the Mamluk sultans. Ibn Khaldun noted how mamluk emirs of high rank disdained the title of vizier. Early on in the Mamluk regime the vizier's authority was mostly confined to financial affairs and a mamluk official, the *na'ib* (deputy), took over as the sultan's deputy. Later, many of the vizier's financial responsibilities were also taken over by a mamluk emir, the *ustadhdar*, or major-domo of the palace, and the vizier was left with restricted authority over taxes.

To take another example, in Tunis, as has been mentioned, Ibn Tafraghin, who held the post of *hajib* (literally "door-keeper"), enjoyed unprecedented power, more indeed than that of the sultans he pretended to serve, but when this strong administrator died, the office dwindled in importance. In Mamluk Egypt, the *hajib* was at first a fairly minor mamluk official within the palace, but over time the office acquired both judicial and military responsibilities and Ibn Khaldun noted that he was ranked just below the sultan's deputy, the *na'ib*.[24] (Incidentally, in the *Muqaddima* Ibn Khaldun claimed that Merinids did not employ *hajib*s, but his own account of Merinid history in the *'Ibar* belies this.) The shaykh of *mazalim* in Tunis had to carry out investigations into alleged cases of misconduct by royal officials. There was nothing exactly corresponding to this in Egypt, though the mamluk emir who held the post of *hajib* seems to have acquired the authority to investigate *mazalim* cases.[25] Again, in North Africa the head of the chancellery who might be termed *sahib al-'alama* or *katib al-sirr* was a powerful figure, usually ranked third in the hierarchy of administrators. In Egypt the office was not as important as that, and, as noted by Ibn Khaldun, this senior secretary was supervised by a mamluk officer, the *dawadar*.[26]

In Egypt the Mamluk sultans kept a puppet caliph, who was a kinsman of the last 'Abbasid caliph of Baghdad (d. 1258) and who was brought out on ceremonial occasions. The pretense was maintained that he was the spiritual leader of the entire Sunni Muslim community. But in North Africa, both the Merinids and the Hafsids had taken caliphal titles (as had the Fatimids and Almohads before them). In the thirteenth century the Hafsid claim to the caliphate had been widely recognized in North Africa. The Hafsids claimed to be heirs of the Almohads and indeed in the *'Ibar* Ibn Khaldun referred to them as "Almohads." Hafsid rulers, who had started out as shaykhs and then promoted themselves to emir, eventually came to use the caliphal title *'Amir al-Mu'minin* (Commander of the Believers), as the Almohads had done before them. Probably because the early Merinids did not want to antagonize the Hafsids, the early Merinids refrained from taking the caliphal title *'Amir al-Mu'minin* and contented themselves with the subtly inferior title of *'Amir al-Muslimin* (Commander of the Muslims), but Abu 'Inan was to take the title *'Amir al-Mu'minim*. It was a marker of his grand ambition to unify the Maghreb. However, the child Salih, who was put on the throne after Abu 'Inan's death, reverted to the title *'Amir al-Muslimin*. But Ibn Khaldun thought that this difference in entitulature did not signify much.[27]

Ibn Khaldun believed that the true caliph's status depended upon his being a successor of the Prophet Muhammad and that his role should be to enforce the Shari'a, since only obedience to the religious law could bring happiness in the afterlife. But the proliferation of caliphs meant that the title had lost its original significance. There was no longer any consensus among the Muslims as to what were the qualifications that a caliph needed to possess. Though many believed that the caliph had to come from the Quraysh, the Prophet's tribe, Ibn Khaldun did not accept this, since the Quraysh no longer possessed sufficient prestige to attract widespread group loyalty. In any case, the age of the true caliphs, the *Rashidun*, had ended in 661 with the death of 'Ali, the Prophet's cousin and the fourth caliph to succeed him as leader of the Muslim community. The "caliphs" thereafter were really kings (*muluk*). It was no longer possible for anyone claiming to be a caliph by virtue of that title to draw on sufficient group feeling (*'asabiyya*).[28]

Besides lecturing and writing, Ibn Khaldun had a sideline in looking after other people's money for safekeeping. In 1396 when a leading emir, Jamal al-Din Mahmud Ibn 'Ali al-Ustadhdar fell from power, Barquq's officers hunted out the places where the emir had deposited or concealed his wealth. It turned out that Jamal al-Din had left various sums of money in what he hoped was the safe keeping of various dignitaries, including twenty thousand dinars with Ibn Khaldun.[29] Ibn Khaldun recorded the event in the *Muqaddima* as an example of the sums that could be accumulated under the Mamluk regime. Barquq "arrested his minister of the interior, the amir Mahmud, and confiscated his property. The man charged with the confiscation informed me that the amount of gold he cleaned out was 1,600,000 dinars."[30] But Ibn Khaldun was reticent about his own involvement. (Incidentally, though it was common practice for wealthy people to entrust sums of money to qadis for safekeeping, Ibn Khaldun was not actually a qadi in 1396.)

TIMUR IN SYRIA

Barquq died in 1399. He had expressed the desire to be buried at the feet of dervishes.[31] His son and designated successor, al-Nasir Faraj, was only ten at the time and was at first placed under the guardianship of two mutually hostile emirs. Sensing an opportunity, Timur (also known in English as Tamerlane), the leader of the Chagatai Turks, moved against Syria. In the closing decades of the fourteenth century Timur had created an empire that included much of Central Asia, Iran, and Iraq. Though Timur was not himself a Mongol, he and his Turco-Mongol following observed the traditions of Genghis Khan and his descendants. Timur had previously threatened Syria in 1394, but on that occasion he had been deterred by the forces that Barquq had been able to muster in the province's defense. This time Timur swiftly captured Aleppo and other cities in northern Syria, and continued his advance on Damascus. At the end of 1400 Faraj was nominally in charge of the Egyptian army that went out to defend that city and, though Ibn Khaldun held no official post at the time, he was one of the civilian dignitaries who were requested by the sultan to accompany him on that expedition. The Egyptian army camped outside the walls of Damascus. There was a brief standoff between the two armies but then some of Faraj's emirs and elite mamluks bolted back to Cairo and Faraj felt obliged to follow them.

Ibn Khaldun however stayed in Damascus, almost certainly because he was curious to meet Timur. Might he be "the man of the century" foretold in recent prophecies? The *Muqaddima* and *'Ibar* had shown only limited interest in the Mongols, despite their being tribal conquerors who might be thought to have owed much of their success to the strength of their *'asabiyya*. (The Mamluk chancellery encyclopedia of al-'Umari had previously served Ibn Khaldun as his main source on the Mongols and their alleged law code, the *yasa*.) But in the *Ta'rif* Ibn Khaldun was to give a detailed and vivid account of Timur.

Ibn Khaldun estimated that Timur's army outside Damascus numbered a million troops. The small number of mamluks remaining in Damascus were incapable of defending the city (though the garrison of the citadel held out for another month). Ibn Khaldun tagged along with the delegation of citizens who went out to negotiate the surrender of the city. Timur made the famous scholar welcome.[32] Theirs was a meeting that can be compared to that of Aristotle and Alexander, or that of Goethe and Napoleon. According to Ibn 'Arabshah, an Arab historian who composed a vituperative life of Timur, when Ibn Khaldun was brought before the monstrous Timur, he addressed him as follows:

> O Lord and Amir! Praise to Allah Almighty! Truly I have had the honour of admission to the kings of mankind and I have restored life to their memory by my chronicles. Of kings of the Arabs I have seen that one and that; to this Sultan and this I have been admitted; I have visited East and West and everywhere talked with Amirs and governors, but thanks to Allah! That my life has been extended and by Allah! That I have lived long enough to see this man, who is truly a king and knows rightly how to rule the Sultanate. But if the food of kings suffice to avert destruction, truly the food of our Lord Amir suffices for this, nay suffices to gain glory and honour.[33]

Timur must have been pleased. According to a later Egyptian chronicler and biographer, Timur was also struck by Ibn Khaldun's good looks.[34]

Given Ibn Khaldun's interest in nomads and their social cohesion, his meeting with this nomadic would-be world conqueror can be compared to a scientist examining a newly acquired laboratory rat. Timur was the vigorous leader of the Chagatai Turks and Ibn Khaldun believed that they had best preserved the old Mongol ways and vigor. They were untouched by luxury and softness and they had preserved their "Bedouin" mode of life.[35] Timur had invaded a settled region to overthrow its regime and in overthrowing it he might establish a new dynasty, which in turn would presumably fall victim to the process of sedentarization and decadence that, in a matter of three or four generations, was supposed to destroy a dynasty.

Timur, for his part, was fond of historians (though they seem to have been less fond of him). For thirty-five days Ibn Khaldun visited Timur in his pavilion. Timur was curious to learn Ibn Khaldun's views on the caliphate. To whom did it rightfully belong? Where were the descendants of Nebuchadnezzar? Timur was most interested in the geography of North Africa. (Perhaps he had hopes of conquering it.) Timur was also keen to buy Ibn Khaldun's exceptionally fine mule. In the circumstances, Ibn Khaldun did not feel that he had any option except to offer it to him as a gift.

Above all, did Ibn Khaldun believe that Timur was destined to rule the world? Ibn Khaldun was able to tell Timur about the prophecies circulating in the Maghreb that seemed to foretell the coming of the nomadic world conqueror and he told Timur how in 1360, while in Fez, he had met Ibn Badis, the *khatib* of Constantine and a great expert on astrology, about the forthcoming conjunction of Saturn and Jupiter in the area of Gemini, Libra, and Aquarius in 1364–65. Ibn Badis replied that "It points to a powerful one who would arise in the northeast region of a desert people, tent dwellers, who will triumph over kingdoms, overturn governments, and become masters of most of the inhabited world." When Ibn Khaldun asked when this man would appear, Ibn Badis replied that this would be in the hijri year 784 (1382–83). In 1382 Timur was to conquer Khorasan. Al-Abili, the scholar who had taught Ibn Khaldun the rational sciences, had made a similar prediction. Ibn Khaldun had also heard that Sufis in the Maghreb were also expecting a momentous event, though they expected the leader of the great conquest to be of Fatimid descent. (Presumably Ibn Khaldun did not pass this alternative version on to Timur.[36]) It may be relevant that in Persian sources Timur was usually designated *sahib al-qiran*, "the lord of the fortunate conjunction of planets."[37] Ibn Khaldun seems to imply that he actually did not believe that the rise of Timur was foretold by conjunction of Saturn and Jupiter, but he did try to use those predictions in order to suggest that Timur was indeed the man of destiny and so put him in a good humor.

Ibn Khaldun's host had made a big impression on him: "This king Timur is one of the greatest and mightiest of kings. Some attribute to him knowledge, others attribute to him heresy because they note his preference for the members of the House [of 'Ali]; still others attribute to him the employment of magic and sorcery, but in all this there is nothing; it is simply that he is highly intelligent and very perspicacious, addicted to debate and argumentation about what he knows and also about what he does not know."[38]

According to Ibn 'Arabshah, Ibn Khaldun had flattered Timur relentlessly and had promised him that he was destined to rule over Egypt: "Egypt refuses to be ruled by any ruler but yourself or to admit any empire but yours." He also boasted of his own learning:

Nothing breaks my back except my books, in which I have spent my life and paid out the pearls of my learning in composing them and extinguished my day and made sleepless my night in writing them. I have set forth in them the annals of the world from its very beginning and the life of the kings of east and west, but I have made you the centre pearl of the necklace and the finest part of their wealth and have embroidered the golden robes of their age with your deeds, and your empire has become a crescent moon on the forehead of their time; but those books are in the city of Cairo and if I recover them, I will never depart from your stirrup or exchange your threshold for another.[39]

But the floridity of the speeches attributed by Ibn 'Arabshah to Ibn Khaldun seem more redolent of Ibn 'Arabshah's own literary style than they are of Ibn Khaldun's. It is most unlikely that Ibn 'Arabshah was actually present at these meetings. He was eleven at the time and was to be taken to Samarkhand as one of Timur's captives. He only returned to Mamluk Syria in 1421. Though Ibn 'Arabshah's portrayal of Ibn Khaldun's obsequiousness and deceit is unflattering, in another shorter account of Ibn Khaldun's encounter with Timur, which appears in a mirrors-for-princes work compiled by Ibn 'Arabshah, Ibn Khaldun is referred to as the "pillar of historians."[40]

Finally, Ibn Khaldun was allowed to leave for Egypt, having falsely given assurances that he would return with his family and books. The encounter with Timur was much less agreeable for the citizens of Damascus. They had paid him several large fines, but he was still not satisfied. When one Damascan delegate offered fulsome flattery, the response was, "You are lying, because I am the scourge of God appointed to chastise you, since no one knows the remedy for your iniquity except me. You are wicked, but I am more so than you are, so be silent!"[41] The city was sacked. According to Ibn Taghribirdi "They were bastinadoed, crushed in presses, scorched in flames and suspended head down; their nostrils were stopped with rags full of fine dust which they inhaled each time they took a breath so that they almost died."[42] By then Ibn Khaldun was on his way back to Egypt. But he too suffered, for he was attacked by thieves in the region of Safed and robbed and stripped of everything.

IBN KHALDUN'S "AUTOBIOGRAPHY"

It was during his years in Egypt that he wrote *Al-Ta'rif bi Ibn Khaldun wa rihlatihi sharqan wa gharban* (Presenting Ibn Khaldun and His Journeys in the East and the West) and it was in this book that he gave an account of his encounters with Timur. Indeed, it seems that he had at first intended the *Ta'rif* to serve as a tailpiece to the *'Ibar* and it was only after his encounter with Timur that he decided to turn the *Tar'if* into an independent work that included a detailed account of his meetings with Timur. Although the *Ta'rif* has been described as an "autobiography," it is decidedly short on self-revelation. Did Ibn Khaldun go for long walks? Did he have red hair? Was he uxorious? Did he like hunting? Did he talk to himself a lot? Did he spend much time hanging out with his mates? Did he keep pets? Did he have more than one wife? We have no idea about any of these things, despite the fact that, late in life, he produced this book, which passes for an autobiography. On the personal level the *Tar'if* is a remarkably unrevealing document. But, more generally, though a number of medieval Muslim "autobiographies" have survived, they did not aspire to be confessional. As Michael Cooperson observes, "much of the so-called biographical literature in classical Arabic, Persian and Turkic has little in common with modern biography . . . the biographies . . . display little interest in how the subject 'came to be who he was.'"[43]

Ibn Khaldun's "autobiography" has the look of a curriculum vitae that has been combined with a chronicle of public events. (*Fahrasa* was the medieval term for an educational curriculum vitae. Ibn Marzuq, for example, had produced such a document about his studies with religious scholars in the eastern Islamic lands.) In the early part of the *Ta'rif*, Ibn Khaldun was particularly assiduous in listing his teachers in order to establish his credentials as a scholar of the religious sciences. As Cooperson, again, has noted: "To better understand pre-modern biographical writing, it is helpful to recall that its primary purpose was often to place individuals within a genealogy of authority and a network of simultaneous relationships."[44] In the culture to which Ibn Khaldun belonged, the oral transmission of knowledge from teacher to student took precedence over the reading of books. Hence the importance of extended and discursive lists of teachers in the first half of the *Ta'rif*.

Ibn Khaldun's self-presentation was overtly without passion and lacks crucial information. He did not name his wife (or should that be wives?) nor his children. He did not mention the ravages wrought by the Black Death in Tunis. He avoided all mention of his early writings. It is from Ibn al-Khatib that we learn that Ibn

Khaldun had written a commentary on the *Burda* (a well-known lengthy poem about the Prophet), a *talkhis* (an abridgement) of the works of al-Razi, another on the works of Averroes, and treatises on jurisprudence, mathematics, and logic, as well as many poems.[45] The *Ta'rif* does not mention al-Maqrizi or any other friends or disciples Ibn Khaldun may have had in Egypt.

The *Ta'rif* is unusually long for a medieval Arab "autobiography." In it, apart from establishing his academic credentials, he perhaps intended to use incidents from his own life in order to illustrate how history worked. If so, it is not obvious what lessons should be taken from that history, much of which consists of a narrative of mamluk infighting. As far as public events are concerned, much of the *Ta'rif* condenses the *'Ibar*. It is also possible that he may have written this semi-memoir partly in order to understand how he had experienced so many reverses in his political career. It is probably also the case that part of the motivation for composing the memoir was emulation of his late friend Ibn al-Khatib, who had included a lengthy autobiography in his *Al-Ihata fi akhbar Gharnata* (The Complete Source on the History of Granada). The *Ta'rif* is bulked out and given a more literary flavor by letters from Ibn al-Khatib and by poetry. In those days poetry was an instrument of politics, for poems were used to declare political allegiances, to solicit political patronage, and to provide diplomats with some of their rhetoric. Much of the poetry in Ibn Khaldun's book is courtier poetry.[46]

Timur withdrew from Syria later in 1401 and he was to die en route to conquer China. The sultan Faraj's prestige had been damaged by his failure to defend Damascus and thereafter he sent Timur gifts that were so extravagant that they should really be accounted as tribute. Faraj was in effect the prisoner of Circassian and Turkish emirs who competed for real power and staged one coup after another against each other. His first reign was to last only six years as he was temporarily deposed in September 1405. The remaining years of Ibn Khaldun's time in Egypt were not good for that region. In 1402 there was a plague of locusts and, as already noted, famine and pneumonic plague struck again in 1403–4. The chronicler Ibn Taghribirdi reported: "During this year [1403] there was a vast extent of uninundated land in Egypt, and extreme scarcity resulted, followed by the plague. And this year was the beginning of a series of events and trials in which Egypt and its provinces were ruined not only because of the failure of the inundation but also because of the lack of harmony in government and the frequent change of officials in the provinces, as well as other causes."[47]

AN OUTSIDER IN EGYPT

As a North African immigrant with idiosyncratic ideas about history, Ibn Khaldun was not popular among the Egyptian civilian elite and he seems to have had only two disciples, one of whom was the chronicler Taqi al-Din Ahmad ibn 'Ali al-Maqrizi (1364–1441), who, besides formally studying with Ibn Khaldun the science of *miqat* (the management of instruments for measuring time, chiefly useful for determining the times of prayers), also attended his lectures on history. Al-Maqrizi had encountered nothing like the latter before and he wrote of the *Muqaddima* as follows: "It is the cream of knowledge and sciences and the pleasures of sound intellects and minds. It informs about the reality of happenings and events. It refers to the representatives of everything in existence in a style which is more brilliant than a well-arranged pearl and finer than water fanned by a zephyr."[48]

Al-Maqrizi was to become a prolific and polemical author whose most notable works included a lengthy chronicle of the Ayyubids and Mamluks, the *Kitab al-suluk fi ma'rifat duwal al-muluk* (The Book of the Ways to Knowing the Dynasties of Kings). In this work he seems to have absorbed his teacher's conviction that history was important, as well as a pessimistic view of the way history developed. In the opening of his topography of Egypt, the *Kitab al-Mawa'iz wa'l-i'tibar fi dhikr al-khitat wa'l-athar* (Book of Exhortations and Considerations Regarding Mention of the Settlements and Monuments), he stated that history was the most important of the sciences "for it contains warnings and exhortations reminding man that he must leave this world for the next." But in the *Khitat* he revealed himself to be far more credulous than Ibn Khaldun, for that work is full of marvels, anecdotes of the supernatural, and speculations about buried treasure. Moreover, neither the *Kitab al-Suluk* nor the *Khitat* shows much sign of being influenced by the methodology of the *Muqaddima*.

But perhaps a little influence of that book can be seen in al-Maqrizi's *Ighathat al-umma bi-kashf al-ghumma* (Book of Help to the People in Disclosing Distress), a treatise on famines and high prices. Ibn Khaldun had got al-Maqrizi interested in the operations of economic and social forces, but al-Maqrizi failed to grasp Ibn Khaldun's underlying methodology and instead presented a version of the operations of economic forces that was even more moralistic than Ibn Khaldun's. Both historians stressed the roles of hoarding and bad government in exacerbating famines, but al-Maqrizi in this work and in others, such as his treatise on coinage, the *Shudhur al-nuqud*, presented what were mostly muddled arguments. According to al-Maqrizi, the high prices and famines of his own times were not due to natural causes, but were due to human mismanagement, corruption, sale of offices, and overtaxation of the peasants. He glumly lamented the vanished glories of the past. He had no special interest in tribesmen or the role of *'asabiyya*. Since copper coinage was not sanctioned by the Qur'an or *hadith*s, al-Maqrizi also wrote a separate treatise on the economic evils of copper coinage. The worsening economic situation was the direct result of bad government.

Al-Maqrizi, like Ibn Khaldun, was taken up by Barquq, though he failed to attract the patronage of later sultans and this led him in later writings to present an embittered portrait of the Mamluk regime.[49] He described the mamluks as "more lustful than monkeys, more ravenous than rats, more harmful than wolves."[50] His eccentric partisanship for the Shi'i dynasty of the Fatimids, who had ruled over Egypt from 969 until 1171, attracted a lot of criticism from his contemporaries.

Muhammad ibn 'Ammar (1367–1441), a professor of Maliki law in Cairo, was also recorded as having studied jurisprudence and the *Muqaddima* with Ibn Khaldun.[51] Al-Sakhawi (on whom see below) quoted Ibn 'Ammar on Ibn Khaldun's espousal of the traditional methods of al-Ghazali and Fakhr al-Din al-Razi and his advice to students to avoid the use of later abridgements. Ibn 'Ammar thought that the *Muqaddima* was one of the great works of literature and a comprehensive survey of scholarship.[52]

Al-Maqrizi and Ibn 'Ammar were the exceptions. Other scholars took a more critical view of Ibn Khaldun. Ahmad Ibn Hajar al-Asqalani (1372–1449) was a youth when Ibn Khaldun arrived in Egypt and, having studied with him, consequently secured an *ijaza* (a certificate granted by a teacher authorizing a student to transmit some or all of what he had learned from him). In time Ibn Hajar became recognized as Cairo's most eminent scholar. He was a prolific author and several times he occupied the post of Shafi'i chief qadi.[53] He had mixed feelings about Ibn Khaldun. He conceded that Ibn Khaldun's lecturing was very good, fluent, and interesting. But in his biographical dictionary of judges he accused Ibn Khaldun of being such a good writer that, like the brilliant tenth-century essayist al-Jahiz, he could make lies seem like truth. Ibn al-Khatib's history of Granada, the *Ihata*, had provided testimony to Ibn Khaldun's excellent literary prose and poetry, but Ibn Hajar was at pains to point out that nothing was said there about Ibn Khaldun's scholarship (*'ilm*).[54] (But it should be borne in mind that Ibn al-Khatib's history had been finished in 1364, well before Ibn Khaldun started work on the *Muqaddima* and the *'Ibar*.) Despite having studied with Ibn Khaldun, when Ibn Hajar came to write history, it took the form of an entirely conventional annal.

Ibn Hajar also accused him of being ignorant of the history of the eastern Islamic lands. Also when Ibn Khaldun presided as a judge he was liable to fly into rages and his neck reddened with anger. He was so high-handed and uncompromising that people used to call him "the spearhead." He refused to wear the official dress of an Egyptian qadi and instead continued to wear the Moroccan burnouse. He acted as he did "because of his love of being contrary in everything." In part, Ibn Hajar had relied on the accusations that had been made by Ibn Khaldun's old enemy, the chief qadi in Tunis, Ibn 'Arafa. When Ibn 'Arafa heard that Ibn Khaldun had been appointed a judge in Cairo, he scoffed that his knowledge of Maliki law was too poor for him to qualify as an *'alim*.

The sometime Malikite chief qadi in Egypt, al-Rakraki, had similarly claimed that Ibn Khaldun had no real knowledge of jurisprudence and that his knowledge of the rational sciences was merely adequate, though he did concede that Ibn Khaldun was superbly eloquent. Ibn Hajar reported that Ibn Khaldun forged a *fatwa* that he attributed to al-Rakraki, but which was subsequently exposed as a forgery. Late in life Ibn Khaldun settled in a house by the Nile where, Ibn Hajar alleged, he delighted in the company of singing girls and young men and he married a woman who had a mentally disturbed younger brother "and the disgraceful things multiplied" (though I find it hard to understand why marrying a woman with a mentally disturbed brother was disgraceful). Al-Maqrizi was quoted on the excellence of the *Muqaddima*, but this was a prelude to Ibn Hajar's speculation that al-Maqrizi was keen on Ibn Khaldun's history because they both believed in the genuineness of the Fatimid genealogy.[55] Ibn Hajar also reported Ibn Khaldun as presciently remarking that "there is nothing I fear more for Egypt than the Ottomans."[56] (The Ottomans were to conquer Egypt in 1517.)

Intellectual life in medieval Cairo was rancorous and Ibn Khaldun was far from being the only victim of libel and polemic.[57] The *hadith* scholar, biographer, and historian Shams al-Din Muhammad al-Sakhawi (1427–97) had been Ibn Hajar's student. Al-Sakhawi was never successful at obtaining a major teaching post and, perhaps as a consequence, had a much more embittered view of his predecessors and contemporaries. His account of Ibn Khaldun is only one of his many sharp and malicious portraits in *Al-Daw' al-lami' fi a'yan al-qarn al-tasi'* (The Bright Light Regarding Important People of the Ninth Century).[58] (Al-Maqrizi was another of al-Sakhawi's victims.) Al-Sakhawi, who recycled most of Ibn Hajar's accusations, denounced Ibn Khaldun as being rude, arrogant, sexually immoral, and a forger. Even so, al-Sakhawi also quoted Ibn al-Khatib, al-Maqrizi, and al-'Ayni in praise of Ibn Khaldun.[59] Incidentally, al-Sakhawi's view of the purpose of history writing was narrower than that of Ibn Khaldun, for he believed history was ancillary to the religious sciences and that its chief purpose was to test the reliability of chains of *hadith* transmitters.[60]

The historian Badr al-Din al-'Ayni (1361–1451) claimed that Ibn Khaldun's knowledge of oriental history was not very good. He also implausibly accused Ibn Khaldun of presiding over an immoral household and of being a homosexual.[61] Al-'Ayni who was a leading enemy and rival of al-Maqrizi, probably libeled Ibn Khaldun because he had been al-Maqrizi's teacher. There were also those who resented his strictness during his tenure of the office of Maliki chief qadi and his refusal to take bribes. The Egyptian biographer and chronicler Ibn Taghribirdi's brief biography was more favorable. He praised Ibn Khaldun for his austerity and incorruptibility and his refusal as qadi to be swayed by the demands of the powerful. It was because of the consequent intrigues against him that he was dismissed from his tenure of the office of chief qadi. Ibn Taghribirdi made no mention of Ibn Khaldun's history (or of any riverside scandals), but instead concluded his short biography by quoting a few lines from a *qasida* (ode) by Ibn Khaldun.[62]

Despite the calumnies of enemies, in his final years Ibn Khaldun was appointed Maliki chief qadi four more times and was dismissed three times before dying in office. He was working on the *'Ibar* and the *Ta'rif* until a few months before his death on March 16, 1406. The fact that he was buried in a Sufi cemetery may suggest that he was a Sufi. This is an issue that will be addressed in the next chapter.

CHAPTER SIX

✦✦✦

The Sufi Mystic

Sufism was classified by Ibn Khaldun as one of the religious sciences. Among other things, it was a way of learning about the world and understanding it. Those Sufis who belong to *tariqa*s (Sufi orders or brotherhoods) trace the origin of their *tariqa* through an initiatory chain of mystical shaykhs, all the way back to 'Ali and through him to the Prophet. But outsiders, and particularly Western scholars who have written about Sufism, have tended to place its origins somewhat later in the eighth or ninth centuries. Some scholars who have written about Sufism have detected Christian, Hindu, Gnostic, and Buddhist influences on Sufism's early development. The earliest Sufis were individual ascetics and there were at first no Sufi *tariqa*s. The *tariqa*s started to form around the early thirteenth century. The Shadhili and Qadiri Sufis were particularly important in North Africa. The first Shadhili *zawiya* had been established in Tunis in 1228. As has been noted, Ibn Khaldun had briefly been appointed shaykh of a *khanqa* in Cairo. *Khanqa*s and *zawiya*s were both Sufi centers, but a *khanqa* was hardly more than a hostel for Sufis and its shaykh was appointed by the secular authority, whereas a *zawiya* was presided over by a shaykh of the *tariqa* whose adherents occupied that particular *zawiya* and he provided a distinctive spiritual teaching and discipline.[1]

The writings of Abu Hamid Muhammad al-Ghazali in the eleventh century had been influential in making a moderate form of Sufism acceptable to mainstream Sunni Muslims and his writings, which had a huge influence on Ibn Khaldun, are much quoted in the *Muqaddima*. Al-Ghazali launched a famous and influential attack on philosophy, the *Tahafut al-falasifa* (Incoherence of the Philosophers). His *Al-Munqidh min al-dalal* (Deliverance from Error) identified the errors in question as being speculative theology, Isma'ilism, and Hellenistic philosophy. His *Ihya''ulum al-din* (Revival of the Religious Sciences) was intended as a complete guide to religious salvation and is in four parts. Part one dealt with acts of worship, part two with social customs, part three with vices or faults leading to damnation, and part four with virtues leading to salvation. In concentrating on what would benefit the Muslim community as a whole, he demonstrated how the Shari'a, or religious law, had been designed to serve the public interest and further the good of the community of the believers. The Shadhili Sufis of North Africa had a particular reverence for the *Ihya'*. Though al-Ghazali did discuss Sufism in the *Ihya'*, he only wrote about the comportment of Sufis and did not discuss *mukashafa*, the removal of the veil of sensual perception, for this matter was not to be written about and was only for initiates.

By the mid-fourteenth century Sufi *tariqa*s were playing a crucial religious, political, and social role in Islamic society. (It is odd that Ibn Khaldun nowhere discusses the importance of the *tariqa*s as political, social, and economic forces in the region.) In North Africa the Merinid ruler Abu 'Inan was a particular patron of Sufis. The leading intellectuals of the age, such as Ibn al-Khatib and Ibn Marzuq, were Sufis. In fourteenth-century North Africa Sufism was so pervasive that it came close to becoming the Sunni orthodoxy. As Michael Cook has observed, "We might be tempted to see Sufism as a kind of alternative Islam, were it not that in many historical contexts it simply was Islam."[2]

Although this was the case, Ibn Khaldun chose not to discuss the social and economic impact of the Sufi orders in the *Muqaddima* and this is a strange omission. Instead, he focused on what was and was not orthodox Sufi doctrine and practice. Al-Ghazali had successfully defended the compatibility of mainstream Sufism with the Shari'a. But, while the *'ulama'* mostly accepted Sufism and many indeed were Sufis themselves, certain of the doctrines and practices of some Sufis were widely condemned as heretical or as unacceptable innovations. Among the practices that attracted the criticism of some Muslims were the practice of *dhikr* (incessant repetition of certain words or formulas in praise of God), singing or dancing in sessions of *sama'* (literally "listening"), the veneration of Sufi shaykhs' tombs, and *shatahat* (ecstatic utterances that might stray into heresy or blasphemous vainglory). Ways in which Sufis might stray into heresy will be discussed in more detail shortly.

IBN KHALDUN A SUFI?

Was Ibn Khaldun a Sufi and, if so, did this shape his view of history? He did after all write in an era when Sufism had become institutionalized.

Many of his colleagues and rivals were Sufis. It would be strange if he was not a Sufi. Yet he never explicitly claimed to have been one, nor did he describe any personal mystical experiences. None of his contemporaries referred to him as a Sufi. And, if he was a Sufi, which *tariqa* did he belong to? And who was his *murshid*? Even so, he was a private man and circumstantial evidence overwhelmingly indicates that he was a Sufi.

First, like Ibn al-Khatib, Ibn Khaldun had studied under the Sufi Abu Mahdi 'Isa Ibn al-Zayyat. In the *Muqaddima*, he refers to him as "our shaykh, the gnostic and chief saint in Spain," before quoting him with approval on the Sufi understanding of the oneness of God. At the end of this lengthy quotation, Ibn Khaldun admits that though he heard this particular Sufi exegesis "from our shaykh Abu Mahdi himself several times," he is actually reproducing it from a treatise of Ibn al-Khatib, entitled *Information on the Noble Love* [of God], since Ibn al-Khatib's writing may preserve the teaching better than Ibn Khaldun's memory, for it was a long time ago.[3] Then when, in 1372, Ibn al-Khatib wrote to Ibn Khaldun a letter in which he announced that he was going to follow the Sufi way, Ibn Khaldun responded enthusiastically.[4]

Secondly, he produced a short treatise on one particular debate among Sufis, *Shifa' al-sa'il li-tadhib al-masa'il* (The Cure of the Questioner through the Clarification of the Problems). This was probably written in the early 1370s, a few years before Ibn Khaldun started work on the *Muqaddima* and it was the response to a query from a scholar in Granada as to whether a Sufi could do

without a *murshid* (a personal spiritual teacher), or whether enlightenment could be achieved just by learning from books. Ibn
Khaldun, after first surveying the technical vocabulary and history of Sufism, stated that it was possible for someone starting out
on the Sufi path to make progress in the early stages by reading
Sufi treatises, but then expressed unease about studying to achieve
'ilm al-mukashafa (the science of unveiling). A *murshid* was necessary for any neophyte who was set upon the path of removing the
veil of sensual perception, for otherwise there was a danger that
the student might drift into self-delusion or heresy. The *murshid*
should guide the disciple "like a blind man on the edge of the sea."
Despite Ibn Khaldun's suspicions about what might be termed extremist Sufis, it seems unlikely that he would have offered an opinion about whether a Sufi neophyte needed spiritual guidance, if he
had not been a Sufi himself.

Even so, Ibn Khaldun was uneasy about recent developments
in Sufism and he detected certain dangers in the writings of Ibn
al-'Arabi, Ibn al-Farid, and al-Buni. *Tajalli* (theophanic self-glori-
fication), monism (the doctrine that all things are ultimately one),
and the practice of letter mysticism could all lead to error. Though,
at this stage, Ibn Khaldun was cautious in his verdicts on these
matters, he thought that Sufism needed quasi-legal supervision
and proper policing. His deployment of a juridical metaphor in his
short treatise on mysticism is striking: whereas mainstream *fuqaha*
(jurists) were competent only in the Shari'a, the Sufi shaykh was "a
faqih competent in the *fiqh* of the hearts." His presentation of the
mystical issues had been that of a religious lawyer. As the editor
and translator of the *Shifa'*, René Pérez has observed, "the juridical
character of this long *fatwa* is all too evident. *Fiqh* shaped its form,
in the vocabulary, the concepts used and the style of argument. But
it unarguably also fundamentally colours the author's vision of the
realities he was dealing with . . . Ibn Khaldun here reveals himself
to be a jurist (*faqih*) and a jurisconsult (*mufti*)."[5] He deplored what
he saw as a gulf between *fiqh* and Sufism.

The *Shifa'* was not a startlingly original work and it was something of a scissors-and-paste job, for it drew heavily on his friend
Ibn al-Khatib's *Rawda*, as well as on al-Ghazali's writings and on

al-Qushayri's *Risala* (letter). (Al-Qushayri (986–1072) had produced the *Risala* as a defense of the orthodoxy of Sufi doctrines
concerning the unity of God (*tawhid*), as well as esoteric interpretations of the Qur'an and other texts and practices.) Ibn Khaldun
spent so long on defining Sufism and outlining its history that it
seems that his contribution to the debate about whether someone
starting on the Sufi path needed a shaykh was really the pretext for
a discussion of more general issues concerning Islamic mysticism.

Thirdly, he presented a highly favorable view of mainstream
Sufism in two chapters in the *Muqaddima*. In chapter 1, in the
course of a wide-ranging discussion of the various ways of obtaining knowledge about the future (many of which were fraudulent
or otherwise dodgy) he came to discuss the Sufis and holy fools
and their ability to pass beyond the veil of sensual perception. He
opened this discussion with these words: "The Sufi institution is a
religious one. It is free from any such reprehensible intentions."[6]
Then, in chapter 6, Sufism was discussed at length as one of the
sciences:

> Sufism belongs to the sciences of the religious law that originated in
> Islam. It is based on the assumption that the practice of its adher-
> ents had always been considered by the important early Muslims,
> the men around Muhammad and the men of the second generation,
> as well as those who came after them, as the path of truth and right
> guidance. The Sufi approach is based upon constant application to
> divine worship, complete devotion to God, aversion to false splen-
> dour of the world, abstinence from the pleasure, property, and posi-
> tion to which the great mass aspire, and retirement from the world
> into solitude for divine worship. These things were general among
> the men around Muhammad and the early Muslims. Then worldly
> aspirations increased in the second [eighth] century and after. At
> that time, the special name of Sufis was given to those who aspired
> to divine worship.[7]

Sufism, unlike theology or philosophy, led to happiness. In his
discussion of Sufism, Ibn Khaldun, as always, looked back with
approval on a time when things were allegedly simpler and more
austere.

Having carefully studied his friend Ibn al-Khatib's treatise on Sufi love, he quoted it in the *Muqaddima*. Ibn Khaldun approved of the practice of the *dhikr*, for this removed the veil of sensual perception and allowed the Sufi to behold divine worlds. "It is like food to make the spirit grow." It makes the spirit ready for "holy gifts."[8] But, having passed beyond the veil of sensual perception, the wisest Sufis kept quiet about what they had learned by doing so.[9]

He believed in miracles. How else could one explain the spectacular triumphs of the early Islamic conquests? Writing about Muhammad's victories over superior numbers of polytheists, Ibn Khaldun observed that "God took care of His Prophet. He threw terror into the hearts of the unbelievers. (That terror,) eventually seized control over their hearts, and they fled. (This, then, was) a miracle wrought by God's Messenger."[10] Ibn Khaldun also accepted that Sufis could work miracles (*karamat*): "Among the Sufis some who are favoured by acts of divine grace are able to exercise an influence upon worldly conditions. This, however, is not counted as sorcery."[11] Adherents of 'Ash'ari theology pointed to the reality of miracles as supporting evidence for their occasionalism. Ibn Khaldun also discussed the miraculous powers of *majdhub*s, or holy fools, in the context of ways of foreseeing future events. These deranged saints have access to supernatural information. It was claimed that holy fools are born, not made.[12] Ibn Khaldun praised ascetic and devotional mysticism. He believed that Sufism had the potentiality to reenergize the Islamic community and serve as a kind of moral rearmament. Even so, his tacit commitment to Sufism contrasted strongly with Ibn al-Khatib's fervent espousal of the mysticism of love.

Moreover, Ibn Khaldun expressed certain reservations and doubts in the *Muqaddima*. Even in the early centuries of Sufism, there were signs of its contamination by Shi'i doctrines. He believed that the Sufi *isnad*s (chains of initiatic transmission from one Sufi shaykh to another) were modeled on the similar Shi'i *isnad*s. More serious was the fact that some Sufi groups had been influenced by Shi'i preaching about the imminence of the Mahdi and this had led to several regional uprisings in North Africa, by pretenders who claimed to be of Fatimid descent. (On beliefs concerning the coming of the Mahdi, see the next chapter.) The wrong kind of Sufism posed social and political danger to the Muslim community. Here and elsewhere Ibn Khaldun's view was shaped by the considerations of general welfare (*istislah*) that played such a large part in Maliki jurisprudence.

Ibn Khaldun had doubts about the *shatahat*, the ecstatic utterances that might be construed as blasphemous. The ninth-century Sufi Abu Yazid al-Bistami had notoriously declared "Glory be to me! How great is my glory!" The famous (or notorious) Sufi al-Hallaj had uttered several *shatahat* and been executed for heresy in Baghdad in 922. Having mentioned this, Ibn Khaldun noncommittally observed that "God knows better."[13] He also expressed doubts about the orthodoxy of the Andalusian Muhyi al-Din Ibn al-'Arabi (1165–1240): "In the East I came across a prediction work attributed to Ibn 'Arabi al-Hatimi. It consists of a long enigmatic discussion . . . The most likely assumption is that the whole work is incorrect, because it has no scientific basis, astrological or otherwise."[14] But the work in question was almost certainly not by Ibn al-'Arabi, and Ibn Khaldun seems to have had little or no direct knowledge of the genuine writings of this mystic. A vast amount of pseudepigrapha was foisted on Ibn al-'Arabi in the middle ages. Ibn Khaldun listed Ibn al-'Arabi and another thirteenth-century Andalusian Sufi, Ibn Sa'bin, as among those Sufis who wrote about the removal of the veil and about suprasensory perception and he went on to accuse such mystics of having been infected by extremist Shi'i ideas.[15] Ibn al'Arabi's writing had also been contaminated by philosophical ideas that had originated in ancient Greece. He was widely attacked for monism. There were influential supporters of Ibn al-'Arabi at the sultan Barquq's court.[16] It may be that in criticizing the esoteric writings attributed to Ibn al-'Arabi, Ibn Khaldun's real target was a group of rival scholar-courtiers. In the *Muqaddima*, Ibn Khaldun also expressed unease about the obscurity of some of the interpretations of the poetry of the controversial Egyptian mystic Ibn al-Farid (1181–1235).[17]

A *fatwa* (legal ruling) reported by a scholar in Fez and apparently issued by Ibn Khaldun when he was in Egypt shows a hardening of his attitude toward speculative and heterodox mystics, particularly the two thirteenth-century Andalusian Sufis, Ibn al-'Arabi and Ibn Sab'in, and their followers. Ibn al-'Arabi was shown to be guilty of immanentism and monism. ("Immanence" designates the belief that the universe is pervaded by the intelligent and creative principle. "Monism" is the doctrine that everything in the universe is ultimately one and in which all plurality is seen as human illusion.) Besides following in the path of Ibn al-'Arabi, Ibn Sab'in had also dabbled with numerology and astrology. Ibn Khaldun accused them of infidelity and reprehensible innovation. Their treatises relied on absurdly complex allegories and should be burned. He also wanted Ibn al-Farid's monistic mystical poems to be burned, together with an equally heretical commentary on them. In this *fatwa* he now stated outright that al-Hallaj had been rightly condemned to death for heresy, since he had been guilty of revealing in a blasphemous form secrets that were only for the initiated. It seems likely that the hardening of his attitude toward speculative Sufism, monism, emanationism, and metaphysical speculation, subsequent to what he had written in the *Muqaddima*, was the result of encounters with heterodox mystics and charlatans in Egypt.[18]

DOES THE *MUQADDIMA* REPRESENT A SUFI INTERPRETATION OF HISTORY?

Recently Allen Fromherz, assistant professor at Georgia State University in Atlanta, in his biography of Ibn Khaldun has emphasized and perhaps overemphasized both the importance of Sufism in Ibn Khaldun's life and its role in shaping his philosophy of history. Fromherz suggests that Ibn Khaldun had a Sufic approach to history writing: "Ibn Khaldun's description of 'awakening' to the hidden truth [of history], of finding meaning behind the surface of events, had parallels in the Sufism or Islamic mysticism that so inspired Ibn Khaldun's grandfather, father, and undoubtedly Ibn Khaldun himself."[19] The historical process of cyclical dissolution and rebirth echoed on a macroscopic scale the individual path of a mystical disciple who "died" in the hands of his master and then was reborn again. Ibn Khaldun was led through Sufism to realize the futility of material power and possessions. Crucially it was Sufism that led him to look beyond the *zahir* (outer appearance) of historical events and intuit the *batin* (inner truth) of the laws that determined those events. One's first response to the above must be, if this is so obvious, why has no one seen it before?

Fromherz has queried the reliability of the report by a scholar based in Fez of the Egyptian *fatwa*. It did not exist, he suggests but, even if it did, it does not say what it seems to be saying. So then he argued that the *fatwa*, if genuine, only dealt with potential misunderstandings of Sufism, or, alternatively, it was an expression of patrician dislike by the leader of a big elite *khanqa*, the Baybarsiyya, for the little *khanqa*s or *zawiya*s that were springing up all over Egypt and which were often popular with the lower orders. It was dangerous to impart higher mystical knowledge to the lower orders. "Ibn Khaldun was a Sufi but he was also an elitist," Fromherz concluded.[20]

There is certainly something in the last point. In writing about al-Ghazali, Carole Hillenbrand has observed that "underlying much of his writing is the belief that knowledge is tiered, that literal interpretations suffice for the masses but that more esoteric interpretations should be for the few."[21] Ibn Khaldun was certainly an elitist and most probably a Sufi and he took his lead from al-Ghazali in holding that certain doctrines were reserved to those who had sufficient education to properly understand them. It is also true that in 1389 Ibn Khaldun had been appointed head of the *khanqa* of Baybars, the greatest and most lavishly endowed of the Egyptian *khanqa*s. However his appointment to run a Sufi institution should not be seen as having mystical significance. His responsibilities there would have been mostly financial.

Moreover Sufis do not surrender themselves to their shaykhs in order to be reborn. A Sufi remains obedient and "like a corpse in the hands of its washer," at least until his shaykh dies. The spring ritual of death and rebirth is a pagan rite that has never had any place in Islam. Also, according to Ibn Khaldun, when one dynasty perishes, it does not get reborn; instead it is replaced by another one. Sufis had no monopoly over the terms *zahir* and *batin*. They were in common use and, for example, they featured frequently in the encyclopedia produced by the Brethren of Purity (a tenth-century group of scholars who were probably Isma'ilis). *'Asabiyya* was not a term bandied about by Sufis. Many historians have struggled to tease out the underlying meaning of history. For example, Oswald Spengler, who was certainly no Sufi, also "found meaning behind the surface of events." The Marxist historian Eric Hobsbawm was not a Sufi either, though he too struggled to find broad explanations for the flow of events. Moreover, though the language of Ibn Khaldun's *fatwa* is somewhat vehement, the content is consistent with what is found in the *Muqaddima* and that vehemence may be a product of Ibn Khaldun's encounters with extremist Sufism in Egypt. Finally, there are, I think, no known instances of other Sufis developing a distinctive historiographical methodology. Although Ibn al-Khatib was a fervent Sufi and he also wrote histories, no one, I think, has tried to argue that his chronicle writing was inspired by Sufism.

Though Ibn Khaldun was almost certainly a Sufi, this was not apparent to nineteenth-century European commentators who mostly preferred to think of him as a rationalist, a materialist, and a positivist. Even later, when scholars abandoned such culture-bound categories and tried to put him in an Islamic context, someone like the great Arabist Hamilton Gibb, who disliked Sufism rather a lot, ignored the possibility of Ibn Khaldun's Sufism altogether.

CHAPTER SEVEN

Messages from the Dark Side

Initially the *Muqaddima* set out to explore the underlying forces behind history and the correct way of understanding them. But the scope of the work expanded as Ibn Khaldun worked on it and so it became looser and baggier and hence the *Muqaddima* includes extensive discussions of such things as secretarial skills, dreams, mystical experiences, the occult, and the principles of pedagogy, as well as a treasury of verses that Ibn Khaldun particularly admired. These things are not strictly relevant to the understanding of historical processes. They were perhaps an advertisement for himself.

The *Muqaddima* comes close to becoming a comprehensive encyclopedia. It was indeed produced in an age when encyclopedias were in fashion in the Arab world, particularly in Mamluk Egypt and Syria. For example, the *Nihayat al-arab fi funun al-adab* (The Heart's Desire in the Arts of Culture) by a former financial administrator, Shihab al-Din al-Nuwayri (1279–1332), is a vast guide to the cosmos, humans and their government, and literature, animals, plants, and history—particularly history. Of the encyclopedia's thirty-one volumes, twenty-one are devoted to history. It was so exhaustive in its coverage that it amounted to a fantasy version of the required culture of a scribe. To take another example, the *Masalik al-absar fi mamalik al-amsar* (Paths of Perception through the Metropolitan Dominions) by a chancery clerk, Ibn Fadl Allah al-'Umari (1301–49), is an encyclopedia in fourteen volumes containing all the information that a secretary might need to know. Al-'Umari devoted a lot of pages to geography and history. One is tempted to ask what Arabic culture was there in the fourteenth and fifteenth centuries other than that of the scribe. Centuries earlier, in the 'Abbasid period, al-Mas'udi's chronicle *Muruj al-dhahab* also had some of the qualities and scope of an encyclopedia.

Although Ibn Khaldun has been presented in recent centuries as the precursor of Comte, Durkheim, and Marx, it must be remembered that he inhabited a different and darker world than the one known to European economists and sociologists. It was one in which plants, stones, and planets had talismanic powers: resemblance "made possible knowledge of things visible and invisible, and controlled the art of representing them. The universe was folded in upon itself: the earth echoing the sky, faces seeing themselves reflected in the stars, and plants holding within their stems the secrets that were of use to man."[1] It was also a world haunted by spirits and presided over by an all-seeing God. Consequently Ibn Khaldun was obsessed with the occult.

THE REALITY OF THE SUPERNATURAL

No believing Muslim could deny the immanence of magic in the world.

The Qur'an attested to the reality of the jinn, as well as the powers of magicians, such as those who appeared before Pharaoh and turned sticks into serpents, or the Arabian witches who blew upon knots.

Sura 113, "Daybreak," runs as follows:

In the Name of God, the Merciful, the Compassionate
Say: I take refuge with the Lord of the Daybreak
from the evil of what he has created,
from the evil of darkness when it gathers,
from the evil of women when they blow upon knots,
from the evil of the envier when he envies.[2]

In the *Muqaddima* Ibn Khaldun quoted a verse from this Sura and gave as its context an account of a woman who used a knot spell against the Prophet to make him imagine he was doing something when he was not. Ibn Khaldun had actually watched a sorcerer using spittle, a knot, and the image of an enemy in order to cast a spell on him.[3]

Sura 114, "Men," is one of several Suras that attest to the reality of the jinn:

In the Name of God, the Merciful, the Compassionate
Say: I take refuge with the Lord of men,
  the King of men,
  the God of men,
from the evil of the slinking whisperer
who whispers in the breast of men
of jinn and men.[4]

But, although the Qur'an attested to the reality of sorcery it also denounced it. According to the second Sura of the Qur'an, in the days of Solomon, Satan descended and taught the people sorcery and unbelief. Ibn Khaldun's attitude to the occult was dictated by what was revealed in the Qur'an.

Although he admitted that there were many confidence tricksters and charlatans among the sorcerers, nevertheless the supernatural was real and he had had personal experience of it. He gave an account of the North African "rippers" who could tear apart the stomach of an animal or a garment just by pointing at it. This black art was used to blackmail a herdsman into paying off the sorcerer with an animal from his flock. Ibn Khaldun had actually talked with these "rippers."[5] Having given elaborate instructions for making the lion seal on a ring that gave its wearer "indescribable power over rulers," he concluded by remarking that "it is attested by experience."[6] The evil eye was something truly malevolent that derived its power from envy.[7] "It should be known that no intelligent person doubts the reality of sorcery."[8] "One cannot deny the actual existence of all the sciences declared illegal by the religious law. It is definite that sorcery is true, although it is forbidden."[9] Sufis were capable of doing things that seemed like magic, but the essential difference between sorcery and Sufi miracles (*karamat*) was moral. There was a clear distinction between a miracle-working Sufi, whose powers came from God and a magician who worked with talismans or magic letters.[10]

Not only had Ibn Khaldun direct experience of the supernatural, but also his belief in its reality was further strengthened by his youthful study of a Maliki work of jurisprudence, the *Risala* (letter) of Ibn Abi Zayd al-Qairouani (922–96). The *Risala*, as Rosenthal has noted, "presupposes the reality of sorcery, the evil eye, and the reality of dreams. On the other hand, it repudiates astrology as being incompatible with Islam. Ibn Khaldun studied this work in his youth and almost certainly must have known it by heart."[11] In line with his Malikism and his stress on the importance of *istislah* (concern for the public interest), Ibn Khaldun also thought that the study and practice of the occult arts had damaging consequences for society. It has been argued that there was an explosion of occultism in the Islamic world beginning in the twelfth and thirteenth centuries.[12] As was the case with his concerns about esoteric Sufism, Ibn Khaldun feared that obscure occult texts might carry veiled Shi'i messages and they might serve as the vehicle for disruptive political programs.

IBN KHALDUN'S EXPLORATION OF THE OCCULT

The literature of medieval Islamic occultism with which Ibn Khaldun was familiar constituted a disordered library, largely composed of forgeries, secretive coded texts, gibberish, ascriptions to imaginary ancestral authors, and with it all a great deal of attendant tedium. As the social theorist Theodor Adorno memorably observed, occult wisdom is "the metaphysics of dopes."[13] In the Middle Ages many Arab and Persian authors self-effacingly sought to secure publicity and circulation for what they had written by claiming that it had actually been composed by someone far more famous, such as Aristotle, the alchemist Jabir ibn Hayyan, the mathematician Maslama al-Majriti, the Sufis al-Buni and Ibn al-'Arabi, the imaginary Indian sorcerer Tumtum, or some other real or legendary celebrity. The names "Jabir ibn Hayyan" and "al-Buni" tended to be used as genre descriptions, giving guidance to the contents of the works in question, rather than designating the real authors. In the case of occult literature there was little or no desire on the part of the writers to put over information in a way that could easily be understood. It seemed better to hint at dark mysteries and to allude to obstacles that the reader would face on his path to enlightenment.

According to the *Muqaddima*, the sorcerer might achieve his results through the exercise of his will. Alternatively, he could draw on the occult powers inherent in the celestial spheres or in letters and numbers. A third way of achieving apparently supernatural effects was for the sorcerer to act upon the imaginations of those watching him. (Perhaps Ibn Khaldun was thinking of hypnotism here, though the word he actually used was *sha'badha*, which usually refers to "conjuring.")[14] Since sorcery involved veneration of spheres, stars, or jinn, it was a form of infidelity. Sorcery, the evil eye, and the divinatory power of dreams could be effective, but they could not interfere with processes of human history. Alchemy and astrology, on the other hand, were merely pseudosciences. Whether efficacious or not, magic was widely regarded by Muslims as something alien to Islam, as something that had either survived from pagan idolatry or that had been imported from neighboring infidel lands. Ibn Khaldun characterized the occult sciences as being, like philosophy, part of the *'ulum al-awa'il* (sciences of the ancients) and their study was seen as primarily an urban phenomenon and, of course, this did not recommend these subjects to him. He thought that the practice of astrology and alchemy had the power to do much damage to religion. The just penalty for sorcery (*sihr*) was death.[15]

The Copts in particular were regarded as the custodians of an ancient and secret Pharaonic wisdom. (Ibn Khaldun does not seem to have made any clear distinction between the Christian Copts and their Pharaonic predecessors.) According to Ibn Khaldun, the Qur'an provided evidence for the long-standing fondness of the Copts for magic, since Harut and Marut were Egyptian sorcerers.[16] (But this was an error on his part. Harut and Marut, who appear in the second Sura of the Qur'an, were two evil angels who taught men sorcery in Babel and Babel was traditionally located in Iraq.) Ibn Khaldun believed that the Egyptian temples were the relics of ancient sorcery and he regarded the Copts, ancient Syrians, and the Chaldaeans as the original specialists in sorcery, astrology, and talismans. In more recent times Indians had acquired renown as practitioners of magic: "We have also heard that in contemporary India, there still are (sorcerers) who point at a man, and his heart is extracted and he falls dead. When someone looks for his heart, he cannot find it among his inner parts. Or they point to a pomegranate. When someone opens it, no seeds are found."[17] He also referred to work on astrology by the (imaginary) sorcerer Tumtum the Indian.[18]

Having described the legendary eighth-century alchemist Jabir ibn Hayyan as the chief sorcerer of Islam, Ibn Khaldun added that Maslama al-Majriti was the only other great sorcerer.[19] Al-Majriti (d. 1057) was a distinguished mathematician, known as the "Euclid of Spain," and he was the teacher of Abu Muslim ibn Khaldun (d. 1057) who was one of Ibn Khaldun's Andalusian forebears. Ibn Khaldun erroneously believed that the sinister sorcerer's manual the *Ghayat al-hakim* ("Goal of the Sage," translated into Latin as *Picatrix*) and an alchemical treatise, the *Rutbat al-hakim* (Rank of the Sage), were both by the distinguished mathematician al-Majriti and therefore to be taken seriously. Ibn Khaldun seems to have been the first person to ascribe the authorship of the *Ghayat* and the *Rutbat* to al-Majriti, but this was certainly an error and it now seems that the real author was not the famous mathematician, but rather a minor sorcerer from Cordova known as Maslama al-Qurtubi (d. 964).[20]

THE PRACTICE OF ALCHEMY AND OF TREASURE HUNTING ARE BAD FOR SOCIETY

Jabir ibn Hayyan was believed to be an alchemist who lived in the late eighth and early ninth centuries, though most of the treatises ascribed to him appear to date from the late ninth and early tenth centuries. (The vast number of bizarre treatises on a wide range of occult subjects that were attributed to this legendary figure has been the subject of a marvelous study by Paul Kraus.)[21] As already noted, Ibn Khaldun described him as "the chief sorcerer of Islam." Having observed that Jabir wrote seventy treatises on alchemy, Ibn Khaldun added "All of them read like puzzles."[22] Later, he delivered a more general verdict: "One can see how all the expressions used by (alchemists) tend to be secret hints and puzzles, scarcely to be explained or understood. This is the proof that alchemy is not a natural craft."[23] Alchemists were either charlatans or self-deluded. Alchemy did not work, but, if it were to work, then the easy production of gold would destabilize economies and societies. (Here again Ibn Khaldun is guided by the principle of *istislah*.) Alchemy tended to be taken up by people who were too lazy to do a proper day's work. Similarly, forgers and treasure hunters should have their hands cut off.

The pseudoscience of treasure hunting was associated with alchemy and sorcery and it was discussed in that context in the *Muqaddima*.[24] The root meaning of *talib* (pl. *tullab*) is "seeker" but the word is commonly used in modern Arabic to mean "student." Unfortunately, in his translation of the section dealing with treasure hunting, Rosenthal has translated *tullab* as "students," whereas these *tullab* should be understood to be treasure hunters. Since treasures were widely believed to be protected by spells and curses, the pseudoscience of treasure hunting had occult resonances. Those brave and gullible enough to follow the professional treasure hunter had to steel themselves to face ancient curses, monsters, death-dealing automata, and lethal trapdoors.

Confidence tricksters used bogus maps and they might salt the alleged site of some great treasure with small quantities of gold and silver. In this way they secured funding for their spurious expeditions from gullible patrons. Underlying the feverish quest for hidden treasures was the sense that both the Maghreb and Egypt had been much wealthier in Pharaonic and Roman times. Where had all the gold and jewels gone? Ibn Khaldun very sensibly suggested much of the past wealth of the Maghreb and Egypt had passed to other regions such as India and Europe, while other treasures had been melted down or crumbled to dust. Treasure hunting was an unnatural way of trying to make a living and it was something that tended to be practiced by the inhabitants of big cities such as Cairo. He was particularly scornful about treasure maps and documents: "Why should anyone who hoards his money and seals it with magical operations, thus making extraordinary efforts to keep it concealed, set up hints and clues as to how it might be found by anyone who cares to?"[25]

LETTER MAGIC AND ASTROLOGY

Though decidedly cynical about alchemy and treasure hunting, Ibn Khaldun believed in the complementary sciences of numerology and letter magic: "The fact that it is possible to be active in the world of nature with the help of the letters and the words composed of them, and that the created things can be influenced in this way cannot be denied. It is confirmed by the continuous tradition on the authority of many (practitioners of letter magic)."[26] But he found the literature on the subject difficult and described it as "an unfathomable subject."[27] (I share his perplexity.)

All the letters had numerical values assigned to them. Although the sophisticated deployment of letter magic and numerology had been pioneered by Shi'is, certain Sufis also wrote on the subject, or had such works falsely ascribed to them, notably Ibn al-'Arabi and al-Buni. "These authors assume that the result and fruit of letter magic is that the divine souls are active in the world of nature by means of the beautiful names of God and the divine expressions that originate from the letters comprising the secrets that are alive in created things."[28] Al-Buni was a Shadhili Sufi mystic who died either in 1225 or in 1232–33 and either he wrote on letter magic and the creation of talismans, or he had such works ascribed to him. According to one of these treatises: "One should not think that one can get at the secret of the letters with the help of logical reasoning. One gets to it with the help of vision and divine aid."[29] In another of the treatises ascribed to al-Buni, letter magic was combined with astrology. But here Ibn Khaldun's commentary was at least as obscure as anything written by the sorcerers that he was so critical of: "The relationship (between star and magic word) is assumed to come from the nubilous ('amal'iyah) presence, which is the purgatory station (barzakhiyah) of verbal perfection and which particularizes itself in the realities in accordance with the relationship they have (to the magic words [?]). They think that those expressions depend on vision to be established. If a person who works with words lacks vision but knows about that relationship through tradition, his actions correspond to those of the person who works with talismans. Indeed, as we have stated, the (latter) is more reliable than he."[30] ("Nubilous" means cloudy, by the way.) In the end, Ibn Khaldun decided that the attempt by al-Buni or pseudo-Buni to distinguish letter magic from sorcery was not entirely convincing.[31]

THE BRETHREN OF PURITY AND THE
GREAT CHAIN OF BEING

Ibn Khaldun's encyclopedic presentation of the various sciences and crafts, as well as his preoccupation with the occult, may have owed something to the writings of the *Ikhwan al-Safa'* (Brethren of Purity). The *Ikhwan* were a secretive body of scholars, probably based in Basra in the tenth or eleventh century, who produced an encyclopedia, entitled simply *Rasa'il* (letters). There are signs of Neoplatonist as well as Isma'ili influence on the fifty-two letters that they produced. They drew heavily on the *Sirr al-asrar*, particularly with respect to occult matters. Cumulatively these letters aimed to guide the reader from concrete subjects to more abstract speculations and ultimately to salvation. Enlightenment would bring spiritual freedom. The *Ikhwan* presented man as a microcosm that corresponded to the macrocosm that was the universe. "As above, so below." The occult sciences featured prominently and the final letter of the encyclopedia, which is on magic and talismans, quoted heavily from the writings attributed to Hermes-Idris, the legendary source of so many magical arts as well as sciences and crafts. The interpretation of dreams was separately discussed in the batch of letters covering religious sciences (and perhaps this led Ibn Khaldun similarly to categorize dream interpretation as a religious science).[32]

The concept of the chain of being, or hierarchy of being, from the lowest to the highest form of existence was central to the

Ikhwan's vision of the universe, and it features also in the *Muqaddima*, where Ibn Khaldun wrote:

> The whole of existence in (all) its simple and composite worlds is arranged in a natural order of ascent and descent, so that everything constitutes an uninterrupted continuum. The essences at the end of each particular stage of the worlds are by nature prepared to be transformed into the essence adjacent to them, either above or below them. This is the case with the simple material elements; it is the case with palms and vines (which constitute) the last stage of plants, in their relation to snails and shellfish, (which constitute) the (lowest) stage of animals. It is also the case with monkeys, creatures combining in themselves cleverness and perception, in their relation to man, the being who has the ability to think and to reflect . . . Above the human world, there is a spiritual world . . . It is the world of the angels.[33]

It is the occasional ability to move from a lower to a higher stage of existence that allowed some individuals knowledge of the future and we must now turn to Ibn Khaldun's meditations on the future.

If, according to the *Muqaddima*, sorcery could not affect history, why did Ibn Khaldun pay so much attention to it? In part, it was, perhaps, because Berber sorcerers and confidence tricksters were perceived to be a social danger in the North African countryside. In part, Ibn Khaldun may have feared the overweening influence of certain ecstatic mystics and soothsayers at the sultan Barquq's court. Barquq relied on the guidance of a Persian Sufi, Shaykh al-Zuhuri. This man usually resided in the sultan's palace. He had foreseen his own death and that of the sultan and he told Barquq that he would not long survive him. Al-Zuhuri died in 1398 and the sultan died a few months later.[34] Another Persian philosopher of the occult, Shaykh Husayn al-Akhlati was also favored by Barquq and was first employed by the sultan as a physician. Perhaps because of the sultan's patronage, al-Akhlati became very wealthy. According to the Mamluk historian al-'Ayni he practiced alchemy and studied astrology, geomancy, and wisdom (*hikma*). He also consumed a lot of alcohol and drugs. Some of his followers believed him to be the expected Messiah. Al-Akh-lati died in 799/1397, aged over eighty.[35] More generally Barquq liked to have Sufis and occultists about him.

IS THE FUTURE KNOWABLE?

But I believe that the chief reason Ibn Khaldun was so obsessed with sorcery was because it overlapped with divination and the power to know the future. The famous historian Hugh Trevor Roper once critically remarked of Thomas Carlyle's way of writing about the past: "History is not prophesy." Nevertheless those who have written about the past often have one eye on the future. According to Sir Lewis Namier, the great historian of Hanoverian England, "Historians imagine the past and remember the future."[36] Though Ibn Khaldun wrote history, he returned again and again to topics that should more appropriately belong to futurology.

Ibn Khaldun was particularly concerned to distinguish between prophets and those who practiced divination. Only the prophets had a perfect vision of unseen things. The diviner had only a partial vision of particular things and sometimes his visions were provided by demons. Mirrors, geomancy, dreams, waking states, and all sorts of other phenomena could reveal glimpses of the future. The diviner, or *kahin*, was ranked below the prophet, and *'arraf*, who deduced the future from knowledge of events in the past, ranked below the *kahin*.

The *'arraf* also used knowledge of past events to do things like deduce the hiding places of stolen property.

Before proceeding to examine divinatory techniques in more detail, it may be worth asking what Ibn Khaldun thought that the future held for his world. First, he believed that techniques and sciences in the Islamic lands had reached their peak in his own time. He was also sure that the great age of the Arabs was over. After all, Baghdad, Samarra, and Rusafa were all now in ruins. The Berbers had taken over in the western Islamic lands and the Turks dominated the east. Also in an early draft of the *Muqad-*

dima he wrote that "we note that in our age civilization seems to be moving from south to north," and so the Franks and Turks and their dynasties had gained in power. He speculated that this shift of the central zone of civilization northwards might be due to the growing power of the sun or other astrological factors.[37] As we have already noted, Ibn Khaldun once observed that "there was no one to fear with regard to Egypt but the sons of Osman [the Ottomans]."

Though he was not so very interested in developments in Christian Europe, he nevertheless showed some signs of marginal unease at the way things were developing. Elsewhere in the *Muqaddima*, he wrote about intellectual developments in Europe: "We further hear that the philosophical sciences are greatly cultivated in the land of Rome and along the adjacent northern shore of the European Christians. They are said to be studied there again and to be taught in numerous classes. Existing systematic expositions of them are said to be comprehensive, the people who know them numerous and the students of them very many."[38] His history of the Franks commenced in the eleventh century and they were eccentrically presented as *badawi* in origin. He noted how Maghribi rulers now preferred to employ European mercenaries because of their superiority in fighting in formation.[39] The Christian merchants who visited the Maghreb seemed to be extraordinarily wealthy.[40] The Christian nations on the shores of the Mediterranean were more versed in the crafts than the Arabs.[41] He also fretted about the decline of Muslim sea power in the Mediterranean, though he concluded his discussion of the admiralty and sea power with these words: "The inhabitants of the Maghrib have it on the authority of the books of predictions that the Muslims will yet have to make a successful attack against the Christians and conquer the lands of the European Christians beyond the sea. This it is said will take place by sea."[42]

But Ibn Khaldun had claimed that "the future resembles the past more than one drop of water resembles another."[43] (The eighteenth-century philosopher David Hume would have begged to differ. In the *Treatise on Human Nature*, he wrote that "The supposition, *that the future resembles the past*, is not founded on arguments of any kind, but is derived entirely from habit.")[44] Despite those occasional misgivings concerning developments in the North, Ibn Khaldun thought that nothing very much was going to change—at least until the Last Days. Although he was preoccupied with knowledge of the future, he had no sense of social or technological progress, and he had no program of reform. Come to that, there was not going to be much future for things to change in, for he believed that he lived close to the End of Time.

THE PROPHET, THE SUFIS, AND THE SOOTHSAYERS

The laws of history, as formulated in the *Muqaddima*, provided no exact guidance to what would happen next. In this they might be thought to differ from certain forms of divination. *Kashf* and *mukashafa*, which have already been mentioned in the context of Sufism, are key terms in Ibn Khaldun's worldview. The ability to see beyond outward appearances was not restricted to Sufis and it might include visions of the future. He devoted many pages to considering the kind of knowledge of the future that was vouchsafed to the Prophet Muhammad and other prophets and how this was to be distinguished from the kinds of foreknowledge that might be available to Sufis, sorcerers, scryers, numerologists, dreamers, people on the point of death, and operators of a device known as the *za'iraja*.

Although it is conventional to describe Muhammad in English as "the Prophet" and indeed as the "Seal of the Prophets," neither of the two Arabic words that might be being translated here foreground prophecy in the sense of knowledge of the future. Rather *nabi* means "lawbringer sent by God" and *rasul* means "messenger." Muhammad's role in the seventh-century Hejaz was that of a messenger delivering warnings, just as the Old Testament prophets before him had delivered warnings to their people. Though Muhammad's knowledge of the future was attested in *hadiths* transmitted from his Companions, Ibn Khaldun did not discuss Muhammad's specific knowledge of future events in the sixth prefatory discussion that forms part of chapter 1 of the *Muqaddima*,

"The various types of human beings who have supernatural perception either through natural disposition or through exercise, preceded by a discussion of inspiration and dream visions."[45] Instead, he concentrated on purported alternative ways of deducing what was to come, particularly with respect to the Last Days. At times he seems to be suggesting that knowledge of the future was reserved to God alone, but at times he seems to be saying that not only are there divinely guided prophets, but there are also people who are not guided by God yet who can see into the future, even though it is immoral and irreligious of them to do so.

Ibn Khaldun reasoned (somewhat strangely) that since the biblical prophets and Muhammad had received knowledge of the future from God, divination carried out by lesser mortals also must be at least partially valid, since there had to be an inferior form of foretelling the future to correspond to the superior form of foreknowledge that was divinely inspired prophecy.

THE LAST DAYS

Some at least of the future was known to Muslims. Muslim ibn al-Hajjaj's *al-Sahih* (The Reliable), a great collection of *hadith*s, which was compiled in the ninth century and which was accepted by Sunnis as authoritative, gave details about the coming of the Antichrist and the Last Judgment as vouchsafed by the Prophet Muhammad. *Al-Bidaya wa'l-Nihaya* (The Beginning and the End), a chronicle compiled by Ibn Kathir (c. 1300–1373), not only recorded past events starting with the creation of the world, but also gave details about the predestined sequence of the Last Days.

In the *Muqaddima*, careful consideration is given to the Last Days and *mashiyyat Allah*, God's plan for the world:

> It has been well known (and generally accepted) by all Muslims in every epoch, that at the end of time a man from the family (of the Prophet) will without fail make his appearance, one who will strengthen the religion and make justice triumph. The Muslims

will follow him, and he will gain domination over the Muslim realm. He will be called the Mahdi [Guided One]. Following him, the Antichrist will appear, together with all the subsequent signs of the Hour (the Day of Judgment), as established in (the sound tradition of) the *Sahih*. After (the Mahdi), Isa (Jesus) will descend and kill the Antichrist. Or, Jesus will descend with the Mahdi, and help him kill (the Antichrist) and have him as the leader in his prayers.[46]

Here Ibn Khaldun presented the popular consensus of his time concerning the Mahdi, but he clearly had doubts about the bases for this consensus and he was very critical about other, more elaborate prophecies concerning the coming of the Mahdi. Belief in the Mahdi was not an essential part of Sunni doctrine. The two most reliable collections of *hadith*s did not mention the Mahdi and al-Ghazali did not concern himself with him. But later Abu 'Abd Allah al-Qurtubi (d. 1273) produced a collection of eschatological prophecies entitled the *Al-Tadhkira fi ahwal al-mawta wa umur al-akhira* (Reminder of the Affairs of the Dead and Matters of the Hereafter) and, faced with this and other eschatological works, Ibn Khaldun felt obliged to write about the various beliefs concerning the Mahdi at some length.[47]

'Ali was not only Muhammad's cousin but was also married to Muhammad's daughter Fatima. According to Shi'i lore, Muhammad revealed to 'Ali knowledge of future events up to and including the End of the World. Consequently, many Shi'is believed that all descendants of Fatima and 'Ali had the capacity to divine the future of dynasties and nations. The knowledge that had been vouchsafed to them was allegedly written down by the sixth Shi'i imam, Ja'far al-Sadiq (d. 765), and it was known as the Great *Jafr*. (The revelation was allegedly written on the skin of a *jafr*, which originally meant "a fat lamb or kid," but the word *jafr* later came to be used in the sense of "a divinatory text.") Its text was both unseen and infallible and its prophecies circulated as rumors. Later, all sorts of speculative texts employing letter magic and other divinatory techniques were also classified as *jafr*. Ibn Khaldun viewed *jafr* with suspicion and hostility, yet he hesitated to condemn it out of hand.

The *Muqaddima* devotes several pages to a prophetic poem, a cryptic example of *jafr* ascribed to a Sufi called al-Bajarbaqi, who attained knowledge of the future by "removal of the veil" (*kashf*). Al-Bajarbaqi's prophecies, like those of the French astrologer Nostradamus, are couched in allusive riddles. Neither Ibn Khaldun, nor his translator, Rosenthal, were able to make much sense of them (and neither can I). But the following lines may refer to Timur who was lame:

> This is the lame Kalbite[?]. Be concerned with him!
> In his time, there will be disturbances, and what disturbances!
> From the East, the Turkish army will come

(Rosenthal's rendering of *Kalbi* as Kalbite, a tenth-century Arab dynasty who ruled in Sicily, is most unlikely to be right. "Canine" or "dog-like" seems more likely.)

Then, as Ibn Khaldun himself noted, another verse seems to refer to the Circassian Mamluk sultan Barquq's bringing his father from Circassia to Egypt:

> His father will come to him after an emigration
> And a long absence and a hard and filthy life.[48]

A late text known as the "Little *Jafr*" contained prophecies that were really propaganda for the Almohad cause. The Little *Jafr* was associated with the founder of the Almohad dynasty, Muhammad ibn Tumart (d. 1130), who was claimed by his followers to be the Mahdi. According to Almohad propaganda, Ibn Tumart had been a pupil of the great Sufi and theologian al-Ghazali, who had recognized the high destiny of Ibn Tumart, since it had been foretold in the *Jafr* and, just before al-Ghazali died, he passed on to Ibn Tumart the prophetic manuscript.

Ibn Tumart was superbly magniloquent:

> If the ignorant rulers take over the world, and if deaf and dumb kings take over the world and if the *dajjalun* ["impostors," "antichrists"] take over the world, then only the Mahdi will get rid of falsehood, and only the Mahdi will carry out the truth. And the Mahdi is known among the Arabs and the non-Arabs and the

Bedouins and settled people. And knowledge concerning him is confirmed in every place and in every collection of documents. And what is known by the necessity of witness after his appearance. And faith in the Mahdi is a religious obligation, and he who doubts it is an unbeliever. And he is protected from error [*ma'sum*] in the matters of the faith which he invokes. No error is conceivable in him. He is not to be contended with, or opposed, or resisted, or contradicted or fought, and he is unique in his time and truthful in his words. He will sunder the oppressors and the impostors, he will conquer the world, both East and West, and fill it with justice as it had been filled with injustice, and his rule will last until the end of the world.[49]

Ibn Tumart, whose prestige was based both on his claim to be the Mahdi and on his supposed association with the Sufi thinker al-Ghazali, succeeded in establishing the Almohad dynasty in Morocco and Andalusia (1130–1269). The Little *Jafr* seems to have been compiled later as propaganda for the dynasty, as Ibn Khaldun rightly deduced from its "forecasts" concerning Almohad rulers, and he added that "the forecasts of the work are right with respect to the preceding period, and they are wrong for the later period."[50] The Fatimid dynasty, like the Almohad dynasty, had been established by a man claiming to be the Mahdi. 'Ubaydallah ibn Husayn, who claimed to descend from Fatima (a claim that Ibn Khaldun spent some time in verifying in book 1 of the *Muqaddima*) declared himself to be the Mahdi in 909 and established a Shi'ite empire that was to extend over Ifriqiyya, Libya, Sicily, and Egypt. But 'Ubaydallah and his descendants kept having to announce the postponement of the promised apocalypse.

Abu 'Abdallah al-Qurtubi's *Tadhkira* had predicted that the Mahdi would first appear in Morocco and go on to lead the Muslims to conquer Christendom. Apart from 'Ubaydallah and Ibn Tumart, other less successful, self-proclaimed-miracle-working Mahdis were the curse of medieval North African politics. The people in remote tribal areas seem to have lived in continuous expectation of the coming of such a figure who would lead them in revolt and bring justice to their world. "The common people, the stupid mass, who make claims with respect to the

Mahdi and who are not guided in this connection by any intelligence or helped by any knowledge, assume that the Mahdi may appear in a variety of circumstances and places."[51] Berber tribesmen expected the leaders of Mahdist rebellions to perform supernatural wonders. Politics and occultism were two sides of a strange coin.

Elsewhere the Hidden Imam of Twelver Shi'ism was equated with the Mahdi (literally "the guided one"). He was held to be the promised charismatic leader who at the End of Time would revive Islam and lead it to worldwide triumph. In several cities in the eastern Islamic lands Shi'is kept a horse saddled, bridled, and ready for the Mahdi when he should appear. While Ibn Khaldun seems to have accepted that the Mahdi would appear and that his coming would herald the end of the world, he was hostile to specific Sufi and Shi'i prophecies about his coming. In particular Ibn Khaldun rejected the notion that the Mahdi would appear in some out-of-the-way place and he also insisted that he would have to possess state-building qualities. Even the Mahdi would need the support of 'asabiyya.[52]

ASTROLOGY AND "SLAUGHTERINGS"

Turning now to astrology, Ibn Khaldun could not deny its validity out of hand, since it seemed to receive support from the Qur'an. "Surely in the creation of the heavens and earth, in the alternation of night and day, there are signs for men possessed of minds" (Qur'an 3:190). As Fromherz has observed: "For Ibn Khaldun, the science of astrology held as many secrets about humanity's actions as his more interesting theories of economy, tribalism and state development. He was keen to show instances in history when astrology worked. For him, the rise of the Almohads was as much a confirmation of astrological theory as historical theory."[53]

But Ibn Khaldun had not been impressed by the predictions made by astrologers and considerations of social welfare (istislah) fuelled his animus against astrology, since predictions could have undesirable political results, as the prophecies of astrologers might inspire rebellions, which in turn might bring about the downfall of dynasties.[54] Yet he was not entirely consistent when dealing with this subject, since he seemed to find nothing objectionable in the use of astrology as an ancillary by geomancers. Moreover, as we have seen, he speculated that the apparent movement of power northwards might have astrological causes and he toyed with the idea that a conjunction of Jupiter and Saturn might have been behind the rise Timur's Turco-Mongol Empire.

Malahim, literally "slaughterings," is the term applied to prophecies, which were usually astrologically based, concerning the fate of dynasties, civilizations, and the end of the world. Ibn Khaldun was sceptical about this genre: "Works in poetry and in prose and in *rajaz* verse dealing with forecasts concerning dynasties were written in considerable quantity. Much of it found its way into the hands of the people. It is called 'predictions' (*malahim*). Some of these works concern forecasts about Islam in general. Others are about particular dynasties. All of these works are attributed to famous persons. But there is nothing to support ascribing them to the persons on whose authority they are transmitted." The *malahim* quoted by Ibn Khaldun were all in verse and dealt with the fates of various North African dynasties.[55] Despite denying the authority and accuracy of these treatises, he was also fascinated and he quoted from them extensively. *Sayahat al-bum fi hawadith al-Rum* (Cry of the Owl Concerning Byzantine Events) was a prophetic treatise that circulated widely. It was spuriously ascribed to Ibn al-'Arabi and it predicted the fall of Constantinople and Rome to the Muslims. Ibn Khaldun became acquainted with this work once he reached Egypt.[56]

Ibn Khaldun was acquainted with other prophetic treatises that were either by Sufis or had a spurious Sufi authorship foisted on them. Abu'l-'Abbas Ibn al-Banna' (c. 1285–1321) was a mathematician, astronomer, and Sufi based in Marrakesh. He was also regarded by Ibn Khaldun as a leading practitoner of astrology and letter magic (*hisab al-nim*), which could be used to predict which king would win when they went to war.[57] It is strange that Ibn al-Banna' was credited both with treatises that expounded the occult sciences and with treatises that refuted those same sciences. As a young Sufi initiate he was granted a vision of the entire celestial sphere and this was taken as a prefigurement of his career as an astronomer and astrologer. Years later he had a second vision, this time of a vast brass dome floating between heaven and earth and within it a man praying. The man praying turned out to be his Sufi shaykh who later revealed to him that this vision signaled his initiation into occult knowledge of the future.[58] Al-Abili, the youthful Ibn Khaldun's teacher, had been a disciple of Ibn al-Banna'. (The idea that the youthful Ibn Khaldun studied only the sober sciences, philosophy, logic, and mathematics with al-Abili may be a mistaken one.)

MORE POSSIBLE WAYS TO KNOW THE FUTURE

Ibn Khaldun interested himself in all the possible techniques for predicting the future. The pre-Islamic sorcerers and soothsayers, the *kahin*s, made use of a special kind of rhymed and rhythmic prose known as *saja'* to stimulate or shape their prophetic utterances.[59] (*Saja'* was first used to refer to the trance that the *kahin* entered into, though in modern Arabic the word refers just to rhymed prose.) Al-Mas'udi had devoted a chapter of the *Muruj al-dhahab* to fortune-telling (*kahana*), in which he stated that its reality was well attested by Arabic and foreign sources. People with pure souls who shunned society and led a nomadic way of life were particularly blessed with this divine gift and the pure-souled Bedouin Arabs were especially endowed with this ability.[60] It was more or less inevitable that Ibn Khaldun should follow up on this theme in the *Muqaddima*. He believed in the stories told about the two most famous pre-Islamic *kahin*s, Shiqq and Satih. The latter "used to fold up like a garment, as he had no bones except for his skull." Satih managed to deduce from someone's dream the coming of Muhammad and the destruction of the Persian Empire.[61] The dictionary meaning of "*satih*" is "flattened on the ground and unable to rise on account of the weakness in his limbs." But, according to other sources, when Satih was inspired to prophesy he would inflate himself and thus be able to stand.

Catoptromancy, divination from reflections, was also featured in the *Muqaddima*. Its practitioners gazed on a mirror until its surface disappeared and was replaced by a white cloud in which images appeared. Ibn Khaldun went on to discuss ornithomancy (*zajr*) and the drawing of auguries from the chance sightings of animals. Here the augur reflects on what he has seen and then lets his imagination work upon it.[62] Some ways of ascertaining the future were decidedly ghoulish: "We have been informed that certain criminal tyrants used to kill their prisoners in order to learn their own future from the words the prisoners would utter when they were about to be killed. It was unpleasant information they received from them."[63]

And, a little later, Ibn Khaldun remarked:

> In the *Ghayah*, Maslamah . . . mentioned that when a human being is placed in a barrel of sesame oil and kept in it for forty days, is fed with figs and nuts until his flesh is gone and only the arteries and the sutures of the skull remain, and is then taken out of the oil and exposed to the drying action of the air, he will answer all special and general questions regarding the future that may be asked. This is detestable sorcery. However, it shows what remarkable things exist in the world of man.[64]

Then he went on to briefly mention the medieval Arab precursors of today's flatliners. These were people who found ways to achieve a near-death state in order to gather information about the future. "It is definitely known that when death descends upon the body, sensual perception and the veil it constitutes disappear, and the soul beholds its essence and the world."[65]

THE BAFFLING *ZA'IRAJA* DEVICE

Ibn Khaldun devoted a lot of space to the *za'iraja al-'alam*, or *za'iraja* of the world. This had been an earlier enthusiasm of his. He encountered this device, half divination machine, half parlor game, during his stay in Biskra in 1370 and, writing about it much later, he described it as "a remarkable technical procedure." It is discussed in two places in the *Muqaddima*.[66] The circular diagram of the *za'iraja* displays concentric circles representing the heavenly spheres, the elements, the sublunary world, existants, and sciences. The names of the zodiacal houses are written in the outermost circle. Chords run from the center out to the circle's circumference. The *za'iraja*'s circle is set within a rectangle divided into numerous compartments and on one side of that square there is a verse ascribed to Malik ibn Wuhayb, one of the greatest diviners of the Maghreb.

In order to question this strange oracle, one first writes one's question and then breaks the question down into its component letters. Then, having taken account of which sign of the zodiac is in the ascendant, one selects the chord that is astrologically indicated and follows its line to the center and thence to the chord that takes one to the opposite side of the circumference. On that chord are letters and numbers in tiny characters known as *ghurab*. The numbers are converted into letters by a process known as *hisab al-jummal*. The total of these letters is added to the letters of the question. Then further procedures, too complicated and tedious to list here, are used to gather yet more letters from the *za'iraja* and in the final procedure certain letters are produced that are in the same rhyme and meter as the verse ascribed to Malik ibn Wuhayb and the verse so formed will give an answer to the initial question.

Ibn Khaldun asked the device to reveal who had invented it and he received the answer in verse that it was the Qur'anic sage, Idris. Idris was identified by Muslims as being the Enoch of the Old Testament, a holy figure who attained immortality. Idris-Enoch was additionally often identified with the Greek Hermes. He was credited with being the inventor of a range of crafts and sciences, and, among other things, he was said to be the first astronomer.

Ibn Khaldun denied that sorcery was involved in the operation of *za'iraja* and he also discounted the possibility that the operators of the *za'irja* device cheated by manipulating the play of letters. He suggested, somewhat doubtfully, that there was nothing supernatural about the procedure and that perhaps the answers were implicit in the questions.[67] But he was not consistent in his skepticism, for he also argued that the *za'iraja* could be consulted for past events, but that it would be wrong and impious to use it for future events (and so sorcery did after all underlie its procedures). Also, there seems to have been something implicitly mystical about the process, since the questioner should prepare himself by reciting Sufi *dhikr*s.[68] Moreover, the lengthy and extremely obscure poem, cited by Ibn Khaldun, which was intended to celebrate and explain the *za'iraja,* refers to the famous Sufis Dhu'l-Nun al-Misri, al-Junayd, and Abu Yazid al-Bistami.

WHAT DREAMS MAY COME

Ibn Khaldun classified dream interpretation as one of sciences of the religious law, since it was akin to religious prophecy.[69] Dreams might offer true visions of the future and the Qur'an legitimized dream interpretation, since in "Joseph," Sura 12 of the Qur'an, Joseph correctly interpreted his own dream and that of Pharaoh. The divinatory power of dreams was also attested in *hadith*s and Ibn Khaldun quoted Muhammad's saying that a good dream was "the forty-sixth part of prophecy." Every morning the Prophet used to ask the men around him if they had had any dreams. "He asked this question in order to derive good news from dream visions, which might refer to the victory of Islam and the growth of its power."[70] Dreams could remove the veil of sensory perception. Clear dreams came from God, allegorical ones from angels, and confused ones from Satan.

Ibn Khaldun had consulted the sorcerer's manual, the *Ghayat al-hakim,* on the category of the dream word, *al-haluma.* This was a word that one said to oneself before going to sleep and then one specified what one wanted and then the thing one asked for would be shown to him in in the person's sleep. "With the help of these words I myself have had remarkable dream visions, through which I learned things about myself that I wanted to know."[71]

HISTORY AND SCIENCE FICTION

For Ibn Khaldun, history was a process that extended into the future.

Distant echoes of Ibn Khaldun's theorizing about the history of the past and the future can be found in twentieth-century science fiction. Isaac Asimov's *Foundation* trilogy, consisting of *Foundation* (1951), *Foundation and Empire* (1952), and *Second Foundation* (1953), was praised in the *Times* as "one of the most staggering achievements in modern SF."[72] At the 1966 World Science Fiction Convention the trilogy was voted "the greatest all-time science-fiction series." The "Foundation" of the title was established by the psychohistorian Hari Seldon. Thanks to his understanding of the laws of history, Seldon had foreseen the collapse of the Galactic Empire and the centuries of violence and barbarism that would follow and therefore he had established the Foundation ostensibly to preserve the sciences and arts and make record of all human knowledge (though the secret long-term aim was to replace the Empire as the maintainer of order in the Galaxy). Seldon taught that psychohistory was "that branch of mathematics which deals with the reactions of human conglomerates to fixed social and economic stimuli."[73] The behavior of humans in the mass could be predicted. The idea of psychohistory, which drew on mathematics, sociology, psychology, and history, shows the influence of the *Muqaddima*, as transmitted and popularized in Arnold Toynbee's *A Study in History* (on which, see chapter 10). Toynbee had mapped out a theory of the rise, decay, and fall of civilizations that relied heavily on challenge and renewal. A leading theme in Asimov's trilogy was the way in which the Foundation met successive challenges and in dealing with them became stronger. The warlord known as "the Mule," who appeared in *Foundation and Empire,* was modeled on Timur who had threatened the rise of the Ottoman Empire. But, though the ideas of Ibn Khaldun and Toynbee have a ghostly presence in this science fiction masterpiece, the influence of Gibbon's *Decline and Fall of the Roman Empire* 1776–88 is more obvious and more influential, even if Gibbon's account was retrospective, while that of Seldon was prospective.[74]

To return to fourteenth-century North Africa, prophets, Sufis, esoteric Shi'is, strangely inspired madmen, and charlatans all claimed to have access to knowledge of the future. The widespread preoccupation with the future and especially the Last Days was perhaps the product of an age of anxiety. Rulers such as Abu'l-Hassan, Barquq, and Timur listened anxiously to what the diviners had to say. Promises of foreordained victories ignited revolts in remote parts of the Maghreb. People waited impatiently for justice and a miraculous solution to their social and economic problems. Medieval futurology was political. No wonder Ibn Khaldun gave the subject so much attention.

CHAPTER EIGHT

✦✦✦

Economics before Economics
Had Been Invented

Not only has Ibn Khaldun been presented as a precursor of such economic thinkers as Marx, Engels, and Pareto, but, at a press conference held in October 1981, Ronald Reagan quoted Ibn Khaldun in support of his view of what is known as "supply side economics." In its early years a regime fixes taxes at a low rate but nevertheless takes in large revenues. But, as the regime decays, it sets high rates of taxation but takes in diminishing amounts of revenue. (This model of higher taxation rates bringing in a lower revenue is known as a Laffer curve.) How marvelous that a fourteenth-century North African thinker should have anticipated American Republican Party fiscal policy! But as we shall see, Reagan (or his speech writers) had misread Ibn Khaldun, and, of course, Ibn Khaldun was not an economist in the modern sense.

It is true that he wrote extensively about economic matters, particularly in chapters 4 and 5 of the *Muqaddima*, and he was original and almost unique among medieval Arab writers in doing so. (The medieval Arabic term for economics was *tadbir al-manzil*, but that literally means "household management.") The importance of economic factors featured prominently in the *Muqaddima*, for economic need was at the basis of all society. He had to work out his ideas on economics from what was practically a standing start. Humans come together and form associations so that they may earn a living.[1] Economic needs create human society and hence underpin all history. A single man on his own cannot support himself. A labor force is necessary to sow the grain, then harvest it, winnow it, and eventually cook it. Civilization will depend on people coming together and producing more food than they need to consume themselves. The division of labor is a prod-

uct of the coming together of people in *'umran* (society or civilization). The more people come together, the more crafts and trades
become possible. Cooperation generates a surplus. Prosperity is
the concomitant of density of population.[2]

Ibn Khaldun's ideas about economics drew upon ethics, *hikma*,
Islamic law, and personal observation. Moral judgments played a
larger part in his deliberations than did the observed movement
of money and goods. As an example of his reliance on *hikma*,
near the beginning of the *Muqaddima*, he had cited the *Sirr al-
asrar* on the role of money and taxation in shaping the circle of
virtue (which we have already encountered): "The world is a garden the fence of which is the dynasty . . . The ruler is supported
by the soldiers. The soldiers are helpers who are maintained by
money. Money is sustenance brought together by the subjects"
and so on.[3]

But the strongest influence on Ibn Khaldun's thinking on the
subject seems to have come from al-Ghazali's *Ihya' 'ulum al-din*, in
which various economic issues had been treated in a religious context. Al-Ghazali regarded commerce as *fard kifaya*—that is to say,
something that was necessary, but not all Muslims were obliged to
engage in it. He denounced the hoarding of foodstuffs, the circulation of debased coinage, and the making of excess profits.

A LABOR THEORY OF VALUE

The right kind of economic theory had to be shaped by moral
considerations and, since Ibn Khaldun so disapproved of luxury
and extravagance, he was hardly going to provide a guide for
rulers and their subjects on how to maximize their incomes. Instead he charted the cyclical rise and fall of urban prosperity. (It is
striking that in his discussion of economic processes, he confines
himself to urban commerce, urban crafts, and long-distance trade
between cities, thereby rather neglecting the agricultural and pas-
toral economies.) Labor produces income and "profit is the value
realised from labor."[4] Here Ibn Khaldun would seem to be anticipating the labor theory of value as propounded by Adam Smith,

David Ricardo, and Karl Marx. But, as we shall see, Ibn Khaldun also recognized that profit was also affected by such factors as demand and scarcity. Moreover, people who owned property might be able to make big profits without laboring at all.[5] (Money lending is not discussed.)

Earned income that is sufficient to provide a livelihood is classified as sustenance (*ma'ash*). Excess income will either be used to buy luxuries or it will be accumulated as capital. Towns and villages enable the division of labor. As the population of a town grows, so does its capacity to produce "luxury and the things that go with it, such as splendid houses and clothes, fine vessels and utensils, and the use of servants and mounts."[6] Even the beggars in big cities are better off than those in small towns. And Ibn Khaldun grimly noted how the premises of the rich attract ants, insects, and rats. "God's secret in this respect should be scrutinized."[7] Industrial workers or craftsmen in large towns find their services in high demand and consequently they charge high prices and become arrogant. City life is expensive, so expensive that the Bedouin and other rural folk find it difficult to accumulate enough wealth to come and settle in a city. But the migration of poor rural folk to cities like Istanbul, Cairo, Beijing, and Shanghai in modern times suggests that Ibn Khaldun was wrong on this particular point. He presented the countryside as being economically dependent on the towns.

God created gold and silver as the measure of value for all things. These metals are not subject to market fluctuations.[8] But an event in recent history should have led Ibn Khaldun to a different conclusion. When in 1324 Mansa Musa, the Emperor of Mali, proceeded on the *hajj* via Egypt he and his entourage brought so much gold dust and bullion with them that in Cairo the value of gold dropped in relation to silver.[9] According to a saying attributed to the Prophet, "A time is certainly coming over mankind in which there will be nothing left of use save a *dinar* and *dirham*." It seems most likely that Ibn Khaldun shared al-Maqrizi's prejudice against the copper coin known as the *fals* (pl. *fulus*). When Ibn Khaldun came to discuss the sultan's prerogative of minting coins, he confined himself to the minting of gold and silver coins, that is, *dinars* and *dirham*s. In Mamluk Egypt and Syria, because coins did not conform to the legal weight prescribed by the Shari'a, they had to be weighed in order to establish their value.[10]

DEPLORABLE WAYS OF MAKING A LIVING

Though the prices of commodities should be determined primarily by the value of labor, other factors had to be taken into account. While commerce must be legal, Ibn Khaldun seems suspicious of it, since "its practices and methods are tricky" and it contains "an element of gambling."[11] He had an intellectual aristocrat's contempt for trading: "This requires cunning, willingness to enter into disputes, cleverness, constant quarrelling, and great persistence. These are things that belong to commerce. They are qualities detrimental to and destructive of virtuousness and manliness, because it is unavoidable that actions influence the soul."[12] Commerce was a necessity, but a regrettable one. Since trading depended on such chancy factors as the weather, shortages, price rises, and so on, it was akin to gambling. (Long before Ibn Khaldun, the jurist Malik ibn Anas had entertained similar suspicions about the legitimacy of buying and selling.)

Various ways of making a living are not natural and Ibn Khaldun provided an oddly assorted list of those who made a living in unnatural ways, including rulers and governors, soldiers, servants, and treasure hunters. By contrast, natural ways of making a living included hunting and fishing, pastoralism, agriculture, craftsmanship, and commerce. It is implied that being paid a salary is not a natural way of earning a living.

Profit is made by laborers producing things that people want. But the common people are not normally aware of needing religious learning and consequently religious office-holding and scholarship, both of which were likely to be salaried, were not the royal road to riches.[13] People could get along fine without *qadi*s, *khatib*s, *faqih*s, and muezzins. It is true that religious officials and scholars are of some use to rulers, but they are not as useful as viziers, generals, and tribal leaders and therefore they are not so well paid. (One feels that here Ibn Khaldun is writing from bitter personal experience.)

Not only was Ibn Khaldun suspicious of commerce, he also deplored the accumulation of excess capital and he cited a *hadith* to this effect: "The Prophet said: 'The only thing you (really) possess of your property is what you ate, and have thus destroyed, or what you wore, and have thus worn out; or what you gave to charity, and have thus spent."[14] Although estates and farms do not provide a decent income, moneyed people nevertheless buy them in the hope that such investments will provide enough income for their offspring to subsist on. But such properties are always liable to be confiscated by the authorities, and so such an investment "spells harm and hardship to its owners." More generally, wealthy city dwellers are likely to attract the jealousy of rapacious rulers and emirs. Tyranny and arbitrary confiscations became the norm in Muslim societies that followed Muhammad and his immediate successors, the *Rashidun* caliphs.[15]

PROSPERITY AND POPULATION DENSITY GO TOGETHER

The more populous a city is the more prosperous it is. Urban conditions allow specialization of labor and, if the consequent labor produces more than is necessary, this will lead on to profit and comfortable living, even luxury. This might seem like a good thing to a modern economist, but not to Ibn Khaldun. Sedentary culture leads to diversification, luxury, immorality, corruption, and death. Because the services of workers, craftsmen, and professional people are much in demand in the cities, they become arrogant.[16] The growing prosperity of a town had the effect of reducing the value of basic necessities and Ibn Khaldun thought that high profits discouraged the artisans from working as hard as they might. The sedentary desire for luxury ruined the urban economy. "Immorality, wrongdoing, insincerity, and trickery, for the purposes of making a living in a proper or an improper manner, increase among them. The soul comes to think about (making a living), to study it, and to use all possible trickery for that purpose. People are now devoted to lying, gambling, cheating, fraud, perjury, and usury."[17] And so the cities, which teem with immoral people, conform to the judgment of God. As the Qur'an has it: "When we want to destroy a village, we order those of its inhabitants who live in luxury to act wickedly therein. Thus, the word becomes true for it, and we do destroy it."[18]

Drawing on his knowledge of North African cities, Ibn Khaldun pronounced that the bigger the city was the richer it was (but, again, if we think of modern cities such as Mumbai, Cairo, or Rio de Janeiro, it is not obvious that he was right). Inflation is an inevitable consequence of city life.[19] Hoarding is not only immoral, but also dangerous for the hoarder, since the grain he stores may not bring a profit. Moreover, and somewhat mysteriously, Ibn Khaldun maintains that this practice brings bad luck to the hoarder and he "is persecuted by the combined psychic powers of the people whose money he takes away, for people's souls cling to their money and they do not readily relinquish it."[20] (Here economic theory slides into occult science.)

Jah (rank or social prestige) has almost as much importance in Ibn Khaldun's thinking as *'asabiyya* and *jah* had economic consequences. The possessors of such prestige find it easier to make money and to retain it. Because of their influence and growing wealth, such people attract both clients and gifts. Traders and artisans need the protection of men who were possessed of *jah* if they were going to be able to work without being robbed, conned, or threatened by hostile legal suits.[21] Agriculture, being a primitive way of making a living, has little or no prestige. Also it is easy to exercise authority over farmers and to tax them.

Ibn Khaldun was extremely hostile to rulers engaging in trade and to their establishment of monopolies. This damaged the wider economy and he cited the wise practice of the ancient Persians, who forbade their rulers to farm or trade. They were also not supposed to use slaves as servants.[22]

He believed that the economic decline of the Maghreb and other regions was chiefly due to population decline. But he allowed that there might also have been astrological factors, for he believed that part of the reason for the greater prosperity of Eastern Islamic lands was due to favorable astrological conjunctions. "The (existence of a) correspondence between astrological judgements and terrestrial civilization and nature is something inevitable."[23] It is certainly plausible that the prosperity of the Maghreb was adversely affected by the coming of the Black Death. But there were other factors that he did not take account of, including the decline of the gold trade route, which reached the Mediterranean via Sijilmasa. Also, European shipping was acquiring a near monopoly over maritime commerce in the Mediterranean. In Egypt Ibn Khaldun paid no attention to the importance to the economy of the Karimi merchants and their importation of spices from the Indies via the Red Sea.

IBN KHALDUN DID NOT INVENT THE LAFFER CURVE

Reagan's praying Ibn Khaldun in aid is at best only partially correct, since Ibn Khaldun's "economic" model placed great weight on the political and moral decline of the dynasty. He did not think that high taxes were the main cause of reduced revenue; rather the high taxes were a consequence of increased expenditure and reduced income. A new dynasty only imposed those taxes that were allowed by religious law: *zakat* (the charity tax), *jizya* (the poll tax), and *kharaj* (the land tax). The new dynasty possesses the virtuous attitudes that have been formed in the desert, including respect for other people's property and a disinclination to appropriate it. Businesses thrive in such circumstances. But city life breeds sophistication and a taste for luxury among the ruling group. Moreover, the ruler needs to recruit and pay armed forces to replace his former support from warrior tribesmen. All this leads to increases in taxation and arbitrary levies. As the tax tariffs increase, people become disinclined to trade or engage in other forms of work. So tax revenue decreases. The dynasty becomes senile and too weak to collect taxes from outlying areas. Sometimes the ruler even tortures his officials and tax collectors in order to force them to disgorge the revenues that they have been holding back. What was just as bad, in Ibn Khaldun's eyes, was that the ruler might set up state monopolies and manipulate the prices for the commodities under his control.²⁴ Early on in the life cycle of a dynasty the ruler distributes most of his revenue to the tribal following who put him in power. Later on a ruler seeks to keep it for himself and his court entourage. In the final stage, large amounts of money have to be spent on dealing with rebels and rivals.

Implicitly at least Ibn Khaldun regarded all taxes that were not sanctioned by the religious law as illegal. After remarking that a hoarder "is persecuted by the combined psychic powers of the people whose money he takes away," Ibn Khaldun recalled how his great teacher, al-Abili, had told him about his acquaintance the chief qadi of Fez who had just been offered a choice of taxes to make up his salary. The qadi chose the tax on wine. When his friends expressed astonishment at his choosing such an immoral source of income, he explained: "All tax money is forbidden. Therefore, I chose the tax that is not haunted by the souls of those who had to pay it. Rarely would anyone spend his money on wine unless he were gay and happy with the experience (of drinking wine), and did not regret it. His soul, therefore, does not cling to the money he has had to spend." Ibn Khaldun added, "This is a remarkable observation."²⁵ (So economic theory again slides into occult science.)

ENGELS AND IBN KHALDUN

Engels had clearly read a translation of Ibn Khaldun and portrayed him in aid of a Marxist and Orientalist account of the backwardness of Islamic societies:

> Islam suits Orientals, especially the Arabs, that is to say, on the one hand, townsmen practising commerce and industry, on the other hand, nomadic Beduin. But there is in this a periodic collision. Townsmen, growing opulent and ostentatious, become lax in the observation of the "Law." The Beduin, poor and hence austere in their manners, contemplate the wealth and enjoyment with envy and lust. They unite under the direction of a prophet, a Mahdi, to

punish the faithless, to re-establish the ceremonial law and the true faith, and by way of recompense to appropriate the treasure of the faithless. A hundred years later, naturally they find themselves at exactly the same point as their predecessors; a new purification is required; a new Mahdi emerges; the game restarts. So it has come to pass since the wars of conquest of the Almoravides and the African Almohads in Spain till the latest Mahdi of Khartoum . . . It was the same, or very nearly, during the convulsions in Persia and other Muslim lands. These movements are born of economic causes even if they have a religious camouflage. But, even when they succeed, they leave the economic conditions intact. Thus nothing has changed, and the collision becomes periodic. By contrast, for the popular risings in the Christian West the religious camouflage is only the banner and mask for an attack on a crumbling social order: in the end, that order is overturned; a new one emerges; there is progress, the world moves on.[26]

Ibn Khaldun, of course, would not have regarded Islam as serving as camouflage for economic greed and he might have found Engels's notion of economically based historical progress hard to grasp.

Though economics was not a recognized science in the Arab world, a few scholars did produce treatises on the subject. As we have seen, al-Maqrizi, who had been strongly influenced by Ibn Khaldun, wrote a treatise on high prices and famines and another on coinage. Maqrizi's economic writings took the form of anti-Mamluk polemics and at one point he remarked that just about the only thing we are allowed to do without paying tax is breathe. The Syrian al-'Asadi, who wrote later in the fifteenth century (we do not have precise dates), wrote a treatise on the economic ills of Egypt and Syria, *Al-Taysir wa'l-i'tibar*, in which he attacked the abusive taxation, monopolies, and corruption of the Mamluk regime. Overtaxation forced the peasants to abandon the land. Like al-Maqrizi, he advocated a return to the religiously canonical gold and silver coinage. At the time he wrote, the coinage was debased and was traded by weight rather than counted.[27] All those who wrote on economics in this period, including Ibn Khaldun, al-Maqrizi, and al-'Asadi, attacked the interventions of the ruling regimes in their economies, but it was only Ibn Khaldun who succeeded in putting his moralizing and religiously based ideas about economic practice within the broader context of a science of society or civilization (*'ilm al-'umran*).

CHAPTER NINE

✦✦✦

What Ibn Khaldun Did for a Living

TEACHING AND WRITING

A later Mamluk historian and biographer, al-Sakhawi, noted that Ibn Khaldun taught in a different way from his contemporaries.[1] Though Ibn Khaldun spent much of his career in both politics and writing, he spent even more of his life in teaching. It was more or less inevitable that he should have devoted a lot of thought to the principles and practice of pedagogy and he covered this in the last chapter of the *Muqaddima*. A number of Arab writers had previously written on this subject, most notably, the brilliant ninth-century essayist al-Jahiz, who in his *Risala fi mu'allimin* (Letter on Teachers) argued that the teaching of arithmetic and writing was of the first importance. It is a little surprising that this elegant and erudite writer argued that the teaching of arithmetic should actually have priority over the teaching of writing. Moreover, he thought students should not be taught the refinements of style and grammar at the expense of a broader knowledge.[2]

The young Ibn Khaldun seems to have been educated at home by his father and various Tunisian scholars. Later, when the Merinid Abu'l-Hasan entered Tunis with his scholarly entourage, Ibn Khaldun's intellectual horizons were greatly widened. The education he received was either on a one-to-one basis or in small groups. Though his studies continued throughout the rest of his life, he never enrolled as a student at a *madrasa* (religious college). As a young man he moved from teacher to teacher, collecting *ijaza*s (licenses to teach what he had learned from a particular teacher). The content of a book was not truly mastered unless it had been commented on by its author, or by someone who had acquired the authority to guide the student through the book. Teaching was usually a mixture of dictation and commentary on what had been dictated. There was a widespread prejudice against the written transmission of knowledge. *Tadris*, meant "study," but it usually referred specifically to the study of religious law. Continuity (*sanad*) was important. Education was a matter of transmitting what was known down the generations and originality was at a discount.

Though the Andalusian scholar Abu Bakr ibn al-ʿArabi (who died in 1148 and who is not to be confused with Muhyi al-Din ibn al-ʿArabi, the thirteenth-century Sufi) had argued that children should be taught texts other than the Qur'an, because the Qur'an was too difficult, Ibn Khaldun regretted that this would hardly be possible, since North African parents would insist on teaching reading skills from the Qur'an, because study of the holy book would be conducive to their salvation. He thought that the Andalusian syllabus overvalued the mastery of style at the expense of religious study. Study of the religious sciences and *hikma* had to be given priority. Such subjects as logic, philology, and arithmetic were auxiliary subjects and one could waste one's life in spending too much time on them. Of course, the Qur'an had to be the basis of all education. But, though teaching of schoolchildren in North Africa was narrowly focused on the Qur'an, Ibn Khaldun in principle seems to have favored studying poetry, philology, and arithmetic as preparation for approaching the holy book.[3] A saying of the Prophet enjoined Muslims to "seek knowledge even as far as China." Ibn Khaldun, who traveled widely in North Africa and Andalusia prior to leaving for Egypt, recommended traveling in search of teachers. North African scholars who had traveled east to study in Mecca, Cairo, Damascus, or Baghdad, such as al-Abili or Ibn Marzuq, gained a great deal of prestige from that fact.

THERE ARE TOO MANY BOOKS.
ORAL TEACHING IS BEST

Oral transmission of knowledge was primary. Rather than praise books as vehicles for the transmission of knowledge, Ibn Khaldun wrote about them as if they were a veil that the student had to strip away in order to properly understand what he was studying.[4] Commentary had been piled upon commentary and he regarded the profusion of commentaries and abridgements as an actual obstacle to scholarship. Brief handbooks were particularly pernicious (this despite the fact that as a young man he had written some of these himself). Already by the fourteenth century it had become obvious that there were too many books and he declared that it would take more than a lifetime just to read all the commentaries on Maliki law. The same applied to Arabic philology.

The best way of teaching was for the teacher to present a brief and simplified presentation of the problems arising from a particular subject and then to go over them again and again, each time in more depth. The student must not be immediately confronted with what was obscure and difficult, but led to those things slowly. Only one subject at a time should be tackled. Logic might be a useful, though not strictly necessary, tool in studying. And there were dangers in over-reliance on logic. There are some who "believe that logic is a natural means for the perception of the truth. They become confused when doubts and misgivings arise concerning the evidence, and they are scarcely able to free themselves from (such doubts)."[5] Inspiration coming from God would be far more effective in guiding a student's understanding.

Ibn Khadun avoided discussing the place of *madrasa*s and *khanqa*s as educational institutions. Nor did he discuss the role of the colleges that were attached to mosques, with their stipends for students and their residential quadrangles, such as the famous one attached to the Qarawiyyin Mosque in Fez. It seems probable that he disliked the excessively restricted curriculum of the *madrasa*s.

Early on in the *Muqaddima* there is a somewhat curious discussion concerning al-Hajjaj's parentage. Under the Ummayad caliphs, al-Hajjaj (c. 661–714) rose to be governor of Iraq, Khurasan, and Sijistan, in which office he was as notorious for his brutality as he was famous for his oratory. Earlier historians had expressed surprise at the apparent low status of his father, who was a teacher, and indeed Ibn Khaldun acknowledges that teachers "are weak, indigent, and rootless," before going on to argue that, though this is the case in his own time, this was not the case in the early centuries of Islam. (Everything was better then.) Scholarship then was not a mere craft. The Prophet relied on his closest companions to spread the teaching of Islam. Al-Hajjaj himself taught the Qur'an, and not as a humdrum way of making a living. Rather his teaching was a sacred calling.[6] (Incidentally, the low status of schoolteachers in the later centuries is confirmed by several stories in *The Thousand and One Nights*.)

THE VIRTUE OF ROTE LEARNING
AND THE PRIMACY OF POETRY

Mastery of the Arabic language and literature involved a huge amount of memorization. The more one memorized, the more one could hold in one's memory. It was best to have by heart the prose and poetry that had been composed in the early centuries of Islam, rather than the later inferior stuff. The content of rote learning and habit shaped the soul.[7] Here I can quote what I have written elsewhere: "Ibn Khaldun, having noted that poetry rather than the Qur'an was used to teach Arabic in Andalusia, went on to urge poets to train themselves in their art by memorizing the poems of their great predecessors, especially those included in the *Kitab al-Aghani*. Ibn Khaldun believed that one was what one had committed to memory; the better the quality of what had been memorized, the better it was for one's soul. For Ibn Khaldun and his contemporaries, rote learning was a source of creativity rather than a dreary alternative to it."[8]

The *Kitab al-Aghani* (The Book of Songs) of Abu'l-Faraj al-Isfahani (897–c. 972) had started out as an anthology of the hundred best poems that had been sung at the court of Harun al-Rashid and a commentary on them, but then expanded to cover the careers of caliphs, poets, and musicians, and further poems which Abu'l-Faraj liked were also added. It was a wonderful guide to the high culture of the 'Abbasid caliphs. As far as Ibn Khaldun was concerned, this was the unsurpassable literary masterpiece: "In it

[Abu'l-Faraj] dealt with the whole of history, poetry, genealogy, battle days, and ruling dynasties of the Arabs."[9]

Although Ibn Khaldun believed that the better the quality of what had been memorized, the better it was for one's soul, he once confessed to Ibn al-Khatib that he thought that in his youth he had memorized so much of the wrong sort of poetry, versified primers and suchlike, that he would never become a good poet himself.[10] But he did write poetry, since poetry in the medieval Islamic lands was, among other things, an instrument of statecraft. He and his political rivals all wrote poetry to recommend themselves and their policies to rulers and, of course, they wrote panegyrics in praise of rulers and other eminent folk. For example, when in Egypt, Ibn Khaldun wanted to regain the favor of the powerful emir Altun-bugha al-Jubani, he pleaded his case in a twelve-page poem. This did not stop him denouncing the practice of composing poetry in order to solicit favors and to beg.[11]

Poetry carried information about language and other matters. In studying poetry, one studied grammar, lexicography, and eloquence. Mastery of these areas was essential for the education of experts in Islamic law. This was a rather prosaic way of looking at poetry. It was also common practice to produced rhymed manuals on such matters as law and philology in order to assist in the memorization of the subject matter.

The *Muqaddima* presented poetry as being subject to rise and decline, just like political regimes. Arab poetry's heyday had been in the pre-Islamic period, when the desert-dwelling Arabs had few other preoccupations. "They made poetry the archive of their history, their wisdom and nobility, and the touchstone of their natural gift for expressing themselves correctly . . . However, (the Arabs) did not know anything except (poetry), because at that time, they practised no science and knew no craft."[12] (Not for the first time, Ibn Khaldun is presenting a romanticized view of the primitive Bedouin of Arabia.)

With the rise of Islam the intellectual elite found distraction in theology and law, but once the main issues in these subjects had been settled, then people turned once more to composing verses and this led to the golden age of 'Abbasid poetry. But, thereafter, a new cycle of decline began. Ibn Khaldun was highly critical of the use of *badi'* in his own time. *Badi'* literally means "new." From the ninth century onwards the term came to be applied to a new and refined style of verse composition that made heavy use of metaphor, paronomasia, and antithesis. By the fourteenth century there was nothing particularly new about this sort of poetry, which continued to be called *badi'*. (But Ibn Khaldun uses the term *'ilm al-badi'* to refer to the science of rhetorical figures.)[13]

Ibn Khaldun's discussion of poetry turned into what was effectively a chrestomathy of extracts from many of his favorite poems. It comprises contemporary Bedouin poetry (much of it extracted from the poetic cycle of the Bani Hilal, which glorified the quasi-legendary Arab invasion of Ifriqiyya in the mid-eleventh century). The verses are by turns boastful, lamenting, or agonistic. They are also often obscure.[14] He also included *muwashshah* and *zajal* poetry from Spain. These were nonclassical compositions. The *muwashshah* was a strophic poetic form with five stanzas. (Ibn al-Khatib had produced a collection of *muwashshah*s, entitled *Jadaka al-ghaythu*, on the theme of the nostalgia of exile.) Several extracts of Ibn Khaldun's selection of *muwashshah*s focused on love and its attendant griefs. The *zajal* was a longer and more colloquial form with a different rhyme scheme. Ibn Khaldun noted its popularity among the common people.

RHETORIC

Bayan can be translated as "style." *'Ilm al-balagha* is rhetoric, or the science of eloquence. Ibn Khaldun discussed it in chapter 6 of the *Muqaddima*.[15] He was proud of his native language: "The Arabic language is vast. The Arabs have a particular expression for each situation, in addition to a perfect use of vowel endings and clarity." There follows an elementary primer on syntax and style that sits oddly in a book that started out as a treatise on history and the underlying principles of historical development. In this discussion it is argued that Arabic "is more concise and uses fewer words and expressions than any other language.[16] He believed that the purest form of Arabic had been spoken by Mudar, a pre-Islamic north Arabian tribal grouping, from which the Prophet's tribe of the Quraysh was said to descend. But over the centuries that form of Arabic was corrupted, because of an admixture of non-Arab elements. Since the study of style (*bayan*) was a luxury, it was more studied in the eastern Islamic lands, where there were larger and more prosperous cities.

Ibn Khaldun praised four works dealing with the "science" of literature: *Adab al-Katib* by Ibn Qutayba, *Kitab al-Kamil* by al-Mubarrad, *Kitab al-Bayan wa al-Tabyin* by al-Jahiz, and *Kitab al-Nawadir* by Abu Ali al-Qali al-Baghdadi.[17] Ibn Qutayba (828–89) wrote a guide to philology for the use of secretaries. The grammarian and philologist al-Mubarrad's *Kitab al-Kamil* mostly dealt with pre-Islamic poetry. Al-Jahiz's *Kitab al-Bayan wa-al-tabyin* (Book of Eloquence and Exposition) is an anecdotal compendium of examples of rhetoric. Al-Qali wrote a guide to pre-Islamic poetry, lexicography, and grammar in the tenth century. But, for Ibn Khaldun, it was more important to acquire the habit of speaking good Arabic, perhaps by living among the Bedouin, than it was to merely know the rules underpinning Arabic. The Bedouin in earlier centuries had no need of written grammars. By contrast, the Arabic spoken by townspeople was, of course, likely to be particularly poor.

Ibn Khaldun had a teacher's dislike of refined and ornate prose, particularly as used by chancellery scribes. In the twelfth century Saladin's secretary Imad al-Din al-Isfahani had popularized a high-flown prose style that came to be widely adopted in the eastern Islamic lands. But Ibn Khaldun described him as an inferior writer.[18]

Adab in modern Arabic can simply be defined as "literature." But in the Middle Ages it had a wider sense. Ibn Khaldun defined adab as "expert knowledge of the poetry and history of the Arabs as well as the possession of some knowledge regarding every science."[19] Yet adab was also used to mean general culture, deportment, or manners. The person gifted with adab would often be expected to possess a fund of instructive or amusing stories. So plainly there is not a perfect match between the medieval sense of adab and "literature." Adab was particularly associated with the culture of scribes and of cup companions.

IBN KHALDUN'S USE OF LANGUAGE

It is worth considering the vocabulary of the *Muqaddima* and the way that vocabulary was used. Style is a major tool of history writing. The examples of Edward Gibbon, Lord Macaulay, Hugh Trevor-Roper, and Eric Hobsbawm may suggest to British readers that style may serve as more than a mere vehicle for the conveying of historical insights; it can actually be their engine. Style carries meaning and shapes thought. Gibbon, like Ibn Khaldun, had favored abstraction.[20] But Ibn Khaldun was less inclined to use rhetoric in order to persuade the reader, nor did he go in for extended descriptions that might evoke the appearance of past cities and monuments. He lacked Gibbon's mischievous humor and penchant for irony and bathos. Gibbon aimed at creating suspense in both the structure of his sentences and his chapters. He was interested in revealing the psychology of the protagonists in the historical events he was describing, whereas Ibn Khaldun envisaged those protagonists as the beneficiaries or victims of broader social forces.

In the Arab world it was generally accepted that the language of the Qur'an provided the best possible stylistic model and Ibn Khaldun subscribed to the conventional view. Yet his own style was less forceful and more pedestrian than that of the Qur'an. For the most part, the masters of style and rhetoric were and always had been located in the eastern part of the Arab world (in Egypt, Syria, and Iraq). As already noted, Ibn Khaldun had described the Baghdadi historian al-Mas'udi as "the imam of historians" and al-Mas'udi's history, the *Muruj al-dhahab*, was one of the models for the *Muqaddima* and the '*Ibar*. But whereas the highly literary al-Mas'udi wrote to entertain as well as instruct and his chronicle is full of fascinating digressions, Ibn Khaldun wrote just to instruct. He only occasionally produced prose that deployed verbal redundancy for rhetorical effect—as in, for example, the much-quoted passages on the ravages of the Black Death and on the glories of Cairo. Though he boasted of his literary style, this was routine practice among medieval Arab writers, whether they were any good at writing or not.

The down-to-earth presentation of his arguments may sometimes be based on the oral delivery of his lectures. He did not hesitate to repeat things in order to make sure that his readers would understand what he had written. *Malaka* means "repetition" or "mastery." There is a lot of repetition in the *Muqaddima* and this too may be the result of transferring lectures to paper, though the difficulty of cross-referencing a manuscript may have been another factor here. When he wished to express a personal opinion, it was often prefaced by the word "perhaps" (*rubbama*).

Religious invocations and brief quotations from the Qur'an are almost invisible to the modern Western reader, but they pervade the text of the *Muqaddima* and this litany is not perfunctory. It serves, as it were, as an extended form of punctuation, marking the end of each section: "Those whom God leads astray have no one to guide them"; "God decides and no one can change his decision"; "This is how God proceeds with his creatures"; "God has no need of the worlds"; "God determines night and day."

Rosenthal and Gibb praised Ibn Khaldun's style (though they seem to have had differing views as to what that style was), but Silvestre de Sacy had found it hard going because it often omitted the necessary conjunctions, as well as sometimes jumping from subject to subject. Vincent Monteil, who did the twentieth-century translation of the *Muqaddima* into French, found the style far too prolix and commented that "it is not the prose of an artist."[21] (On Silvestre de Sacy, Gibb, Rosenthal, and Monteil, see the next chapter.) Not only have modern scholars differed over the quality of Ibn Khaldun's prose, but they have also come to wildly different conclusions about the meaning and significance of what he wrote and these disagreements will feature largely in the next chapter.

CHAPTER TEN

✦✦✦

The Strange Afterlife of the *Muqaddima*

Quot homines, tot sententiae.

Beyond the obvious facts that he has at some time done manual labour, that he takes snuff, that he is a Freemason, that he has been in China, and that he has done a considerable amount of writing, lately, I can deduce nothing else.
—Conan Doyle, "The Red-Headed League"

Ibn Khaldun had only a slight influence on his contemporaries and immediate successors who wrote histories in the Mamluk Sultanate, Andalusia, and the Maghreb. A few Maghribi historians read and used the *Muqaddima*. The fifteenth-century Andalusian scholar Ibn al-Azraq quoted from Ibn Khaldun's writing extensively in his *Bada'i' al-silk*, a treatise on politics, but despite mining it for facts and insights, he did not absorb its underlying methodology.[1] Ibn Khaldun created no school of Khaldunian historians and his work was all but forgotten in the Arab world. In the early sixteenth century Leo Africanus, a Moroccan scholar, after being captured by pirates and converted to Christianity in Italy, tried but failed to introduce Ibn Khaldun to the West and cited him in his *Description of Africa*, published in 1550 in Italian.

Ibn Khaldun's earliest serious admirers were to be found among the Ottoman Turks. It is likely that copies of the *Muqaddima* were among the looted manuscripts taken back to Istanbul after Selim's conquest of Mamluk Egypt in 1517. In the sixteenth century the Ottoman Empire was expanding and triumphing everywhere. A century later doubts began to arise among the Turkish intelligentsia about the eternity of their rule. In 1653 Katib Celebi, who is also known as Hajji Khalifa, included Ibn Khaldun's works in

Kashf al-Zunun, a catalog that listed 14,500 titles of books in Arabic, Turkish, and Persian. He also produced a memorandum, *The Rule of Action for the Rectification of Defects*. The memorandum outlined the organic life cycle of regimes: rise, stagnation, and decline on the Khaldunian pattern. Katib Celebi suggested that the Ottoman Empire was showing the early symptoms of old age. Then Na'ima (?–1716), a historian and disciple of Katib Celebi, produced a history that opened with a general discussion of the rise and fall of societies and, during this discussion, he paid glowing tribute to Ibn Khaldun, "the greatest of all historians." The *Münejjimbashi*, or court astrologer, Ahmed ibn Lutfullah (?–1702) also relied heavily on Ibn Khaldun in his universal history. The Turks, unlike Ibn Khaldun, entertained hopes that the decline of their regime could be arrested. In 1749 the first five chapters of the *Muqaddima* were translated into Turkish by Shaykh al-Islam Piri-zade Mehmed Effendi.[2] Muhammad 'Ali, the ruler of Egypt between 1805 and 1848, read Ibn Khaldun and had him retranslated into Turkish. Together with writings of Machiavelli and accounts of the campaigns of Napoleon, the political and social thought of Ibn Khaldun may have had a role in shaping Muhammad 'Ali's statecraft.

Ibn Khaldun had made a brief appearance in Barthélémy d'Herbelot's *Bibliothèque orientale* (first published in 1697), a compilation that drew heavily on Hajji Khalifa's *Kashf al-Zunun*. Under the heading "Tarikh Ebn Khaledoun" one finds the statement that *"c'est une histoire forte curieuse,"* which is fair enough, but the entry also informs one that this Ibn Khaldun came from the Hadramawt, became chief qadi in Aleppo, and was taken as a captive by Timur to Samarkand where he died in the hijri year 808. At least the death date is correct.[3] The *Muqaddima* was properly discovered and publicized in the West by the great Orientalists, Antoine Isaac Silvestre de Sacy and Joseph von Hammer-Purgstall, at the beginning of the nineteenth century and the editing and translating of the text was undertaken by Quatremère and De Slane respectively (both of them students of De Sacy). Though Silvestre de Sacy was first to publish translations of small excerpts from the *Muqaddima* in his chrestomathy, it seems likely that it was Hammer-Purgstall who first came across references to Ibn Khaldun, thanks to his wide reading of Turkish historians.

Joseph von Hammer-Purgstall (1774–1856) was an Austrian who first pursued a career as a dragoman (an interpreter in Eastern countries). Later he inherited a title and a castle in Styria and thereafter he devoted himself to scholarly matters. He is chiefly famous for his massive multi-volume history of the Ottoman Empire. He was a prolific and careless translator of Turkish, Persian, and Arabic. Hammer-Purgstall got the erroneous impression that Ibn Khaldun was a Berber (as did Silvestre de Sacy) though, given Ibn Khaldun's enthusiasm for the Berbers, this was an understandable mistake.[4]

In *Uber den Verfall des Islam nach den ersten drei Jahrhunderten der Hidschrat* (On the Decline of Islam after the First Three Hijri Centuries) Hammer-Purgstall called Ibn Khaldun "an Arab Montesquieu," a label that would stick and would be elaborated on by later commentators.[5] There is indeed some justice in the comparison. Charles de Secondat, baron de Montesquieu (1689–1755) is most famous for *De l'espirit des lois* (1748), a book that presented a wide ranging survey of different sorts of social organization throughout the world and the factors governing the making of laws, as well as how laws governed the formation and maintenance of states. Montesquieu placed particular emphasis on the shaping role of the physical environment and climate on culture (as Ibn Khaldun had done in the second prefatory discussion of the *Muqaddima*). Montesquieu also wrote *Considérations sur les causes de la grandeur des Romains et de leur decadence* (1734) in which he looked for the underlying social causes of the historical rise and fall of the Roman Empire. The Roman state grew due to its size and economy. Its decline was due to corruption that was brought about by excessive expansion. He had sought in this story to find general historical principles and lessons of universal relevance.[6] Al-Tahtawi, an Egyptian who was studying in Paris in the 1820s, made the following (possibly ironical) observation: "Among the French Montesquieu is known as the European Ibn Khaldun, whereas the latter is known as the Eastern Montesquieu or the Montesquieu of Islam."[7]

FRENCH READINGS AND FRENCH COLONIALISM

Hammer-Pugstall kept in close scholarly contact with Silvestre de Sacy with whom, however, he did not always agree. It was Antoine Isaac Silvestre de Sacy (1758–1838) who first published translations of selections from the *Muqaddima*. Al-Tahtawi described Silvestre de Sacy as being "famous among the Franks for his knowledge of Oriental languages, especially Arabic and Persian. . . . He is one of the notables of Paris and a member of several scholarly societies of France as well as of other countries." But while al-Tahtawi praised Silvestre de Sacy's ability to read and translate Arabic, he noted that he could not speak Arabic "unless he has a book in his hands."[8] Silvestre de Sacy was indeed a grand figure. He was professor at the Ecole spéciale des langues orientales vivantes. The Ecole had been established in 1795 with the aim of furthering international commerce and diplomacy. But, despite these utilitarian aims, Silvestre de Sacy does not seem to have cared much for living languages and instead used extracts from the Qur'an and *The Thousand and One Nights* as his basic teaching texts. He was also a member of the Académie des Inscriptions et Belles-Lettres from 1785 and a founder of the Societé Asiatique (1822). He edited al-Hariri's famous work of belles-lettres, the *Maqamat*, and he produced a grammar of classical Arabic. He occasionally translated official documents into Arabic and was created a peer of France in 1832. Though there had been individual erudite Orientalists before him who specialized in the languages and cultures of Islam, he was the real founder of this branch of institutionalized academic Orientalism and he taught most of the next generation of leading Orientalists, not just in France, but across Europe.

Silvestre de Sacy introduced Ibn Khaldun to Europe with his *Chrestomathie arabe*, which included heavily annotated translations from the *Muqaddima*, covering the excellence of history and its underlying principles, the places that are subject to the authority of the caliph, the various insignia of royal rule, and calligraphy. According to Silvestre de Sacy, the *Muqaddima* "enjoys great celebrity in the Levant, and indeed deserves this renown." He prefaced his annotations with a short biography of Ibn Khaldun that quotes Hajji Khalifa on how Ibn Khaldun was a qadi in Aleppo who was taken by Timur back to Samarkhand as a captive and further pieces of misinformation from him and other sources about Ibn Khaldun, before correctly plumping for the Egyptian chronicler Abu al-Mahasin Ibn Taghribirdi's information as being the most reliable. Silvestre de Sacy worked from four manuscripts of the *Muqaddima* and his annotations to his chosen extracts display impressive erudition. He noted that the *Muqaddima* had been translated into Turkish and this suggests that Hammer-Purgstall had first drawn his attention to this text.[9] Silvestre de Sacy subsequently published further extracts from the *Muqaddima* on treasure hunting, the patronage of architecture by powerful regimes, linguistic sciences, dialectic, and Sufism.[10] Silvestre de Sacy's students and successors, including Coquebert de Montbret, Quatremère, de Slane, and Garcin de Tassy, continued the work of putting Ibn Khaldun on the European intellectual map. For a long time most of the work on Ibn Khaldun was done by the French, since their conquest of Algeria (which began in 1830) and the protectorate they subsequently established over Morocco meant that there were French experts who were very interested in what Ibn Khaldun had to say about the Arabs and Berbers of North Africa, though it should be noted that Silvestre de Sacy had been primarily interested in the *Muqaddima* from a philological point of view.

De Sacy's star pupil, Etienne-Marc Quatremère (1782–1857), was what is known as an *orientaliste de cabinet*, that is to say he preferred to read about the Orient rather than actually to go there. Like his mentor, Silvestre de Sacy, he was a Jansenist and his first interest was in the Bible and those languages that might assist in studying the sacred text. In 1819 he became a professor at the Collège de France. Later, his interests broadened and he edited Arabic, Turkish, and Persian texts. His primary interest in those texts was philological. Austere and introverted, he was a stern critic of other people's work. He fell out with De Sacy, he ridiculed Champollion's claim to have deciphered Egyptian hieroglyphics, and he was widely disliked. Rosenthal described Quatremère as "a scholar of great merits but one who it seems was at odds with his colleagues and the world in general."[11] In

1858 Quatremère's three-volume edition of the *Muqaddima*, entitled *Prolégomènes d'Ebn Khaldoun*, was posthumously published, uncorrected and without an introduction. His edition had been preceded by an inferior Arabic edition produced by Nasr al-Hurini based on only two manuscripts. But Quatremère had been able to use four manuscripts, one of which was the oldest extant manuscript of the *Muqaddima*, which dated from the 1390s. There were many misprints in the posthumous printing and Reinhart Dozy, the distinguished Dutch Arabist who loved getting into polemical scraps, made detailed criticisms of the edition and suggested that Quatremère's edition was a product of senility.[12]

William Mac-Guckin, baron de Slane (1801–78) was born in Belfast, but pursued a scholarly career in Paris, where he was a student of Silvestre de Sacy. In the 1840s he was employed by the French administration and army on several missions in Algeria. In Algiers he first translated the *Ta'rif*, which he published in a series of issues in the *Journal asiatique* and then he translated large extracts of the *'Ibar* as *Histoire des Berbères et des Arabes* (1852–56). This last work had been commissioned by the French Ministry of War. In the years 1862, 1865, and 1868 he published a translation of Quatremère's edition of the *Muqaddima* as *Prolégomènes historiques*. De Slane used the annotation of his translation as a vehicle for attacks on the competence of Quatremère's edition. But De Slane omitted those bits of the *Muqaddima* that he found too difficult to translate, especially the poetry, and he was reduced to summarizing Ibn Khaldun's exposition of the workings of the *za'iraja* (which, in the circumstances, was an understandable strategy, since Ibn Khaldun's exposition of that device was very obscure). De Slane rendered the keyword *'asabiyya* as "esprit de corps," which catches some of the sense of the word, but then in the hands of later French commentators "esprit de corps" acquired Bergsonian overtones of élan vital and *'asabiyya* was misleadingly transmuted into a kind of life force that, ever striving upward, powered humanity's creative evolution. Though De Slane's translation has been criticized by some as being rather free, the usually combative and hypercritical Reinhart Dozy was enthusiastic about it.[13] While the twentieth-century historian of the Islamic lands Marshall Hodgson had muted praise for De Slane's translation of the *Muqaddima*, he was more critical of De Slane's version of the *'Ibar*, observing that he "seems to have had difficulty with passages of Arabic above the level of 'who killed whom'" and he added that De Slane had a tendency to simply omit the more analytical or philosophical passages.[14]

De Slane's translation had received official funding, presumably because it was thought that a thorough understanding of the *Muqaddima* and the *'Ibar* might assist the French colonial project in North Africa, and indeed these books were appropriated and misinterpreted by French academics teaching in Algiers and Oran. Émil-Félix Gautier (1864–1940), who taught in the University of Algiers for over thirty years, was a geographer who sought to make links between geology and history. His *L'Islamisation de l'Afrique du Nord: Les siècles obscures du Maghreb* (1927) posed the question: how was it that after the fall of the Roman Empire North Africa was never again united? As far as Gautier was concerned, most of the blame fell upon the Arabs. He equated Arab with nomad and nomad with nihilist destroyer. Since he did not register that Ibn Khaldun used the word "Arab" in two different senses, he was able to quote De Slane's translations in support of his argument and he gave an almost apocalyptic dimension to a centuries-old conflict between the nomad and the settled, allegedly corresponding to a conflict between the Arab and the Berber. According to Gautier, the Arabs had no sense of country, only of lineage. In particular, he used quotations from Ibn Khaldun to argue that the Hilali Arab invasion of Ifriqiyya in the eleventh century was, like Ibn Khaldun's "swarm of locusts," a catastrophe for the Maghreb and that its aftereffects were still being felt in the twentieth century. The Berbers had been unable to resist the Arab invasion because of rivalry between the Zanata nomads and the Sanhaja peasants. The whole history of the Maghreb was a "*salade bigarée*" and a culture that had failed to evolve in the way Europe had.

Arabs were like children and their *ta'rikh* was not proper history. But Ibn Khaldun was special: "*il est unique, il écrase tout, il est génial.*" (When Gautier described him as *génial*, he did not mean that he was cheerful and easy going, but merely that he was a genius.) Ibn Khaldun was a gentleman historian, like Joinville and the Duke de Saint Simon. He had a Western view of history and there was "a perfume of the Renaissance" about him. The aim of Gautier and of several scholars who came after him was to strip Ibn Khaldun of his superficially medieval Arab identity and reveal him to be in reality a modern Frenchman and one, moreover, who would have approved of the French Empire in North Africa.[15] Somewhat similarly, William Marçais (1872–1956), an academic Arabist who taught in Algeria and who was an enthusiastic supporter of French colonialism, deployed his scholarship to disparage both Arab and Berber culture. The Arabic language with its diglossia between *fusha* (classical) and *ammi* (colloquial) versions was "incurable." Berbers had no social sense or individual creativity.[16]

In the 1950s and '60s the French were fighting to retain their hold on Algeria. But a significant number of experts on the Arabist world, including Louis Massignon, Yves Lacoste, and Maxime Rodinson, campaigned for Algerian independence. Vincent Monteil (1913–2005) who was to retranslate the *Muqaddima* was of their number. He had an extraordinary career. A graduate of the military college of Saint-Cyr, he served in Morocco where he became fluent in Arabic, before being attached to French embassies in various Middle Eastern capitals as military attaché. He fought for the Free French during the Second World War and later saw service in Korea and Indochina. In 1955 he was briefly a member of Jacques Soustelle's cabinet in Algiers, where he was employed to put out feelers to the insurgent National Liberation Front (FLN), but he soon resigned in protest at the French use of torture. He denounced repression in Algeria and Morocco and had secret contacts with Algerian rebels and he favored negotiating with the FLN commandant in Algeria. Eventually he left the army and took up academic posts in Lebanon and Senegal. As well as translating the *Muqaddima*, he wrote on Arab travelers. He had met the charismatic Orientalist and devout Christian Louis Massignon in 1938 and came to regard him as his revered master and in 1987 he published a book on him. Monteil converted to Islam in 1976 at the age of 64. He campaigned on behalf of the Palestinians and supported the Iranian revolution. In his last years he taught at the University of Vincennes.[17]

Monteil produced a three-volume translation of the *Muqaddima* under the title of *Discours sur l'histoire universelle* (Beirut, 1967–68) with the aim of replacing De Slane's version by being closer to the spirit of the Ibn Khaldun's ideas rather than the letter. Monteil's introduction presented Ibn Khaldun as an inspired precursor not only of Machiavelli, but also of French Enlightenment thinking. As if that was not enough, Ibn Khaldun had invented sociology, as well as anticipated Darwin. (Monteil here was relying on those two passages in the *Muqaddima* in which Ibn Khaldun placed monkeys just below men in the Great Chain of Being.) Having noticed the reticences and self-effacing quality of Ibn Khaldun's writings, Monteil resorted to astrology in order to better understand the author's personality. Ibn Khaldun was, it seems, a typical Gemini—that is to say, subtle and curious and capable of combining reason with imagination. He must have been benign and sociable, yet also inclined to irritability, pessimism, authoritarian intransigence, and vanity. He would have been good at the sciences, letters, politics, and high administration.[18] One has to wonder how much of this Monteil got from the stars and how much from his reading of the *Muqaddima* and the various short biographies produced by medieval Arabs.

THE GERMANS

The nineteenth-century Germans had no colonies in the Arab world to which they might apply insights derived from the *Muqaddima*. Instead, their readings of Ibn Khaldun tended to encourage them to move away from fact-driven positivism and scissors-and-paste chronologies. It is hard to think back to nineteenth-century ways of looking at the past. Cultural history was something new in the nineteenth century—that is to say, the history not just of kings, queens, and battles, but an account of broad social phenomena, customs, and economic developments, as well as artistic and literary productions. Pioneering examples include Macaulay's famous chapter on England in the Reign of Queen Anne in his *History of England* (1855–61) and Jacob Burkhardt's *Civilization of the Renaissance* (1860). Perhaps the Western discovery of Ibn Khaldun would not have been possible before the nineteenth century, since earlier it would have been difficult to find analogies and precedents for his ideas.

It is possible that German and Austrian scholars were particularly enthusiastic about Ibn Khaldun, because of the widespread influence of Hegel on German history writing. Hegel had forced history into a grand philosophical system. Certainly the Austrian Arabist Alfred von Kremer (1828–89) in his approach to Islamic culture was strongly influenced by Hegel, as well as by the philosopher, theologian, poet, and literary critic Gottfried Herder. Von Kremer was one of the leaders of the movement away from narrowly philological preoccupations in German Orientalism. He sought rather to produce a grand overview of Islamic culture and to compare it with other cultures. In 1879 he produced *Ibn Chaldun und seine Kulturgeschichte des islamischen Reiche*, which was published in the proceedings of the Viennese Imperial Academy of Sciences. In this study he relied on Arabic manuscripts of the *Muqaddima*, rather than on De Slane's translation. Culture or civilization was seen by him as the total expression of a people. Von Kremer sometimes translated *'asabiyya* as civic spirit and sometimes as national idea (which he saw as the motor of history). Eccentrically he argued that Islam was not really important in Ibn Khaldun's thinking. Ibn Khaldun was *sui generis* in the Arab world, without Arab precursors and totally original. He was then a man born out of his time (and several more modern interpreters of Ibn Khaldun have followed Von Kremer in this). But Von Kremer, who believed in the Hegelian advance of the state and the human spirit, found the cyclical model of history unattractively pessimistic.[19]

Like many in the nineteenth century, Von Kremer had seen Ibn Khaldun as a positivist and a materialist. It soon became commonplace in studies of Ibn Khaldun to acclaim him as a precursor of Comte. Auguste Comte (1798–1857), the founder of positivism and perhaps the founder of sociology in the West, had taught that all true knowledge is scientific and based on observable phenomena. But sociology is secular and inductive, while Ibn Khaldun's account of society was not.

TOYNBEE AND HIS ADMIRERS

The English-speaking world paid little attention to the ideas of Ibn Khaldun until the world historian Arnold Toynbee (1889–1975), having discovered him, identified him as one of his intellectual ancestors. Having described the *Muqaddima* as "undoubtedly the greatest work of its kind that has ever been created by any mind in any time or place," Toynbee went on to patronize Muslim culture: the *Muqaddima* "shines the more brightly by contrast with the foil of darkness against which it flashes out." Ibn Khaldun was the one outstanding personality in the history of a civilization whose social life on the whole was "solitary, poor, brutish, and short."[20]

Like Vico, Toynbee was steeped in the reading of the classics. He began life as a classicist and at the outbreak of the First World War he had been lecturing on Thucydides. After the war he briefly held the Koraes Chair in Greek at London University, before becoming director of studies at the Royal Institute of International Affairs (also known as Chatham House). He has been described by the Middle East specialist Albert Hourani, who knew and revered him, as "warm, a mixture of warmth and distance, his mind was always far away thinking great thoughts of the history of the world." Hourani also made this observation about Toynbee's historico-spiritual quest: "It is impossible not to hear, in the voice of Toynbee brooding on civilisation, the anguish of a man brooding on himself. *A Study of History* is a spiritual autobiography, but one of a peculiar sort."[21]

As with Ibn Khaldun and Edward Gibbon, ruins provided much of the initial impetus for Toynbee's meditations on the decline of civilizations and its causes. In a draft of his *Memoirs* Gibbon had written that "it was at Rome on the fifteenth of October 1764, as I sat musing amidst the ruins of the Capitol, while the barefooted fryars were singing Vespers in the temple of Jupiter, that the idea of writing the decline and fall of the City first started to my mind."[22] And the initial inspiration for *A Study of History* came from Toynbee's sight of the ruins of a Crusader castle in Greece: "Mistra had continued . . . to reign for . . . 600 years as the queen of the broad landscape that could be surveyed from her topmost battlements; and then, one April morning, out of the blue the avalanche of wild highlanders . . . had overwhelmed her . . . and her ruins had been left desolate from that day to this."[23] He started by thinking about the causes of the fall of Greek civilization and then moved on to consider the reasons for the decline and fall of the Roman Empire and slowly he moved on to think about the underlying causes for the rise and fall of all civilizations. As he did so, he began to hunt out intellectual ancestors, thinkers who were ready to make generalizations about historical processes—Thucydides, Polybius, St. Augustine, Roger Bacon, Vico, Volney, Spengler, and H. G. Wells. This intellectual genealogy might go some way to legitimizing the vast scope and ambitions of *A Study in History*. Toynbee was delighted with Ibn Khaldun and the *Muqaddima*. It was like discovering a long-lost relative.

A Study of History appeared in twelve fat volumes between 1934 and 1961. It is a comparative study of civilizations and their cyclical rise and fall. Toynbee was a deeply religious though idiosyncratic Christian and one of his leading aims was to overturn Gibbon's verdict that the Roman Empire was destroyed by barbarism and religion. Toynbee thought he could see a pattern in history and he formulated a series of developmental laws. He developed the idea that civilizations develop or fail due to a cycle of challenges and responses. A member of a cultured elite himself, he also had ideas about the role of elites in imposing civilization on the mindless proletariat. And Toynbee, who grew more mystical as he aged, eventually identified God as the ultimate mover of the cycles of civilizations and he came to view the primary function of civilizations as to be the bearers of religions. "History is a vision of God's creation on the move."[24]

Toynbee's *A Study of History* derived some of its initial impetus from a reading of Spengler and, like *The Decline of the West* and most cyclical theories of history, Toynbee's schema was somewhat pessimistic. He thought that in the wake of two world wars he could already detect the signs of the waning of Western civilization. Only a higher religion might save it. I have previously (and perhaps rather unkindly) characterized Toynbee's theoretical model in the following terms:

> Toynbee's notion of civilization can be visualised (perhaps fancifully and rather unsympathetically) as an array of automata, which have been set in motion at various times, but which independently go through what are broadly the same motions. Creative minorities drive the civilizations, guiding the arms in a characteristic see-saw of challenge and response and, at the same time, spraying out threads of affiliation and apparentation to neighbouring civilizations. But, as the creative minorities decay into dominant minorities, the machines run down and their movements become increasingly circumscribed. A civilization whose engine has run down restructures itself as a universal state. Thereafter a fixed and doomed rhythm sets in—rout, rhythm—rout, rhythm—rout, rhythm.[25]

And there is more. He at first postulated that there had been twenty-one civilizations, but later he upped the estimate to thirty-one.

For a time Toynbee's ideas were fashionable and much talked about, but, long before he had finished publishing *A Study of History*, his grand theories and his detailed evidence, or supposed evidence, were savaged by professional historians, including A.J.P. Taylor, H. R. Trevor-Roper, R. H. Tawney, and Pieter Geyl. The Marxist-leaning historian E. H. Carr dismissed Toynbee's cyclical theory as "the characteristic ideology of a society in decline" and backed this up with a quotation from Marcus Aurelius reflecting on the decline of the Roman Empire: "How all things that are now happening have happened in the past, and will happen again in the future."[26]

But Toynbee had done an immense amount to popularize a reading of Ibn Khaldun in the Anglophone world in advance of the Rosenthal translation into English. (Toynbee had relied on Quatremère's French.) Ibn Khaldun's life was presented as matching Toynbee's law of withdrawal, since Ibn Khaldun had withdrawn from politics to embrace a period of lonely scholarship in Qalʿat

Banu Salama. Then the production of the *Muqaddima* obeyed the law of etheralization, as it extracted the laws of history from the politics of experience. Finally, he exemplified the law of return, as he returned to practical politics in the Maghreb. As Toynbee continued to labor on his grand scheme of history, he did find some things to complain about in the *Muqaddima*. Ibn Khaldun had formed his philosophy on the basis of too narrow a territorial and chronological basis. Most empires had not been founded by nomads.[27] Toynbee, who had came to Ibn Khaldun via the French translators and commentators, was much influenced by Gautier's patronizing and polemical presentation of the Arabs.

Ibn Khaldun's pessimism was attractive and so was the moralizing portrait of the inevitable cycle of political decay brought about by luxury and greed. Toynbee liked the grand sweep of the *'Ibar* and praised it for not stopping with merely human affairs. The processes of history can only be properly understood by a believer in God. Ibn Khaldun "gave a vision of history bursting the bounds of this World and breaking through into an Other World." However, Toynbee rejected the view that *'asabiyya* was a nomadic monopoly. Italian citizens in the Renaissance, for example, also possessed *'asabiyya. 'Asabiyya* was "the basic protoplasm out of which all bodies politic and bodies social are built up." Moreover, Toynbee thought that the precise Khaldunian model of rise and decay applied only to empires founded by nomads. And nomads could not create civilizations. Rather, nomads were a symptom of the decay of civilization. Thus the invasions of the Goths and Vandals were a symptom of the decline of the Roman Empire, not its cause.

Despite Toynbee's unsuccessful attempt to learn Arabic and his friendship with the Arabist Hamilton Gibb, he did not know all that much about Muslim history and culture. He stressed the now-discredited importance of the Banu Hilal invasions for North Africa. As Toynbee read him, Ibn Khaldun had compared the beneficent Arab invasion of North Africa in the seventh century with the destructive invasion of the Banu Hilal and Banu Sulaym in the twelfth century. Both the first group of tribal invaders and the second have the force conferred upon them by *'asabiyya*, but in the first case the invaders gained additional unity and the ability to establish a new kingdom from their fervent belief in the new religion. Ibn Khaldun's perception of the inadequacy of a secular-sociological explanation of the history of North-West Africa in the Islamic Age thus led him to present God as the ultimate driving force of history and, in so doing, to give history itself a new dimension.[28]

Toynbee's ideas, which are almost entirely discredited now, were immensely influential in the early years of the volumes' publication and he did a huge amount to popularize Ibn Khaldun in the English-speaking world. Hamilton Gibb, Marshall Hodgson, Albert Hourani, and Ernest Gellner were among those who fell under his spell. Sir Hamilton Alexander Rosskeen Gibb (1893–1971), who published copiously on Islamic history and Middle Eastern current affairs, was successively professor at London University's School of Oriental African Studies, Oxford, and Princeton. Though Gibb was at first chiefly interested in medieval Islamic history, international developments in the 1930s had made him feel that it was his duty to take an interest in contemporary Middle Eastern politics and society. This preoccupation with the contemporary Arab world resulted in such books as *Whither Islam?* (1932) and *Modern Trends in Islam* (Chicago, 1947).

During the Second World War Gibb was for a time head of the Middle East section of the Foreign Office Research Department. Toynbee was at that time the director of the whole department, and Gibb and Toynbee became friends. Gibb, like Toynbee, was a strong Christian who believed in God as the ultimate mover in history. Gibb's *Arabic Literature: An Introduction* was first published in 1926. One of the interesting features of this book is its slightly drab assessment of Ibn Khaldun: "His independent work will certainly stand comparison with that of any other Muslim historian, however much it may fall short of the standard he himself demanded." And Gibb's verdict on the *Muqaddima* was that the "work refers to and has value only for the political conditions of his age and community, but for those it is inestimable."[29] Later, and doubtless under the influence of Toynbee, Gibb was to revise his opinion upwards.

In 1933 "The Islamic Background of Ibn Khaldun's Political Theory" was published in the *Bulletin of the School of Oriental and African Studies*.[30] Here Gibb argued that Ibn Khaldun's primary purpose in the *Mudqaddima* was not to set himself up as the medieval father of sociology or of political science. Rather he sought to show how Islamic history was the product of the incompatibility of the demands of the religious law (the *Shariʿa*) with men's fallible desires, but "since mankind will not follow the *Shariʿa* it is condemned to an empty and unending cycle of rise and fall, conditioned by the 'natural' and inevitable consequences of the predominance of its animal instincts." Only close adherence to the *Shariʿa* would free people from the Yin and Yang of history, the cyclical rise and fall of regimes. He also sought to demonstrate that Ibn Khaldun's thinking was modeled on that of earlier Muslim jurists and hence rather orthodox and conventional. This fitted with Gibb's general view that law was the central core of Islam. That Islam was primarily a legal religion was one of his *idées fixes*. Like many of Gibb's works, the essay is undereferenced and Gibb's view of Ibn Khaldun has since been challenged by other specialists. Gibb disregarded the detailed history and treated the historian as if his primary concern was with divine things. Nevertheless Gibb's focus on the importance of the religious law in shaping Ibn Khaldun's historical thinking is most plausible.

Elsewhere, the influence of Ibn Khaldun is most clearly seen in Gibb's grand-sweep essay "An Interpretation of Islamic History" and in his various essays on Saladin, for Ibn Khaldun presented Saladin as an exceptional figure who had used jihad to revive the social cohesion of the Islamic community and Gibb was happy to go along with this interpretation.

The historian of the Middle East Albert Hourani (1915–93) became director of the Middle East Centre at St Antony's College, Oxford, and in his lifetime he was one of the most influential figures in Arabic studies. During the Second World War he worked at the Royal Institute of International Affairs with Toynbee and Gibb and it seems likely that those two aroused his interest in Ibn Khaldun, though his understanding of the historian was deepened through reading and reviewing Marshall Hodgson's *The Venture of Islam.* A Khaldunesque preoccupation with the cyclical rise and decline of dynasties permeates Hourani's masterpiece, *A History of the Arab Peoples* (1991), and his prologue to that book consists of a four-page summary of the turbulent, perilous, and highly mobile career of Ibn Khaldun before ending with these characteristically eloquent words:

> Something was stable, however, or seemed to be. A world where a family from southern Arabia could move to Spain, and after six centuries return nearer to its place of origin and still find itself in familiar surroundings, had a unity which transcended divisions of time and space; the Arabic language could open the door to office and influence throughout that world; a body of knowledge transmitted over the centuries by a known chain of teachers, preserved a moral community even when rulers changed; places of pilgrimage, Mecca and Jerusalem, were unchanging poles of the human world even if power shifted from one city to another; and belief in a God who created and sustained the world could give meaning to the blows of fate.[31]

In *A History of the Arab Peoples* Hourani had tried to present that history in terms of an internal dynamic, rather than repeatedly relating Arab history in terms of responses to developments in Europe.

ROSENTHAL

In a scorching review published in 1960 of Franz Rosenthal's translation of Ibn Khaldun's *Muqaddima*, Gibb had denounced Rosenthal for having comprehensively failed to capture Ibn Khaldun's style. Ibn Khaldun's "ideas stream out in long cascades, sometimes indeed tumbling into excited incohesion, but for the most part held together by a taut and beautifully modulated structure of prose, controlled by precise mechanisms of coordination and subordination, and articulated with a trained elegance that gives to every word the exact degree of emphasis required by his argument." As the very structure of the above sentence suggests, Gibb was writing about Ibn Khaldun's literary style but, I believe, actually thinking about his own style, or at least the style that he aspired to. Others have judged Ibn Khaldun's prose style to be plain and straightforwardly didactic. Gibb attacked Rosenthal's "low-keyed and monstrous distortion, this moronic staccato in which a subordinate clause is almost a crime." Rosenthal was judged to have broken the flow and complexity, by chopping up Ibn Khaldun's meandering sentences.[32]

The victim of Gibb's review, Franz Rosenthal (1914–2003), a German Jew, fled Nazi Germany in 1938 and eventually ended up in the United States where, after the war, he became professor of Semitic languages at Yale. He wrote prolifically on medieval Islamic culture and his books in that area include studies of humor, hashish consumption, historiography, and the classical heritage in Islam. Yet, if the only thing he had published had been his heavily annotated translation of the *Muqaddima*, this would have been enough to establish his reputation as an Orientalist of the first rank. There was (and is) no properly established critical edition of the *Muqaddima* in Arabic and so Rosenthal's translation is the best substitute for the Arabic edition we do not have. It is based on a range of manuscripts, including one in Istanbul, which is in Ibn Khaldun's own hand. In cases where there are important variants in the manuscripts, these are either translated or signaled in the footnotes. The annotation, which registers possible sources or parallels for what Ibn Khaldun had written, is of enormous value. Indeed the range and depth of scholarship is downright intimidating and Gibb was full of praise for Rosenthal's elucidation of difficult passages as well as for the learned annotation.

The translation was published by Bollingen Foundation in three volumes in 1958 (and reprinted in 1967 with corrections by Princeton University Press). Though most scholars praised the translation, there were some who criticized Rosenthal's translation strategies. De Slane, when faced with tricky words such as *'asabi-yya* or *'umran badawi*, had rendered them differently according to context. But Rosenthal when faced with such problematic words usually footnoted their first appearance and thereafter tended to give those words the same English rendering throughout the text.

Though this way of translating lacks flexibility, the uniformity of his translation makes it easy to work out the Arabic lying behind his rendering of a particular word.

His literal version of the Arabic reads less comfortably than De Slane's or Monteil's French, but it is more accurate. Aziz al-Azmeh (on whom see below) was hostile to this literal translation, which "reduced interpretation to the minimum."[33] But one senses that, if Rosenthal had chosen a freer, more idiomatic translation, he would have been criticized for that too. Moreover, it is difficult to see how Azmeh's complex, nuanced, and wordy exegesis of certain key terms could have been inserted into any translation that would remain readable.

As T. S. Eliot observed in *Burnt Norton*:

Words strain,
Crack and sometimes break, under the burden,
Under the tension, slip, slide, perish[34]

SOME FURTHER CRITICISMS OF ROSENTHAL

The historian Marshall Hodgson (1922–68) was an enthusiast for the *Muqaddima*, which "is no doubt the best general introduction to Islamicate civilization ever written." But he was as critical as Gibb and Azmeh of Rosenthal's translation, though for different reasons. His great three-volume work *The Venture of Islam: Conscience and History in World Civilization* was posthumously published in 1974. In it he had sought to present the history of Islamic civilization, or, as he preferred Islamicate civilization, from a non-Eurocentric point of view. *The Venture of Islam* is a wide-ranging, brilliant, and stimulating work that draws extensively on the thinking of Ibn Khaldun, but Hodgson found fault with both the French and English translations of the *Muqaddima*.[35] He was somewhat captious in his criticisms of Rosenthal's translation decisions. He claimed that Rosenthal was in error when he rendered 'Arab as "Arab," as if it were a racial and linguistic term. Hodgson wanted it to be translated as "camel nomad" (an ecological term). But the trouble is that Ibn Khaldun did sometimes use "Arab" in a racial or linguistic sense and sometimes in the sense of Arab nomad, but he would not have referred to camel-rearing nomadic Berbers or Turks as "Arabs." Again, Hodgson claimed Rosenthal was in error when he translated *ghayb* as "supernatural," rather than as "invisible." Well *ghayb* does mean "invisible," but according to Wehr's *Arabic Dictionary* it also has the sense of "that which is transcendental, the supernatural; divine secret."

Probably the underlying ground for Hodgson's discontent with the translation was that Hodgson was determined to present Ibn Khaldun as a fully fledged philosopher (*faylasuf*) in the Graeco-Islamic tradition and Rosenthal's renderings gave little support for this. Hodgson's version of Ibn Khaldun would have had no truck with the supernatural. He went further and argued that while in Granada Ibn Khaldun had tutored Muhammad V in philosophy and had hopes of turning the ruler, "his ward," into a philosopher-king. There is no evidence for this and, apart from anything else, by the time Ibn Khaldun arrived in Granada in 1362 Muhammad was twenty-four and perhaps a little too old for philosophical grooming at the hands of someone who was only six years older than he was.[36] Hodgson's reading of the *Muqaddima* took its acknowledged lead from Muhsin Mahdi's "epochal" book on Ibn Khaldun. (On Mahdi's book see below.)

Abdesselam Cheddadi, a later translator of the *Muqaddima* into French (on whom see below), was kinder, describing Rosenthal's translation as "*assez complete et rigoureuse bien que parfois un peu rigide, accompagné d'un appareil critique très riche.*"[37] And Stephen Dale in a recent study of Ibn Khaldun has described Rosenthal's edited translation as "superb."[38]

SOME CRITICISMS OF THE FRENCH COLONIALIST VERSION OF IBN KHALDUN

As we have seen, Ibn Khaldun's insights had been looted to provide a naive form of ethnography that might be of service to the colonialists. But eventually the colonialist reading of Ibn Khaldun attracted criticism. In Robert Brunschvig's great work, *La Berbérie orientale sous les Hafsides*,[39] which was effectively a history of medieval Tunisia, he opposed the misreading of Ibn Khaldun that claimed that he had envisaged an eternal antagonism between Arabs and Berbers. Fiercer criticism came from Yves Lacoste. This Marxist geographer and expert on geopolitics was born in Fez in 1929. (Geopolitics deals with the politics of states that are affected by geographical factors, such as frontiers, as well as the importance of geography in international relations.) He had been a professor in Algiers, but he was a militant anti-colonialist, who supported Algeria's struggle to be free and he opposed the American intervention in Vietnam. In *Ibn Khaldoun: naissance de l'histoire passé du tiers-monde* (1965) his aim was "to assist the people of North Africa in the liberation of their past."[40] In it he presented Ibn Khaldun as primarily a sociologist. Lacoste began by describing the economic background of the region Ibn Khaldun lived in, focusing particularly on international commerce and the social and economic structures of tribal life. Then, after giving a brief account of Ibn Khaldun's life, Lacoste presented a Marxist version of the *Muqaddima* and claimed that this had relevance for the Arab nations of the 1960s.

Lacoste denounced French colonialists and their academic stooges for creating a fictional Ibn Khaldun who offered them ammunition for their presentation of North Africa as ruined by centuries-old conflicts between the nomads and the sedentary and between the Arabs and the Berbers. Lacoste argued that the Hilali migration was a deportation rather than an invasion. He saw Ibn Khaldun as a materialist and as a Marxist manqué who could be used as a vital source on the mode of production in the medieval Maghreb. Ibn Khaldun had described a society that was run by a military democracy and a mercantile aristocracy and he had criticized a society in which the bourgeoisie had failed to monopolize the means of production. This was the Asiatic mode of production: "The Asiatic mode is characterised by the existence of a class capable of appropriating a surplus and exploiting the population without necessarily owning the means of production which for the most part, remain in the hands of tribal or village communities."[41]

Ibn Khaldun's work, which was based on direct observation rather than theory, was a contribution to the history of underdevelopment. Lacoste drew on it to suggest that underdevelopment existed in the region centuries before the coming of colonialism. When the colonialists did arrive, tribal divisions of the type described by Ibn Khaldun handed control over Algeria and Morocco to the French.

Ibn Khaldun was a reactionary religious thinker (and Lacoste impatiently dismissed his "mystical obscurantism"). Nevertheless, Ibn Khaldun had come close to producing a materialist analysis of economic and social developments. But Lacoste criticized him for failing to recognize that the economic crisis of the fourteenth century was due to the decline in international commerce. Ibn Khaldun had attributed the decline he perceived to purely internal factors. Lacoste's study aimed to liberate the Maghreb from a past that had been imposed on it by colonialists and Orientalist scholars, but from the perspective of the twenty-first century, Lacoste's reading of Ibn Khaldun looks as anachronistic and culture-bound as Gautier's. Certainly his presentation of the fourteenth-century Maghreb as any part of a "Third World" is questionable. Lacoste went on in 1976 to publish the highly controversial *La géographie, ça sert d'abord à faire la guerre* (Geography's Primary Purpose Is to Make War). In this book he denounced traditional ways of doing geography as being typical of prescientific knowledge. If geography did not serve left-wing aims then it was useless or worse.

THE PHILOSOPHER MUHSIN MAHDI
AND HIS IBN KHALDUN, THE PHILOSOPHER

Muhsin Mahdi (1926–2007) was a professor of Arabic at Harvard. He specialized in Arab philosophy and political theory and he was also a great expert on manuscripts of *The Thousand and One Nights*. He was a colleague of Gibb, and Gibb, as we have seen, had presented Ibn Khaldun as a man who had given faith priority over reason, but the contrary-minded Mahdi argued that Gibb had failed to provide any evidence at all for his thesis and Mahdi went on in *Ibn Khaldun's Philosophy of History* to present

Ibn Khaldun as a rationalist and a political philosopher.[42] Mahdi's early study of the tenth-century political philosopher, al-Farabi, had persuaded him that all Islamic philosophy must be political. Mahdi's approach to the life and writings of Ibn Khaldun had been strongly influenced by the distinguished political scientist Leo Strauss (1899–1973). Strauss had advocated the application of classical philosophy to modern politics. Recourse to Plato and Aristotle should serve as guides to modern political realities and provide warnings about the limits of Enlightenment values. In *Persecution and the Art of Writing* (1952) Strauss had argued that great minds express their thoughts esoterically, in order to conceal their true meanings from those lesser minds who dully subscribed to whatever the prevailing ethos of the time might be. Following this Straussian line, Mahdi argued that Ibn Khaldun really was a philosopher in the Graeco-Islamic tradition, but, given the hostility to philosophy in the fourteenth-century Maghreb, he had to present his philosophic arguments obliquely. He was then an elitist who had no interest in gaining a mass audience. The important thing for Mahdi was to seek out "the deliberate intentions" of Ibn Khaldun, rather than his surface meaning. According to Mahdi, Ibn Khaldun had attempted to resolve the conflict between philosophy and theology and he had deployed an Aristotelian methodology in order to liberate philosophy from its union with theology. Ibn Khaldun was a philosopher of the same type as Averroes.

Yves Lacoste was one of those who challenged this argument that Ibn Khaldun was a *faylasuf* who wrote in the Graeco-Islamic philosophic tradition, even though he had allegedly refrained from making that explicit: "According to Muhsin Mahdi, the explanation for this discretion is that Ibn Khaldun thought that the philosophical basis of his work was obvious, that it was pointless to specify it and hence any statement of principles was superfluous. There is nothing in Ibn Khaldun's writings to support this dubious hypothesis. There is no obvious link between his theses and those of philosophers who were solely concerned with normative arguments and who never tried to apply their theories to history."[43] Lacoste went on to reject Mahdi's notion that Ibn Khaldun was deploying Platonist philosophy in order to diagnose what was wrong with Islamic society and suggest how it could be reformed. Lacoste rightly points out that at no point does Ibn Khaldun propose any reforms.

Mahdi had also intriguingly suggested that the *Muqaddima* could be read as an attempt by Ibn Khaldun to understand why he was a political failure. This may be worth thinking about, even though it is not immediately clear how the *Muqaddima* answers this particular question. As already noted, Hodgson had taken from Mahdi the idea that Ibn Khaldun in Granada had tried to bring up the young Muhammad V as a philosopher-king, though there is little to support this thesis. Mahdi also assigned unexpected meanings to various terms. Thus he held that the primary meaning of *badawi* was not "nomadic" or "rural," but "primitive," as the root verb from which the adjective was derived was *bada'a,* "to begin."[44] But surely there is nothing intrinsically primitive about agriculture or bee-keeping, nor, for that matter, nomadism, and there is no indication that Ibn Khaldun thought of these things as primitive. To take another example, Mahdi argued that *'ibar,* when used in connection with history, "indicated essentially the activity of looking for the unity of the plan underlying the multiplicity of events."[45] But though "looking for underlying unity" is indeed what Ibn Khaldun was doing, there is no evidence that he was using the word *'ibar* in this new sense to describe what he was doing and, had he done so, it is unlikely that his readers would have understood that this was the case.

THE SOCIOLOGIST ERNEST GELLNER AND HIS IBN KHALDUN, THE SOCIOLOGIST

Ernest Gellner (1925–95) began academic life as a philosopher, and early on in his career became famous, or notorious, for his attack on linguistic philosophy in *Words and Things* (1959) and the resulting controversy with Gilbert Ryle. But already in the 1950s he was turning enthusiastically to anthropology. He did his fieldwork among the Berbers in the High Atlas Mountains of Morocco—fieldwork that resulted in a book, *Saints of the Atlas*

(1969). If there was a problem with Gellner's research, it was that he extrapolated from his research among the Berber saints, the *igumaren*, to make generalizations about Berber and Arab Sufis in other regions and periods where his insights did not apply. When Rosenthal's translation of the *Muqaddima* appeared, Gellner's review acclaimed it as "a magnificent production." He also suggested that Ibn Khaldun should be seen as a precursor of Maynard Keynes and Max Weber.[46] Like so many who have studied Ibn Khaldun, Gellner created an Ibn Khaldun in his own image: he was allegedly "a superb inductive sociologist, a practitioner, long before the term was invented, of ideal types, a brilliant account of *one* extremely important kind of society." Ibn Khaldun was presented as a value-free sociologist and his theoretical models were relevant for twentieth-century North Africa and the Middle East.

"The past is a foreign country," as the novelist L. P. Hartley observed, "they do things differently there" and Gellner was only a tourist in that country.[47] When he came to compare Ibn Khaldun with Machiavelli, he stated that "What the two share, apart from their greatness, is a marked inclination towards dispassionate analysis, instead of pious moralising."[48] But as earlier chapters in this book have indicated, there was a great deal of pious moralizing in Ibn Khaldun's writings. Indeed piety and the need to deliver religious warnings were the primary impetus behind what he wrote. But Gellner was determined first to secularize Ibn Khaldun and then to make him relevant to the modern Middle East.

Gellner was even keener than Ibn Khaldun in positing general rules and structures to explain how Islamic societies functioned. For example, he proposed that premodern North African regimes could be understood as being based on three rings: first, at the center, settled government (sheep); secondly, tribes employed by the government (sheepdogs); and, thirdly, rebellious and uncontrollable tribes (wolves). In the cyclical progression, the wolves became sheepdogs and then the sheepdogs became sheep. In describing this process, Gellner used Toynbee's phrase "the circulation of elites."[49] (Toynbee in turn probably took the term from the *Treatise on General Sociology* by the Italian sociologist Vilfredo Pareto.) But, as the example of the Dawawida tribe's shifting loyalties in the late fourteenth century surely shows, there was not much of a distinction between the latter two categories. The Dawawida were sheepdogs when they were paid and wolves when they were not. They never became sheep. Gellner also posited an over-schematized opposition within Islamic societies between learned, urban, puritan Muslims and the superstitious and illiterate followers of rural saints. In particular, this presentation of townspeople as puritanical and sober is very much at odds with Ibn Khaldun's stress on the comfort and ultimate decadence of life in the cities and conversely Gellner has ignored Ibn Khaldun's praise for the puritanism and strict monotheism of Arab and Berber nomads.

In *Muslim Society* Gellner quoted the *Muqaddima* on how peaceful Egypt and Syria were without strong tribes, in order to explain why the Mamluk and Ottoman dynasties were exceptional in his historical sociology of Muslim society, unaware that Ibn Khaldun had misrepresented the situation in Mamluk Egypt and Syria.[50] Similarly, he mistakenly believed that the Ottoman regime did not have trouble containing nomadic tribesmen. Also, Gellner entirely missed how positive Ibn Khaldun was about the mamluks and instead stated that it "is part and parcel of the world of Ibn Khaldun that recruiting non-tribal mercenary or slave armies only aggravates the disease of a declining state."[51] Though Gellner may be correctly representing Ibn Khaldun's views on mercenaries, the historian had a very high regard for the slave-soldier mamluks (as we have seen in chapter 5) and he had presented them in a positive light.

Gellner thought that only kinship, whether real or fictitious, could produce *'asabiyya*, but Ibn Khaldun thought that living in close proximity could also do so and he was also explicit that the close bonds formed in mamluk barracks also generated *'asabiyya*. In the *Ta'rif* Ibn Khaldun described how the Ayyubid sultan al-Salih Ayyub boosted the cohesion (*'isaba*) of his regime by purchasing and training large numbers of mamluks.[52]

Gellner linked the theoretical model advanced in the *Muqaddima* with the ideas of various Western philosophers and sociologists, thereby Europeanizing and secularizing that model and, in the opening chapter of *Muslim Society*, "Flux and Reflux in the

Faith of Men," he sought to combine the theories of Ibn Khaldun with those of Plato and David Hume. Hume's *A Natural History of Religion* (1757) had put forward the idea that throughout history there was a pendulum swing between polytheism and monotheism and Gellner reapplied this pendulum swing to the Maghreb. Gellner also claimed that Ibn Khaldun intended his theorizing about society to be universally applicable: "He evidently thought he was describing the only kind of human society, society *as such*, anywhere."[53] In general, Gellner's brilliant theorizing was metaphor-driven. For example: "From time to time the wheel of fortune would turn and a new dynasty would emerge from the reservoir of the tribal proletariat." ("Tribal proletariat" was another term that he had borrowed from Toynbee.)[54]

Gellner was a friend of the brilliant Islamic scholar, Patricia Crone. Crone (1945–2015) taught successively at Oxford, Cambridge, and the Princeton Institute of Advanced Studies. Crone's *Slaves on Horses* begins as a study of 'Abbasid prosopography but then turns to addressing much larger questions. One of those questions was how is it that the mamluk or slave soldier institution has been so pervasive throughout the Islamic lands? Another question was how did the medieval Chinese and Muslim perceptions of tribal conquerors compare? Confucian historians were, like Ibn Khaldun, proponents of a cyclical theory, but theirs was a very different sort of cycle. In the Confucian historical cycle the settled state had vigor that it slowly lost, a kind of oozing out of the life force, and it reached its nadir when it succumbed to tribal conquest. The tribal conquerors were barbarians without virtue. They needed to be civilized before they could run a state. But for Ibn Khaldun "tribal conquest marks the high point of the cycle." He took it for granted that settled government could never become stronger by overmastering the tribes. Unlike Chinese theorists of cyclical history, "Ibn Khaldun, in short, saw the cycles from the barbarians' point of view" and he worried about the inevitable decay of their primitive vigor. His was a particularly elaborate example of "the Muslim fixation on the tribal past," something that was religiously fixed (though Ibn Khaldun also praised the mamluks as institutionalized tribal conquerors). "Politics in Islam remained the domain of the tribal barbarians." Settled society by contrast was nonpolitical and effeminate. He was an urban man whose great history was a product of his disappointment at being unable to fulfill his political ambitions under a tribal regime.[55]

"The systematic lack of comprehension and the resolute hostility which this nonconformist thinker of genius encountered among his own people forms one of the most moving dramas, one of the saddest and most significant pages in the history of Muslim culture."[56] Though Brunschvig exaggerated the neglect of Ibn Khaldun by his Arab contemporaries and immediate successors, it was only a slight exaggeration and the belated rediscovery of Ibn Khaldun by Arab intellectuals in the nineteenth and twentieth centuries was made possible by European publications. Like the *Thousand and One Nights* and the *Rubaiyat of Umar Khayyam*, the writings of Ibn Khaldun can be seen as a Western cultural reexport to the Middle East.

The Arab rediscovery of Ibn Khaldun is part of the background to the *Nahda*, or Arab renaissance of the nineteenth and early twentieth centuries, and also a product of that renaissance. This was a cultural revival that drew variously upon secularism, nationalism, and Islamic revivalism. In part, it was a reaction against European colonialism, but it was also the case that this renaissance drew on Western values and genres.

In 1826 Rifa'a al-Tahtawi (1801–71) was dispatched from Egypt to Paris on an educational mission—a part of Muhammad 'Ali's drive to modernize and Europeanize Egypt. He read widely in the arts and sciences and, as already noted, he came to know the Orientalist Silvestre de Sacy. He recorded his experiences in a fascinating book, *Takhlis al-ibriz fi talkhis Bariz* (The Extraction of Pure Gold in the Abridgement of Paris). In 1831 he returned to Egypt where he was to play a leading part in overseeing the translation of European writings into Arabic. In 1857 he got the government press in the Cairo suburb of Bulaq to publish the *Muqaddima*. He held that one of education's chief goals should be to encourage love of one's country and he was much preoccupied with *hubb al-watan* (love of the country, or patriotism), which he seems to have regarded as a kind of *'asabiyya*.

Two leading pioneers of Islamic modernism, Jamal al-Din al-Af-ghani (1839–97) and Muhammad 'Abduh (1849–1905), made a special study of the *Muqaddima* at a time when it was not much read in the Islamic world.

The pan-Islamic anti-imperialist campaigner al-Afghani used the *Muqaddima* as a teaching text when he was in Egypt in the 1870s.

His disciple 'Abduh lectured on Ibn Khaldun at the Dar al-'Ulum College in Cairo and wrote what seems to have been a Khaldun-ian history of philosophy and society. He denounced luxury and loose living in Khaldunian terms. Though he lectured a lot on Ibn Khaldun, we do not know the details because in 1879 the Egyptian government seized his lecture notes and burned them.[57] 'Abduh's disciple, Rashid Rida (1865–1935) was, however, less fond of Ibn Khaldun's ideas. Rida was one of the founders of modern Salafism and he preached a return to the practices and standards of the pious first generation of Islam (*al-salaf al-salih*) and he advocated the revival of the caliphate. He denounced Ibn Khaldun for having given more importance to *'asabiyya* than to religion. The very con-cept of *'asabiyya* seemed to him to be un-Islamic.

MODERN ARAB READINGS

Taha Husayn (1889–1973), critic, essayist, novelist, scholar, and jack-of-all-literary-trades, was Egypt's leading intellectual in the twentieth century. Born blind, he nevertheless attended both the al-Azhar (where he heard 'Abduh who also lectured there) and the more secular Egyptian National University and he shone in both places. At the National University the Italian Arabist, Carlo Nallino, had introduced him both to Ibn Khaldun and to positiv-ism. In 1916 Husayn won a scholarship to study at the Sorbonne where he encountered other positivists and sociologists, including the greatest sociologist of the age, Emile Durkheim. Almost all his teachers at the Sorbonne were positivists—that is to say that they held the view that all true knowledge is scientific and must be based on observable phenomena.

In 1917 he was awarded a doctorate for his thesis entitled *Étude analytique et critique de la philosophie sociale d'Ibn Khaldoun* (and some years later the thesis was published in Arabic). This was a fairly astringent piece of work as, though he praised Ibn Khaldun as a genius, he denied that he was either a scientific historian or a sociologist, or, for that matter (as Kremer had had him) a *Kulturhistoriker*. Ibn Khaldun was not a modern-style historian since he neglected the actual traces of the past, in the form of either documentary or archaeological evidence. Instead he had relied on information that was ultimately oral. He was not a sociologist either, since he only concerned himself with the state and ignored other social groups such as the Sufi orders. Insofar as he studied societies, it was to shed light on social events. His *'ilm* was not science, but a body of knowledge. He was an Arab historian of the fourteenth century and, as such, bound by the conventions of his time and place. Taha Husayn thought that Ibn Khaldun's apparent religiosity was only precautionary. The *Muqaddima* was a work of self-promotion. Still, the man was brilliant and his successors in the Arab world only failed to follow up on his insights because of the coming of the Turks who had turned the Arab world to dust.

A later book of his in 1926 that questioned the authenticity of *jahili* (pre-Islamic) poetry caused a storm of controversy. Taha Husayn was tried for apostasy and lost his academic job. However, he was too grand and clever to be kept down for long and later he became minister of education. In more modern times Ibn Khaldun has been belatedly adopted by the Egyptians as a national hero though, of course, rival claims have been made by Tunisia and Morocco and all three countries have organized conferences devoted to his life and thought.

Unsurprisingly, in recent decades many of the most important scholarly studies of Ibn Khaldun's thought have been produced by Arabs. An early study, *Ibn Khaldun, hayatahu wu turathuhu al-fikri*, was published in Cairo in 1933 by an Egyptian lawyer and university lecturer, Mohammad 'Abdullah Enan, and later translated into English. This book summarized the life and writings of Ibn Khaldun. Enan presented him as being so hostile to the Arabs that he was practically a Berber: "Although claiming to be of Arab origin, he belongs, in fact to that Berber race whose country the Arabs conquered . . . Ibn Khaldun was born and bred in this Berber society, burning with its feelings, traditions and memories. His family lived in it a hundred years before and enjoyed the patronage of the Berber Almohades. It is not strange, therefore, to see Ibn Khaldun condemning the Arabs in this most severe and cruel manner."[58]

Enan presented him as "the founder of modern sociology," but, though a case can be made for Ibn Khaldun as a precursor of the modern science of sociology, it is hard to see him as its actual founder, since the necessary continuity between the ideas of an Arab in the fourteenth century and those of certain French and German thinkers of the nineteenth century is not there. Enan's Ibn Khaldun was brilliant and fluent, but also an opportunist.

Enan also made much of the parallels between the career and writings of Ibn Khaldun and those of Machiavelli.[59] The same comparison has been made by others, including Abdesselam Cheddadi (on whom see below).[60]

Niccolò Machiavelli (1469–1527) had served the Florentine regime in war-torn Italy before withdrawing from politics to write his great work, *The Prince* (1513). Like Ibn Khaldun, he had previously operated in a politically complex environment and carried out diplomatic missions. *The Prince* was born out of political disappointment and written in the hope of regaining princely patronage. History was of central importance to Machiavelli and he mined it in order to formulate general laws of politics and society as they might be deduced from Greek and Roman history, as well as from more recent Italian history. Study of particular events furnished the basis for generalizations that might be of use to princes and generals. Like the *Muqaddima*, *The Prince* is a gloomy and pessimistic work.

But the differences between the two authors are more striking than the resemblances. Machiavelli asked how power could be won and retained and in doing so, he placed much stress on *fortuna*, or chance, in politics. The ability to call in a foreign army might also be an important factor in helping a ruler to retain or extend his power. History provided a guide to statecraft. Ibn Khaldun studied history in order to understand its underlying laws and, though the *Muqaddima* does include a letter written by Tahir ibn al-Husayn in the mirrors-for-princes genre, Ibn Khaldun did not write a guide to statecraft that might be of service to a ruler. Machiavelli interested himself in the psychology of rulership, the quest for glory, and the role that personality played in high politics. These things did not interest Ibn Khaldun. Machiavelli wrote a lot on the arts of war. Ibn Khaldun did not. Machiavelli argued that vices had their uses and that the ruler might act immorally if necessity demanded it. The intensely religious and moralistic Ibn Khaldun would have found such cynicism abominable. Machiavelli, on the other hand, wanted to keep religion out of politics. He dreamt of the unification of Italy. Ibn Khaldun had no such dreams for North Africa. There is nothing like *'asabiyya* in *The Prince,* or in the *Discorsi,* Machiavelli's later commentary on Livy's history of Rome. Ibn Khaldun did not come close to anticipating Machiavelli's concept of *virtu* (literally "manliness"). *Virtu,* as Machiavelli conceived of it, was compounded of cunning, decisiveness, force, and, above all, courage. Livy's formulation "Fortune favours the brave" was Machiavelli's watchword. And, as another enthusiast for Livy put it, "Fame is the spur" (Milton, *Lycidas*).

Finally, as Enan did note, Machiavelli "surpasses Ibn Khaldun in the fluency of his logic, the precision of exposition and conclusion, and the beauty of his style."[61] In Machiavelli's writings the record of great deeds had to be matched with a high style, and consequently the deployment of aphorisms, epigrams, carefully structured antitheses, and even accounts of historical incidents that were invented for rhetorical effect. Rhetoric in this sense was alien to Ibn Khaldun.

Aziz al-Azmeh, born in Damascus in 1947, is a former student of Hourani. He has taught at various universities and, at the time of writing, he is a professor at the Central European University in Budapest. He has published two studies that are most relevant here, *Ibn Khaldun in Modern Scholarship: A Study in Orientalism* and *Ibn Khaldun, an Essay in Reinterpretation.*[62] In these books his declared aim was to liberate Ibn Khaldun from the Orientalists and their philological and historicist preoccupations. (Historicism refers to the doctrine that all sociological phenomena are historically determined.) But al-Azmeh seems to have also wished to cut Ibn Khaldun down to size since he believed that his reputation mostly rested on the acclaim of Orientalists. Ibn Khaldun was not so very original and he was neither a sociologist, nor the propounder of a general theory of history. Al-Azmeh argues that Ibn Khaldun's philosophy of history consisted mostly of a series of unsupported generalizations and he had in fact failed in the quest for underlying principles that would explain historical events. There was usually a gap between what Ibn Khaldun logically deduced and the actual run of events. Moreover, when Ibn Khaldun came to write dynastic history, it turned out to be pretty conventional stuff. In a review in the *Bulletin of the School of Oriental African Studies*, Michael Brett, a historian of North Africa, criticized al-Azmeh's excessively downbeat account in the following terms. Ibn Khaldun's writings had been presented as "a freak or satyr." "This monster is exhibited for what it is, the brainchild of a medieval man who put it together for no known reason and to no great effect." Indeed, according to al-Azmeh, his writings were forgotten about "until rescued by representatives of an alien culture." Brett judged Azmeh's prose to be "inspissated."[63] Certainly neither of his books makes for easy reading and this may have limited their influence.

Al-Azmeh disputed Mahdi's Aristotelian reading of Ibn Khaldun's thinking and argued, surely correctly, that, for Ibn Khaldun, philosophy was a marginal science. But, having rejected Mahdi's argument that Ibn Khaldun was a crypto-rationalist, al-Azmeh also rejected Gibb's view that Ibn Khaldun supported faith against rationalism. We shall return to the view that Ibn Khaldun was in some important sense a creation of the Orientalists toward the end of this chapter.

Abdesselam Cheddadi, born in 1944, was a professor in the History Department of the University Muhammad V in Rabat from 1980 until 1998. He has held other distinguished posts and has received numerous awards. He is a translator of Ibn Khaldun into French and commentator on him. His translation of the *Ta'rif* was published as *Le Voyage d'Occident et d'Orient* and he published some reflections on the writings as *Ibn Khaldoun revisité*.[64] His French translation of the *Muqaddima*, as well as the North African section of the *'Ibar*, was published by Gallimard in 2002 and his *Ibn Khaldûn: L'homme et le théoricien de la civilisation* appeared in 2006 with the same publisher. Cheddadi has comprehensively surveyed Ibn Khaldun's writings and, in doing so, has tended to emphasize Ibn Khaldun's importance as a medieval ethnographer and anthropologist, and consequently he has paid particular attention to Gellner's writings, though he has criticized Gellner's attempt to Europeanize Ibn Khaldun's thinking. But, while Ibn Khaldun may have been an anthropologist in a loose sense, he did not interest himself in the sorts of things that modern anthropologists usually get interested in: elaborate kinship systems, marriage rules, local rituals, gift exchanges, taboos, the details of material life, and so on.

Though *ta'rikh* is conventionally translated as "history," Cheddadi warns against confusing *ta'rikh* with history, since *ta'rikh* in its medieval usage was no more than the chronological arrangement of miscellaneous information. Many of Ibn Khaldun's contemporaries in the Maghreb and Egypt produced such compilations. He did not. Unlike al-Azmeh, Cheddadi sees race rather than dynasty as being the primary organizing principle in Ibn Khaldun's history. Cheddadi stresses the universality of Ibn Khaldun's message and argues that it is still relevant today.

AMERICAN READINGS

Ibn Khaldun, Life and Times (2010), by the American academic Allen James Fromherz, is a biography that seeks to present Ibn Khaldun's thought in the context of his life in fourteenth-century North Africa. Fromherz believes that he has found more self-revelation in Ibn Khaldun's *Ta'rif* than earlier readers of Ibn Khaldun. He has paid close attention to Ibn Khaldun's political career in the Maghreb and his specialist status as a negotiator with Arab and Berber tribesmen. More controversially, as noted in chapter 6, Fromherz is confident that not only was Ibn Khaldun a Sufi, but that Sufism crucially shaped his cyclical theory of history. Although he was probably a Sufi, a case for his theory of history being underpinned by a Sufi methodology or any kind of Sufi inspiration would have to be made in a lot more detail in order to be convincing.

Cheddadi was emphatic that Ibn Khaldun was not a philosopher in the Graeco-Islamic tradition and that he saw some aspects of that kind of thinking as harmful to religion.[65] But Stephen Dale's monograph, *The Orange Trees of Marrakesh: Ibn Khaldun and the Science of Man* (2015) has more recently argued the contrary case. To quote from the blurb of the book: "His methodology was derived from Aristotelian notions of nature and causation, and he applied it to create a dialectical model that explained the cyclical rise and fall of North Africa dynasties . . . His strikingly modern approach to historical research established him as the pre-modern world's preeminent historical scholar. It also demonstrated his membership in an intellectual lineage that begins with Plato, Aristotle, and Galen; continues with the Greco-Muslim philosophers al-Farabi, Avicenna, and Averroes; and is renewed with Montesquieu, Hume, Adam Smith, and Durkheim." Indeed, Dale believes that it is precisely because Ibn Khaldun owed so much to Greek philosophy that his writings have been so readily acclaimed by Western thinkers who were comfortable with that tradition.[66]

Though Dale's case that Ibn Khaldun wrote in the Graeco-Islamic philosophical tradition is carefully and persuasively argued, it is clearly not the one that is being advanced in *Ibn Khaldu: An Intellectual Biography*. It can be conceded that early on in his education Ibn Khaldun had absorbed much of the vocabulary of the philosophers and he made extensive use of that vocabulary when he came to write the *Muqaddima*.

But when he did so, he did not necessarily give those words their full philosophical meaning. Thus the word *muqaddima* can have the philosophers' meaning of "a premise, proposition or axiom that is an inductively derived statement of a generally recognised truth," but it can also mean "prolegomena." *'Ibara*, a word that derives from the same root as *'ibar*, was the word used by medieval Arabs to translate Aristotle's work on hermeneutics (known in the

West as *De interpretatione*), but *'ibara*'s primary meaning in Arabic was "explanation" and Ibn Khaldun's use of the related word *'ibar* surely reflects the way it is used in the Qur'an. Similarly, Dale argues that when the word *burhan* appears in the *Muqaddima*, it specifically means "apodictic proof," one that is necessarily true, but *burhan* was more widely used to mean proof in the more general sense. And so on.

The evidence for Ibn Khaldun being turned into a full-blown philosopher by his teacher, al-Abili, is thin. Al-Abili seems to have taught as much theology as philosophy and he was not the totally dedicated rational thinker that Dale (and Mahdi) would have liked him to be. In his youth al-Abili had studied with the mystic Ibn al-Banna' and Ibn Khaldun may have gained much of his extensive knowledge of the occult from al-Abili. He cited al-Abili on the impending coming of the man of destiny foretold by the conjunction of Saturn and Jupiter.[67] Al-Abili also taught Ibn 'Abbad al-Rundi, a man who was to become a leading Sufi master and who had a great deal of influence on the Shadhili Sufi order. Ibn 'Arafa was another student and he went on to achieve fame not as a philosopher, but as a leading authority on Maliki law. Moreover, as has been noted, Ibn Khaldun's access to the genuine works of Aristotle was restricted, even though he seems to have been familiar with the content of Aristotle's eight books on logic, known as the *Organon*.[68]

Dale also claims that Ibn Khaldun was deeply familiar with the thinking of the Greek physician Galen (AD 129–199), "the third most influential Greek or classical rationalist thinker after Plato and Aristotle."[69] Galen's approach to medicine entailed "a philosophical understanding and method that proceeded from a knowledge of the nature or essence of the body as the necessary first step in identifying the underlying or hidden causes of disease. Comprehending the essential nature of things, whether physical objects or human beings, was an Aristotelian principle."[70] But there is no direct evidence that Ibn Khaldun had grasped Galen's underlying methodology and he is mentioned only a handful of times in the *Muqaddima*. Ibn Khaldun, in a listing of estimable medical authorities, briefly praised Galen's anatomical treatise *De usu partium* (Of the Use of Different Parts [of the Human Body]). This may have been the only work of Galen that he knew of and he may only have known of it through citations in other authors. He also cited *De usu partium* on man's use of swords and lances as a substitute for claws and horns.[71] In Ibn Khaldun's somewhat obscure discussion of the function of dreams, he attributed dreaming to the activity of the corporeal animal spirit when we are sleeping: "This spirit is a fine vapour which is concentrated in the left cavity of the heart, as stated in the anatomical works of Galen and others."[72] Elsewhere Ibn Khaldun criticized al-Mas'udi's citation of Galen in order to explain excitability and emotionalism of the Negroes, which Mas'udi asserted was due to "the weakness of their brains."[73] In rejecting Mas'udi's explanation, he was also implicitly rejecting that of Galen.

Dale sees Ibn Khaldun as primarily a deductive thinker. "Deduction" means the inference of a particular truth from a general truth previously known. "Induction," by contrast means reasoning from particular cases to general conclusions. Today the words "deduction" and "deduce" are widely misused. "Ask anyone at the Drones, and they will tell you that Bertram Wooster is a fellow whom it is dashed difficult to deceive. Old Lynx-Eye is about what it amounts to. I observe and deduce. I weigh the evidence and draw my conclusions."[74] It is no surprise to find the silly ass, Bertie Wooster, misusing the verb "deduce." But Sherlock Holmes should have known better. Holmes was actually using induction and Wooster was trying to.

According to Dale, Ibn Khaldun systematically relied on the top-down logic of deduction. But in when one considers how deduction and induction work in practice, it becomes evident that for most thinkers the distinction between the two processes cannot be hard-edged. It is true that the *Muqaddima* is, in large part, set out as a deductive treatise in which general historical laws are announced and then particular examples are adduced to illustrate those laws. Yet it is hard to conceive how Ibn Khaldun could, for example, have formulated his cyclical thesis, in which vigorous tribal warriors overcome a sedentary urbanized dynasty and establish a new dynasty that in turn becomes weakened by being sedentarized and consequently is overthrown by a new tribal wave, without his having first induced this law from his reading about what actually happened in the early period of the caliphate, as well as in the later histories of the Almoravids and Almohads.

In presenting Ibn Khaldun as a philosopher working in the Graeco-Islamic tradition, Dale can claim Mahdi as a supporter. But Gibb, Lacoste, Azmeh, Cheddadi, and Fromherz have emphatically rejected this hypothetical intellectual lineage. Of course, this is not a matter that should be decided by a show of hands. But I believe that enough evidence has been presented in the previous chapters of this book to suggest that there were strict limits to Ibn Khaldun's rationality. He had limited access to the genuine writings of Aristotle and though he conceded that logic certainly had its uses he thought that the practice of philosophy was dangerous. Maliki jurisprudence furnished a more important model for his historical methodology.

KHALDUNIAN NOVELS

Bensalem Himmich (b. 1949 in Meknes) is a prolific and distinguished novelist, poet, and philosopher who teaches philosophy at the Mohammed V University in Rabat. In 1998 he published *Khalduniyya fi daw' falsafat al-ta'rikh*. Himmich does not believe that the mature Ibn Khaldun wrote in the Graeco-Islamic philosophical tradition, but he is equally unhappy with the presentation of him as primarily a legalistic thinker and a moderate partisan of Sufism. Like Lacoste and Cheddadi, Himmich finds lessons in the *Muqaddima* that are relevant for today, especially regarding underdevelopment in most of the world and, like Lacoste, Himmich has been strongly influenced by the writings of Marx and Engels, though he also cites Saussure, Derrida, Foucault, Levi-Strauss, and Deleuze and Guattari. There is an extended comparison of Ibn Khaldun's economic thought with that of Marx. Ibn Khaldun was judged to be both a materialist and a positivist. But Himmich rejected Lacoste's imposition of an "Asiatic mode of production" on North Africa. For Himmich, the messages found in the medieval treatise give potential guidance to today's Third World on how to free itself belatedly from the medieval evils of tribalism, despotism, clientage, and nepotism.

Himmich presents Ibn Khaldun as an intensely depressed person who wrote in an age of obvious crisis and decline. Research and thinking for his nonfiction book fed into the novel that he worked on at around the same time. His novel *Al-'Allama* was first published in Beirut in 1997. Subsequently it won the Naguib Mahfouz Award in Egypt, was republished there, and then translated into English as *The Polymath*. The novel deals with Ibn Khaldun's last years in Egypt and Syria and quotes extensively from the *Muqaddima* and the *Ta'rif*. Indeed, in the (excessively didactic) first half, Ibn Khaldun expounds his philosophy of history to his scribe. A philosopher, Himmich, reflects then on how a philosopher, Ibn Khaldun, writes. It is a novel about the intellectual's difficulties with the authorities, how rulers manipulate history, and, finally, about loneliness and the approach to death. "Having reached its end, I then saw myself plunging into a bottomless abyss possessed of total control over the forces of fusion and attraction. At its very bottom, twixt earth and dust, it had the power to restore the falling soul to its original clay. The only one to escape its depths was the soul that in its ascent clung to the rope extended by God from heaven to earth."[75]

The ideas of Ibn Khaldun have fed into other novels. The case of Isaac Asimov's *Foundation* trilogy has already been mentioned. In the *Dune* cycle of novels by the science fiction writer Frank Herbert (1920–86) the debt to Ibn Khaldun is implicit, but fairly obvious. *Dune* (1965), *Dune Messiah* (1969), and *Children of Dune* (1976) deal with medieval-style intergalactic politics. In an anticipation of *The Game of Thrones*, a lot of the plot swings around vendettas between noble households. Fremen, Bedouin-like dwellers on the desert planet of Arrakis, are masters of the spice trade. They travel not on camels but on sandworms. The Fremen language is explicitly based on Arabic and in the novel one finds such familiar words as *jihad, adab,* and *Shari'a*. Most significantly, the Fremen's survival manual is entitled the *Kitab al-Ibar*. The Fremen are the descendants of the Zen*sunni* Wanderers. The spice that the Fremen mine and trade in conferred prescience and how the future could be known is a leading theme in the *Dune* novels, as it was in the *Muqaddima* (on which see chapter 7). Though the Fremen support the revolt led by the prophet Paul Mu'ad Dib of the Atreides clan, their traditional and austere way of life will be doomed by their rise to power under Mu'ad Dib's leadership. He and his descendants will convert the Fremen into an intergalactic conquering army and their conquests make them rich, wasteful, and corrupt. The messianic figure of Mu'ad Dib is modeled in part on Muhammad and it is clear that Herbert must have read Montgomery Watt's two volumes on the career of the Prophet, *Muhammad at Mecca* (1953) and *Muhammad at Medina* (1956), but above all, as Herbert confirmed in a radio interview, he had read the *Muqaddima*.

IBN KHALDUN, A PRODUCT OF ORIENTALISM?

According to Bruce Lawrence, an American academic specializing in Islamic studies, "Ibn Khaldun was a product of Orientalism, and the extent to which he can now be assessed apart from the Orientalist interest evoked by him is highly questionable. Yet Orientalism took its implicit, if not explicit, beginnings from the promptings of power, when colonizing European nations ruling over Muslim peoples needed to know more about their subjects so as to better predict their behaviour, and thus perhaps control them. Ibn Khaldun provided a unique resource." Lawrence goes on to argue that it was Ibn Khaldun's critical approach to Islamic ways of thought and of doing politics that attracted Western scholars.[76]

I think that Lawrence's generalization overstates the complicity of Orientalism with colonialism. Until well into the twentieth century religious motivations were far more important than political ones in inducing scholars to study the Middle East and Islam. Some learned Arabic in order to translate the Gospels into that language and to prepare to go out as missionaries. Some produced translations of the Qur'an and commentaries on it in order to refute it. Some regarded Arabic as a useful handmaiden in the study of the Hebrew of the Bible. Some went out to the

Arab lands to study the doctrines of the Eastern Christians in the hope that some of those doctrines might serve as ammunition in the various polemics in Christian Europe between Catholics and Protestants, or, within Catholicism, between Jesuits and Jansenists. Some studied the way of life of Arab tribesmen for the light that this might shed on the material culture of the ancient Israelites.[77]

More specifically, Ibn Khaldun was discovered by Hammer-Purgstall and Silvestre de Sacy decades before the French colonization of North Africa got under way, and Silvestre de Sacy's short translations and commentaries on Ibn Khaldun do not seem to offer much to the prospective colonialist. Then Quatremère was a religiously driven scholar who seems to have had little or no interest in the French Empire. The Austrian Von Kremer was a citizen of an empire that possessed no territories in the Middle East or North Africa and he was apparently interested in cultural history for its own sake. Later yet, Monteil and Lacoste were avowed anti-imperialists. Furthermore, most of the books that have been written about Ibn Khaldun have been written by Arabs.

It must be conceded that De Slane was commissioned by the French Ministry of War to produce his translations of Ibn Khaldun. Later, Gautier and other French professors teaching in the universities of Algiers and Oran quoted Ibn Khaldun selectively and inaccurately in order to highlight the allegedly destructive effects of the Arab invasions on North Africa and they also misquoted him to suggest that there was an eternal antagonism between Arab and Berber. Even so, Khaldunian scholarship has not been dominated by a single colonialist agenda, but by many agendas. There has perhaps been a tendency among some scholars to create an Ibn Khaldun in their own individual image. So the intensely pious Christian Hamilton Gibb discovered in Ibn Khaldun an intensely pious Muslim. The Marxist Lacoste recognized in Ibn Khaldun a fellow traveler, if one of a rather primitive kind. Muhsin Mahdi discovered a Straussian Ibn Khaldun who had been careful to expound his political philosophy in such a way that it could not be understood by the masses. (I suppose that I may well be guilty of some similarly questionable proceeding.)

The study of Ibn Khaldun has, if anything, intensified in the post-colonial period. In part this may be because of the hunger of political scientists, sociologists, anthropologists, ethnologists, and economists to find an intellectual ancestor or precursor for what they practice. This sort of ancestor worship has its dangers and the keenness of modern Western Christian or secular thinkers to legitimate their thinking by drawing on the writings of a strict Muslim who lived in the fourteenth century is most curious. Awarding him a gold star for modernity is odd.

After a while, a subject that has been much studied—the rise and fall of Hitler, the Bloomsbury Group, the magical realist novel, the life and times of Richard III—begins to exert its own gravitational pull. The books and articles breed more books and articles. The availability of good translations of Ibn Khaldun and the abundance of secondary literature on Ibn Khaldun makes it an attractive option for academic courses and sometimes the academics who teach such courses begin to develop their own ideas about how Ibn Khaldun should be read and in this way the Khaldunian literature proliferates. Michael Brett, an expert on medieval African history and, more specifically, on Ibn Khaldun, has come to the following conclusion: "That Ibn Khaldun continues to mean all things to all men is a measure of his greatness as well as of his ambiguity."[78]

CHAPTER ELEVEN

Ending Up

The Liberal historian H.A.L. Fisher made the following confession in the preface to his *History of Europe*, published in 1934:

> Men wiser and more learned than I have discerned in history a plot, a rhythm, a predetermined pattern. These harmonies are concealed from me. I can see only one emergency following up on another as wave follows upon wave, only one great fact with respect to which, since it is unique, there can be no generalisations, only one safe rule for the historian; that he should recognise in the development of human destinies the play of the contingent and the unforeseen . . . The ground gained by one generation may be lost by the next.[1]

Well, Ibn Khaldun was wiser and more learned than Fisher. He was able to contemplate the complexity, unpredictability, and bloodiness of politics as practiced by the Merinids, Hafsids, 'Abd al-Wadids, and Nasrids, and, having considered all that, he was able to generalize and draw from it laws that governed the formation and dissolution of communities. His version of history was less narrowly political than that of Fisher and gave more weight to such factors as the economy, climate, kinship bonds, and the operations of the supernatural. The laws he had discovered would, he believed, explain not only what had happened, but what would happen.

Fisher's lament had surely been a critical response to the publication of the first three volumes of Toynbee's *A Study of History*, which had been published a few years earlier. Doubtless, the pessimistic tone of Fisher's response also reflected the disillusionment that was widely felt in the wake of the First World War, as well as anxiety about the rise of Nazism and Communism in Europe. But there is something a touch disingenuous about Fisher's disavowal of any ability to see a pattern. If his *History of Europe* really had no plot, no shaping pattern, and was just a blurred concatenation of events without any special significance, then this would make for hard reading (but it is not so and I read it several times as a schoolboy). His book does have a plot, even if this is not admitted by its author. And indeed, having penned his despair at history's failure to deliver easy lessons, he then added: "This is not a doctrine of cynicism and despair. The fact of progress is written plain and large on the page of history."[2] And, as one would expect from a Liberal historian writing in the tradition of the Whig version of history, a pattern of sorts does appear in the narrative of his *History of Europe*. Under the Romans civilization flourished for three hundred years in much of Europe, before being destroyed by the Teutonic invasions. The story thereafter is one of slow and bumpy progress toward a new civilization. The Renaissance, the Reformation, and the French Revolution were milestones on that progress. But as Fisher wrote, civilization was once again under threat from the Teutons and "Nordic paganism." Fisher took it for granted that European history had a meaning, unlike that of the rest of the world: "But of all that human misery which prevails in the vast spaces of Asia, Africa and South America where thousands of millions of men and women have lived, worked and died, leaving no memorial, contributing nothing to the future, these volumes are not concerned."[3]

To return to Ibn Khaldun, writing this book has been the culmination of a necromantic pursuit. I have spent most of my life communing with a man who has been dead for over six hundred years, a man whose ways of thinking are very different from my own. It has been a kind of séance and, as is so often the case with séances, it has sometimes been difficult to interpret the messages coming across the centuries. I am conscious that I have sometimes failed to understand what Ibn Khaldun is saying. I am not the first person to be defeated by his account of the operations of the *za'iraja*, but I also found his exposition of physiology, psychology, dreaming, and soothsaying somewhat obscure. Then, setting aside topics on which he seemed to have difficulty in expressing himself clearly, more generally the sheer depth and elaboration of the man's thinking is challenging. Even when what he is saying seems to be perfectly clear, it is still difficult. Otherwise there would not be so many different interpretations of the message of the *Muqaddima*. Wordsworth's lines on Isaac Newton come to mind:

The marble index of a mind
Voyaging through strange seas of thought, alone.

Those "seas of thought" are indeed strange and to modernize Ibn Khaldun and to elide the strangeness of his thinking is to denature him. Previous accounts of his life and works, in the course of seeking to demonstrate that he was the world's first sociologist, or an early Marxist, or a philosopher in the Aristotelian tradition, or a forerunner of the political philosopher Leo Strauss, have exaggerated Ibn Khaldun's rationality and posited an essentially secular frame of mind. (In many cases they have also presented him as being guilty of what the Surrealists used to term "anticipatory plagiarism.") He has been stretched out on a Procrustean bed, in which certain parts of him have been lopped off in order to make him fit on a piece of furniture that is of modern design. The discarded parts include, among other things, his devotion to Maliki jurisprudence and his preoccupation with occultism and futurology, as well as some of his bizarre scientific ideas.

Who was Ibn Khaldun writing for? Well, certainly not for me. Nor come to that, for the massed academics of the twenty-first-century world. Moreover, though he dedicated copies of the *Muqaddima* to the ruler of Tunis and to the sultan of Egypt, it does not seem that he wrote the book in order to guide a ruler. It is unlikely that Ibn Khaldun was seeking readers among his fellow jurists and teachers of whom he had a rather low opinion. We have also seen that he was suspicious of merchants and shopkeepers. Most of the tribesmen he had dealings with could not read. I suspect that Ibn Khaldun's ideal destination audience was himself and that he wrote to clear his head of all those ideas and insights that boiled and seethed within it.

Some of our problems in reading Ibn Khaldun arise from trying to make him a more systematic thinker than he really was. He was inconsistent in the use of certain keywords, including *'asabiyya, badawi,* and "Arab." He was inconsistent on whether the Mamluk system was immune from the historical cycle of decay or not. He was inconsistent on whether his cyclical theory of history applied outside the Maghreb or not. He was inconsistent on the causes of the plague. That he often seems to contradict himself in the *Muqaddima* is not surprising. The book was written over a long period of time in various locales. While at times he had access to large libraries, at other times he did not. Moreover, as Aristotle observed, "Great men may make great mistakes."

Does what Ibn Khaldun wrote have relevance today? Many Arab academics have argued that he does. Cheddadi believes that modern anthropologists can learn from him. Himmich finds support for the tenets of Marxism in the *Muqaddima*. Other Arab scholars have hailed Ibn Khaldun as an early Arab nationalist. To take a different kind of example, the ghostly presence of Ibn Khaldun can be detected in The *Arab Human Development Report 2004*, which had this to say about the Gulf and, more generally, about the Arab world in the twenty-first century: "Clannism ['*asabiyya*] in all its forms (tribal, clan-based, communal, and ethnic) . . . tightly shackles its followers through the power of the authoritarian patriarchal system. This phenomenon . . . represents a two-way street in which obedience and loyalty are offered in return for protection, sponsorship and a share of the spoils . . . Its positive aspects include a sense of belonging to a community and the desire to put its interests first."[4] For all its reference to "positive aspects," the *Report* is clearly using '*asabiyya* in a pejorative sense and moreover applying it in an urban context. Ibn Khaldun's sense of the word always had a positive and dynamic quality, whereas the *Report* implicitly presents '*asabiyya* as something that contributes to the stagnation of contemporary Arab society.

Few today would share Ibn Khaldun's positive vision of tribal loyalty as an engine of social change. Much of the *Muqaddima's* fascination lies in the fact that its author, starting from medieval premises and working on medieval data, went on to create powerful theoretical models to explain how things worked in the world he lived in. In that sense Ibn Khaldun can indeed be compared to Darwin, Marx, and Durkheim, even though Ibn Khaldun's theoretical models and conclusions cannot apply to modern societies. As Mark Zuckerberg observed when selecting the *Muqaddima* as one of his books of the year in 2015, "While much of what was believed then is now disproven after 700 years more progress, it's still interesting to see what was understood at the time and the overall world view when it's all considered together."[5]

Perhaps the ultimate purpose of the *Muqaddima* was to prepare Muslims for the Last Judgment. Ibn Khaldun quoted a saying of the Prophet: "Be in this world as if you were a stranger and a passing traveller." The bleakness and loneliness of this historian are striking. It can be argued that Ibn Khaldun was unreasonably prejudiced against luxury and today there must be many who would argue from their experience, and against Ibn Khaldun, that living in luxury can be conducive to health and contentment. He was austere. He was also arrogant, as both his contemporaries and his own writings bear witness, but then he had a lot to be arrogant about. On quite a few issues the Qur'an and Maliki law books did his thinking for him. In so many ways he was outstanding and exceptional; yet in other ways his thinking was that of a thoroughly conventional Muslim. Consequently this book has served not only as an account of the workings of genius, but also as a guide to perfectly ordinary Muslim beliefs.

Finally: "We almost strayed from our purpose. It is our intention now to stop . . . Perhaps some later scholar, aided by the divine gifts of a sound mind and solid scholarship, will penetrate into these problems in greater detail than we did here . . . God knows and you do not know."[6]

NOTES

Preface

1. Arnold Toynbee, *A Study of History* (London, 1935), vol. 3, p. 322.
2. Hugh Trevor-Roper, "Ibn Khaldoun and the Decline of Barbary," in Trevor-Roper, *Historical Essays* (London, 1957), p. 28.
3. Marshall Hodgson, *The Venture of Islam: Conscience and History in a World Civilization* (Chicago and London, 1977), vol. 2, p. 55n.
4. Ernest Gellner, *Muslim Society* (Cambridge, 1981), p. 88.
5. Ibn Khaldûn, *The Muqaddimah: An Introduction to History* (1967, London; reprinted Princeton, NJ, 1980), vol. 1, pp. 77–78 (hereinafter cited as *Muq.*).
6. *Muq.*, vol. 1, p. 83.
7. Aziz al-Azmeh, *Ibn Khaldun in Modern Scholarship: A Study in Orientalism* (London, 1981).
8. *Muq.*, vol. 3, p. 288.
9. Patricia Crone, *Pre-Industrial Societies* (Oxford, 1989), p. 1.
10. Ibn Khaldun, *Le Livre des exemples* (Paris, 2002).
11. Franz Rosenthal, "Ibn Khaldun in His Time," in Bruce B. Lawrence, ed., *Ibn Khaldun and Islamic Ideology* (Leiden, 1984), p. 14.

Chapter One. Ibn Khaldun among the Ruins

1. *Arabian Nights: Tales of 1001 Nights* (London, 2008), vol. 2, p. 523.
2. *Arabian Nights: Tales of 1001 Nights*, vol. 2, pp. 518–46; cf. Andras Hamori, "An Allegory from the *Arabian Nights*: The City of Brass," in Hamori, *The Art of Medieval Arabic Literature* (Princeton, NJ, 1974), pp. 145–63; David Pinault, *Story-Telling Techniques in the Arabian Nights* (Leiden, 1992), pp. 148–239; Jocelyne Dakhlia, "Un miroir de la royauté au Maghreb: la ville d'airan," in Patrice Cressier and Mercedes García Arenal, eds., *Genèse de la ville islamique en al-Andalus et au Maghreb occidental* (Madrid, 1998), pp. 17–36; Ulrich Marzolph and Richard van Leeuwen, *The Arabian Nights Encyclopedia* (Santa Barbara, CA, 2004), vol. 1, p. 146–50; Bruce Fudge, "Underworlds and Otherworlds in *The Thousand and One Nights*," *Middle Eastern Literatures* 15 (2012), pp. 257–72.
3. *Muq.*, vol. 2, p. 351.
4. *Muq.*, vol. 1, p. 305.
5. Jaroslav Stetkevych, *The Zephyrs of Najd: The Poetics of Nostalgia in the Classical Arabic Nasib* (Chicago, 1993), p. 63.
6. Michael Brett and Werner Forman, *The Moors: Islam in the West* (London, 1980), p. 66.
7. Ibn Jubayr, *The Travels of Ibn Jubayr* (London, 1952), p. 226.
8. Muhsin Mahdi, *Ibn Khaldûn's Philosophy of History* (Chicago, 1964), p. 68.
9. Ibn Khaldun, *Peuples et Nations du Monde* (Paris, 1986), vol. 1, p. 144.

10. Jonathan P. Berkey, *Popular Preaching and Religious Authority in the Medieval Islamic Near East* (Seattle and London, 2001), p. 80.

11. *Muq.*, vol. 1, p. 4.

12. *Muq.*, vol. 1, p. 386.

13. *Muq.*, vol. 1, p. 305.

14. Jean-Claude Garcin, *Les Mille et Une Nuits et l'Histoire* (Paris, 2016), pp. 38–43.

15. *Muq.*, vol. 2, pp. 104–5.

16. Ibn Khaldun, "Autobiographie," in Khaldun, *Le Livre des exemples* (Paris, 2002), vol. 1, p. 111; cf. Allen James Fromherz, *Ibn Khaldun, Life and Times* (Edinburgh, 2001), p. 79.

17. Alexander Knysh, "Ibn al-Khatib," in Maria Rosa Menocal, Raymond P. Scheindlin, and Michael Sells, eds., *The Cambridge History of Arabic Literature: The Literature of Al-Andalus* (Cambridge, 2000), p. 366.

18. *Muq.*, vol. 1, p. 64.

19. Ahmed Shboul, *Al-Mas'udi and His World* (London, 1979); Tarif Khalidi, *Islamic Historiography: The Histories of Mas'udi* (New York, 1975).

20. Gustave E. von Grunebaum, *Medieval Islam* (Chicago, 1946), pp. 339–40n.

21. Chase F. Robinson, *Islamic Historiography* (Cambridge, 2003), p. 36.

22. On Ibn Khaldun's debt to al-Mas'udi, see Fischel, *Ibn Khaldun in Egypt: His Public Functions and His Historical Research* (Berkeley and Los Angeles, 1967), pp. 111–14.

23. Al-Mas'udi, quoted in Peter Webb, *Imagining the Arabs: Arab Identity and the Rise of Islam* (Edinburgh, 2016), p. 329.

24. *Muq.*, vol. 1, pp. 75–76.

25. Al-Mas'udi, *Les prairies d'or* (Paris, 1966–79), vol. 1, p. 149.

26. *Arabian Nights*, vol. 1, pp. 898–903.

27. *Muq.*, vol. 1, pp. 25–28.

28. Masudi, *Meadows of Gold: The 'Abbasids* (London, 1989), pp. 44–46.

29. H. P. Lovecraft, "The Nameless City," in T. Joshi, ed., *Lovecraft, The Complete Fiction* (New York, 2008), p. 147.

30. *Lovecraft, The Complete Fiction*, p. 368.

31. *Muq.*, vol. 1, pp. 73–74; cf. al-Mas'udi, *Muruj al-dhahab wa-ma'adin al-jawhar* (Paris, 1861–77), vol. 2, pp. 425–27.

32. *Tales of the Marvellous and News of the Strange* (London, 2014), p. 139–40.

33. Hugh Kennedy, *The Court of the Caliphs: The Rise and Fall of Islam's Greatest Dynasty* (London, 2004), pp. 71–77.

34. *Muq.*, vol. 1, p. 28–33; al-Mas'udi, *Muruj al-dhahab*, vol. 6, pp. 387–89; al-Mas'udi, *The Meadows of Gold*, pp. 115–20.

35. Marzolph and Van Leeuwen, *Arabian Nights Encyclopedia*, vol. 2, p. 488.

36. *Muq.*, vol. 1, pp. 33–34.

37. *Muq.*, vol. 1, pp. 39–40.

38. *Arabian Nights*, vol. 1, pp. 903–4; cf. Marzolph and Van Leeuwen, *Arabian Nights Encyclopedia*, vol. 1, p. 232.

39. *Muq.*, vol. 1, p. 359.
40. *Muq.*, vol. 1, pp. 356–57; cf. vol. 2, p. 239.
41. *Muq.*, vol. 1, pp. 357–58; cf. vol. 2, p. 240.
42. *Muq.*, vol. 1, pp. 357–58; cf. vol. 2, pp. 240–41.
43. *Muq.*, vol. 3, p. 277.
44. *Muq.*, vol. 2, p. 432.
45. *Muq.*, vol. 2, p. 136; cf. Michael W. Dols, *The Black Death in the Middle East* (Princeton, NJ, 1977), p. 90.
46. *Muq.*, vol. 2, p. 245.
47. *Muq.*, vol. 2, p. 86.
48. *Muq.*, vol. 1, p. 4.
49. Al-Maqrizi, *Mamluk Economics: A Study and Translation of al-Maqrizi's Ighathah* (Salt Lake City, 1994), p. 53.
50. *The Arabian Nights*, vol. 1, pp. 902–3.
51. *Muq.*, vol. 3, pp. 36–37.

Chapter Two. The Game of Thrones in Fourteenth-Century North Africa

1. Hugh Kennedy, *An Historical Atlas of Islam* (Leiden, 2002), p. 1; Henri Bresc and Annliese Nef, *Idrisi; La première géographie de l'Occident* (Paris, 1999).
2. *Muq.*, vol. 1, pp. 167, 172.
3. *Muq.*, vol. 1, pp. 161–63; cf. pp. 110, 137, 149, 157–58, 166, 172.
4. *Muq.*, vol. 1, p. 138.
5. Fernand Braudel, *The Mediterranean and the Mediterranean World in the Age of Philip II* (London, 1972), vol. 1, p. 174.
6. *Muq.*, vol. 2, pp. 27–28.
7. The following works have been most useful in providing an outline of his career: Franz Rosenthal, "Introduction," in *Muq.*, vol. 1, pp. xxxix–lvii; M. Talbi, "Ibn Khaldun," in *The Encyclopedia of Islam* (Leiden, 1960–2009), vol. 3, pp. 825–31; Fromherz, *Ibn Khaldun.*
8. Anselm Adorno, *Itinéraire d'Anselme Adorno en Terre Sainte (1470–1471)*, pp. 101, 103, 141.
9. Mohammed B. A. Benchekroun, *La Vie intellectuelle Marocaine sous les Mérinides et les Wattasides* (Rabat, 1974), p. 38.
10. On al-Abili, see Nassif Nasser, "Le maître d'Ibn Khaldun: al-Abili," *Studia Islamica* 20 (1964), pp. 103–15.
11. Ibn Khaldun, *Le Voyage d'Occident et d'Orient* (Paris, 1980), p. 48–49, 54–58, 72.
12. *Muq.*, vol. 2, pp. 189, 198, 339.
13. Maya Shatzmiller, *The Berbers and the Islamic State: The Marinid Experience in Pre-Protectorate Morocco* (Princeton, NJ, 2000), p. 92.
14. *Muq.*, vol. 3, p. 264.
15. Ahmed Khaneboubi, *Les Institutions gouvernmentales sous les Merinides (1258–1465)* (Paris, 2008), p. 110; Ibn Khaldun, *Voyage*, p. 47.
16. Since I found no single narrative history of the Merinid dynasty and Ibn Khaldun's involvement with it, the following account is based on many and vari-

ous sources. But the following books were particularly useful: Benchekroun, *La vie intellectuelle*; Khanenoubi, *Les institutuions gouvermentales*; Maya Shatzmiller, *L'historiographie Merinide: Ibn Khaldūn et ses contemporains* (Leiden, 1982).

17. Ibn Khaldun, *Voyage*, p. 84.

18. Shatzmiller, *L'historiographie Mérinide*, pp. 36–43; Benchekroun, *La vie intellectuelle*, pp. 283–93.

19. Ibn Khaldun, *Voyage*, pp. 85–86.

20. Ibn Khaldun, *Voyage*, p. 86.

21. *Muq.*, vol. 3, p. 459. On the life and works of Ibn al-Khatib, see D. M. Dunlop, *Arab Civilization to AD 1500* (London, 1971), pp. 146–48; Anwar G. Chejne, *Muslim Spain, Its History and Culture* (Minneapolis, 1974), passim; Knysh, "Ibn al-Khatib," pp. 358–72; Emilio Molina López, *Ibn al-Jatib* (Granada, 2001); Robert Irwin, *The Alhambra* (London, 2004), pp. 82–86.

22. Alexander D. Knysh, *Ibn 'Arabi in the Later Islamic Tradition: The Making of a Polemical Image in Medieval Islam* (Albany, NY, 1998), pp. 171–84.

23. Ibn Khaldun, *Voyage*, pp. 69–70.

24. On Ibn Khaldun in Granada, see Ibn Khaldun, *Voyage*, pp. 89–93; Rachel Arié, *l'Espagne Musulmane au Temps des Nasrides (1232–1492)* (Paris, 1973), passim.

25. Muhsin Mahdi, *Ibn Khaldûn's Philosophy of History: A Study in the Philosophic Foundation of the Science of Culture* (Chicago, 1964), p. 42.

26. On Hafsid history, see Robert Brunschvig, *La Berbérie orientale sous les Hafsides: des origins à la fin du XVe siècle* (Algiers, 1940, 1947); Ramzi Roughi, *The Making of a Mediterranean Emirate: Ifriqiyya and Its Andalusis, 1200–1400* (Philadelphia, 2011).

27. On Yahya ibn Khaldun, see M. Talbi, "Ibn Khaldun," in *Encyclopedia of Islam*, vol. 3, pp. 831–32.

28. Ibn Khaldun, *Voyage*, p. 103.

29. Michael Brett and Elizabeth Fentress, *The Berbers* (Oxford, 1996), p. 139.

30. *Muq.*, vol. 3, p. 366.

31. Knysh, *Ibn 'Arabi*, p. 176.

32. Patricia Crone, *Medieval Islamic Political Thought* (Edinburgh, 2004), p. 315.

33. Enoch Powell, *Joseph Chamberlain* (London, 1977), p. 151.

34. *Muq.*, vol. 3, pp. 308–10.

Chapter Three. The Nomads, Their Virtues, and Their Place in History

1. Max Weber, *Weber Political Writings*, P. Lassman and R. Spiers eds. (Cambridge, 1994), p. 358.

2. Brett and Fentress, *The Berbers*, pp. 148–49.

3. Jacques Berque, "Ibn Khaldoun et les Bédouins," in Berque, *Maghreb, histoire et société* (Algiers, 1974), pp. 48–52.

4. Ibn Khaldun, *Le Voyage*, p. 142; Rosenthal, "Introduction," in *Muq.*, vol. 1, p. liii.

5. *Muq.*, vol. 1, pp. 77–78.

6. *Muq.*, vol. 1, p. 82.

7. Fromherz, *Ibn Khaldun*, p. 84.

8. Ibn Khaldun, *Le Livre des exemples*, vol. 2, p. 746.

9. *Muq.*, vol. 1, pp. 177–78.

10. Bruce Chatwin, *The Songlines* (London, 1987), p. 196.

11. T. E. Lawrence, *Seven Pillars of Wisdom: The Complete 1922 "Oxford" Text* (Fordingbridge, Hampshire, 2004), p. 184.

12. H.R.P. Dickson, *The Arab of the Desert: A Glimpse into Badawin Life in Kuwait and Sa'udi Arabia* (London, 1949), p. 505.

13. Wilfred Thesiger, *Arabian Sands* (London, 1959), pp. 112–13.

14. Donald P. Cole, "Bedouin and Social Change in Saudi Arabia," *Journal of Asian African Studies* 16 (1981), p. 140.

15. *Muq.*, vol. 1, p. 182.

16. John Wiseman, *SAS Survival Guide* (Glasgow, 1993), p. 27.

17. Thesiger, *Arabian Sands*, p. 94.

18. Thesiger, *Arabian Sands*, p. 97.

19. *Muq.*, vol. 1, p. 286.

20. *Muq.*, vol. 1, p. 438.

21. *Muq.*, vol. 1, p. 305.

22. Gellner, *Muslim Society*, p. 38.

23. *Muq.*, vol. 1. p. 343.

24. *Muq.*, vol. 1, p. 281, citing Exodus 20:5.

25. *Muq.*, vol. 1. p. 438.

26. *Muq.*, vol. 1, p. 437.

27. *Muq.*, vol. 1, pp. 418–19.

28. *Muq.*, vol. 1, p. 386.

29. Crone, *Medieval Islamic Political Thought*, pp. 318–19.

30. Jim Penman, *Biohistory: Decline and Fall of the West* (Newcastle on Tyne, 2015) p. 156.

31. *Muq.*, vol. 1, p. 253.

32. *Muq.*, vol. 1, p. 255.

33. Qur'an quoted in *Muq.*, vol. 1, p. 293; vol. 2, p. 294.

34. *Muq.*, vol. 1, p. 249.

35. *Muq.*, vol. 2, p. 357.

36. *Muq.*, vol. 1, p. 302.

37. *Muq.*, vol. 1, pp. 304–5.

38. *Muq.*, vol. 1, pp. 302–5, vol. 2, p. 289; *'Ibar*, vol. 6, pp. 13–16.

39. *Muq.*, vol. 3, pp. 415–20; cf. Malcolm C. Lyons, *The Arabian Epic: Heroic and Oral Storytelling* (Cambridge, 1995), vol. 2, pp. 136–211, vol. 3, pp. 237–300.

40. J. Poncet, "Le mythe de catastrophie hilalienne," *Annales Economies, Societés, Civilisations*, vol. 22 (1967), pp. 1099–120; Claude Cahen, "Quelques mots sur les hilaliens et le nomadisme," *Journal of the Economic and Social History of the Orient* 11 (1960), pp. 130–33; Michael Brett, "The Flood of the Dam and the Sons of the New Moon," in *Mélanges offerts à Mohammed Talbi* (Tunis, 1993), pp. 55–67.

41. Ibn Khaldun, *Le Livre des exemples*, vol. 2, p. 746.

42. Ibn Khaldun, *Le Livre des exemples*, vol. 2, p. 352.

43. Ibn Khaldun, *Le Livre des exemples*, vol. 2, p. 58.

44. Ibn Khaldun, *Le Livre des exemples*, vol. 2, pp. 151–57.

45. On genealogy, see *Muq.*, vol. 1, pp. 264–73.

46. *Muq.*, vol. 1, pp. 21–22; Brett and Fentress, *The Berbers*, pp. 124, 130; Shatzmiller, *The Berbers and the Islamic State*, p. 149n.

47. *Muq.*, vol. 1, p. 24.

48. Ibn Khaldun, *Le Livre des exemples*, vol. 2, pp. 747–48.

49. H. T. Norris, *Saharan Myth and Saga* (Oxford, 1972), pp. 58–60.

50. *Muq.*, vol. 1, p. 272.

51. *Muq.*, vol. 1, p. 54.

52. *Muq.*, vol. 1, pp. 41–43.

53. María Rose Menocal, *The Ornament of the World: How Muslims, Jews, and Christians Created a Culture of Tolerance in Medieval Spain* (New York, 2002), p. 230.

54. R. B. Serjeant, review of Rosenthal's translation of the *Muqaddima* in *Bulletin of the School of Oriental and African Studies* 24 (1961), p. 143.

55. *Muq.*, vol. 2, pp. 138–56.

56. Edmund Bosworth, "Mirrors for Princes," in Julie Scott Meisami and Paul Starkey, eds., *Encyclopedia of Arabic Literature* (London and New York, 1998), vol. 2, p. 528.

57. *Muq.*, vol. 1, p. 81.

58. *Muq.*, vol. 1, pp. 81–82.

59. *Muq.*, vol. 1, pp. 235–36.

60. *Muq.*, vol. 2, p. 48.

61. Dunlop, *Arab Civilization*, p. 138.

62. Talbi, "Ibn Khaldun," p. 829.

63. Brunschvig, *La Berbérie orientale*, vol. 2, pp. 385–92.

64. Donald Presgrave Little, *An Introduction to Mamluk Historiography: An Analysis of Arabic Annalistic and Biographical Sources for the Reign of al-Malik an-Nasir Muhammad ibn Qala'un* (Wiesbaden, 1970), pp. 75, 76.

65. On the Ayalon thesis, see Robert Irwin, "Gunpowder and Firearms in the Mamluk Sultanate Reconsidered," in *The Mamluks in Egyptian and Syrian Politics and Society* (Leiden, 2004), pp. 114–39.

66. Jean Froissart, *The Chronicles of Froissart* (London, 1908), p. 1.

67. Jan Huizinga, *The Waning of the Middle Ages: A Study of the Forms of Life, Thought and Art in France and the Netherlands in the Fourteenth and Fifteenth Centuries* (London, 1955), p. 252.

Chapter Four. Underpinning the Methodology of the *Muqaddima*: Philosophy, Theology, and Jurisprudence

1. *Muq.*, vol. 1, p. 6.

2. On *hikma*, see, *Muq.*, vol. 1, pp. 80–83; cf. Mahdi, *Ibn Khaldûn's Philosophy of History*, pp. 158–59.

3. *Arabian Nights*, vol. 2, pp. 195–96.

4. *Arabian Nights*, vol. 2, pp. 325–26.

5. *Arabian Nights*. vol. 2, pp. 326–27.

6. *Muq.*, vol. 1, pp. 82–83.

7. *Muq.*, vol. 1, p. 83.

8. *Muq.*, vol. 2, pp. 139–56.

9. *Muq.*, vol. 1, p. 82.

10. *Muq.*, vol. 3, p. 250.

11. Rosenthal, "Introduction," in *Muq.*, vol. 1, p. xliv.

12. *Muq.*, vol. 3, pp. 290–91.

13. *Muq.*, vol. 3, p. 54.

14. *Muq.*, vol. 1, pp. 108–9.

15. *Muq.*, vol. 1, pp. 275–76.

16. *Muq.*, vol. 3, p. 254.

17. Majid Fakhry, *Averroes (Ibn Rushd): His Life, Works and Influence* (Oxford, 2001), pp. 112–14; Crone, *Medieval Islamic Political Thought*, p. 191.

18. *Muq.*, vol. 2, p. 53.

19. *Muq.*, vol. 1, p. 36.

20. Bernard Lewis, "Islamic Concepts of Revolution," in Lewis, *Islam in History; Ideas, People, and Events in the Middle East* (Chicago and La Salle, IL, 1993), pp. 311–12.

21. *Muq.*, vol. 2, pp. 218–19: Lewis, "Islamic Concepts," p. 312.

22. Patricia Crone, *Slaves on Horses: The Evolution of the Islamic Polity* (Cambridge, 1980), pp. 89–91.

23. Peter Burke, *Vico* (Oxford, 1985).

24. Oswald Spengler, *Der Untergang des Abendlands,* 2 vols. (Munich, 1922); Spengler, *The Decline of the West* (London, 1932).

25. Bertrand Russell, tr. C. F. Atkinson, *A History of Philosophy* (London, 1946), p. 724.

26. Naguib Mahfouz, tr. Catharine Cobham, *The Harafish* (New York, 1993), p. 119.

27. Paul Valéry, "The Crisis of the Mind," in Valéry, *History and Politics* (London, 1963), p. 23.

28. *Muq.*, vol. 3, p. 38.

29. *Muq.*, vol. 3, pp. 137–47.

30. *Muq.*, vol. 3, pp. 152–55.

31. *Muq.*, vol. 3, p. 249.

32. Robinson, *Islamic Historiography*, p. 85 and n.

33. *Muq.*, vol. 3, p. 257.

34. *Muq.*, vol. 3, p. 143.

35. *Muq.*, vol. 3, pp. 113–14.

36. *Muq.*, vol. 3, pp. 113–14; cf. Dmitri Gutas, *Greek Thought, Arabic Culture: The Graeco-Arabic Translation Movement in Baghdad and Early 'Abbasid Society (2nd–4th/8th–10th Centuries)* (London, 1988), pp. 36–41.

37. *Muq.*, vol. 1, p. 78.

38. *Muq.*, vol. 3, p. 14.

39. *Muq.*, vol. 3, p. 143.

40. Oliver Leaman, *An Introduction to Classical Islamic Philosophy* (Cambridge, 1985), p. 94; Massimo Campanini, "Al-Ghazzali," in *History of Islamic Philosophy*, pt. 1 (London, 1996), pp. 262–63.

41. *Muq.*, vol. 3, pp. 36–37.

42. *Muq.*, vol. 3, p. 29.

43. *Muq.*, vol. 3, p. 54.

44. *Muq.*, vol. 3, pp. 41–42.

45. *Muq.*, vol. 3, p. 54.

46. *Muq.*, vol. 3, pp. 6–7.

47. *Muq.*, vol. 1, pp. 79–80.

48. *Muq.*, vol. 3, p. 23.

49. Ibn Khaldun, *Voyage*, pp. 46, 47, 48, 177–85.

50. *Muq.*, vol. 2, p. 373.

51. Hamilton Gibb, "The Islamic Background of Ibn Khaldun's Political Theory," in Gibb, *Studies on the Civilization of Islam* (Boston, 1962), p. 171.

52. Gibb, "Islamic Background," pp. 173–74.

Chapter Five. Ibn Khaldun's Sojourn among the Mamluks in Egypt

1. Saad Ghrab, *Ibn 'Arafah et le Malikisme en Ifriqiya au VIII/XIVe siècles* (Tunis, 1996).

2. *Muq.*, vol. 2, pp. 99–100.

3. *The Arabian Nights*, vol. 1, pp. 198–99.

4. Ibn Khaldun, *Voyage*, pp. 148–49.

5. *Muq.*, vol. 2, p. 274.

6. *Muq.*, vol. 2, p. 435.

7. *'Ibar,* vol. 5, p. 371; David Ayalon, "The Position of the Yāsa in the Mamlūk Sultanate," *Studia Islamica* 36 (1972), p. 119.

8. Crone, *Slaves on Horses*, p. 90.

9. Rosenthal, "Introduction," in *Muq.*, vol. 1, pp. xliv–xlv.

10. Abu al-Muhasin Ibn Taghribirdi, *Al-Nujum al-zahira fi muluk Misr wa al-Qahira* (Berkeley, 1915–60), vol. 5, p. 603.

11. On Ibn Khaldun's tenure of the post of Maliki chief qadi on five occasions and his relations with other members of the judiciary, see Morimoto Kosei, "What Ibn Khaldun Saw: The Judiciary of Mamluk Egypt," *Mamluk Studies Review* 6 (2002), pp. 109–31.

12. Ibn Khaldun, *Voyage*, pp. 177–85.

13. Leonor Fernandes, *The Evolution of a Sufi Institution in Mamluk Egypt: The Khanqah* (Berlin, 1988), p. 48.

14. Ibn Taghribirdi, *Nujum*, vol. 5, p. 422.

15. Ibn Khaldun, *Voyage*, p. 160; cf. pp. 162, 164.

16. *Muq.*, vol. 1, p. 334.

17. Robert Irwin, "Tribal Feuding and Mamlūk Factions in Medieval Syria," in *Texts, Documents and Artefacts: Islamic Studies in Honour of D .S. Richards* (Leiden, 2003), pp. 251–64.

18. On these events, see P. M. Holt, *The Age of the Crusades: The Near East from the Eleventh Century to 1517* (Harlow, Essex, 1986), pp. 127–29; Jean-Claude Garcin, "The Regime of the Circassian Mamluks," in Carl Petry, ed.,

The Cambridge History of Egypt: Volume One, Islamic Egypt, 640–1517 (Cambridge, 1998), p. 291; Irwin, "Tribal Feuding."

19. Al-Maqrizi, *Mamluk Economics,* pp. 4, 51; Dols, *The Black Death,* p. 232.

20. *Muq.,* vol. 1, pp. 299–300.

21. Ibn Taghribirdi, *Nujum,* vol. 5, p. 598.

22. *Muq.,* vol. 1, p. 12.

23. Walter J. Fischel, *Ibn Khaldun in Egypt: His Public Functions and His Historical Research* (Berkeley and Los Angeles, 1967), pp. 71–108; Sami G. Massoud, *The Chronicles and Annalistic Sources of the Early Mamluk Circassian Period* (Leiden, 2007), pp. 14–22, 90–95, 193.

24. *Muq.,* vol. 2, p. 14.

25. Robert Irwin, "The Privatisation of 'Justice' under the Circassian Mamlūks," *Mamluk Studies Review* 6 (2002), pp. 63–70.

26. *Muq.,* vol. 2, pp. 14, 28. On office-holding the Mamluk Sultanate, see P. M. Holt, "The Structure of Government in the Mamluk Sultanate," in P. M. Holt, ed., *The Eastern Mediterranean Lands in the Period of the Crusades* (Warminster, Wiltshire, 1977), pp. 44–61. On office-holding in North Africa, see Khaneboubi, *Les Institutions gouvermentes.*

27. Khaneboubi, *Les Institutions gouvermentales,* pp. 42–43.

28. *Muq.,* vol. 1, pp. 385–402, 414–28, 448–51.

29. Ibn al-Furat, *Ta'rikh al-duwal wa'l-muluk* (Beirut, 1936–42), vol. 9, pp. 435–36; al-Maqrizi, *Kitab al-suluk* (Cairo, 1956–73), vol. 1, p. 326.

30. *Muq.,* vol. 1, p. 368.

31. Ibn Taghribirdi, *Nujum,* vol. 5, p. 594.

32. On Timur's siege of Damascus and Ibn Khaldun's meetings with him, see Walter J. Fischel, *Ibn Khaldūn and Tamerlane: Their Historic Meeting in Damascus, 1401 A. D. (803 A. H.): A Study Based on Arabic Manuscripts of Ibn Khaldūn's "Autobiography," with a Translation into English, and a Commentary* (Berkeley and Los Angeles, 1952); Hilda Hookham, *Tamburlaine the Conqueror* (London, 1962), pp. 229–40.

33. Ahmed Ibn Arabshah, *Tamerlane or Timur the Great Amir* (London, 1936), pp. 144–45.

34. Ibn Taghribirdi, *Al-Manhal al-safi wa al-mustawfi ba'd al wafi* (Cairo, 1994), vol. 7, p. 208.

35. Ibn Khaldun, *'Ibar,* bk. 5, pp. 230–31; Ibn Khaldun, *Voyage,* p. 225.

36. Ibn Khaldun, *Voyage,* pp. 232–33; Fischel, *Ibn Khaldūn and Tamerlane,* p. 35–36; cf. *Muq.,* vol. 2, pp. 226–27, for al-Bajarbaqi's enigmatic versified prophecy, which also seems to hint at the coming of Timur.

37. Fischel, *Ibn Khaldūn and Tamerlane,* p. 50n.

38. Ibn Khaldun, *Voyage,* p. 246; Fischel, *Ibn Khaldūn and Tamerlane,* p. 47.

39. Ibn 'Arabshah, *Tamerlane,* pp. 296–98.

40. Ibn 'Arabshah, *Fakihat al-khulafa' wa mufakahat al-zurafa'* (Cairo, 2001), p. 357.

41. Walter J. Fischel, "A New Latin Source on Tamerlane's Conquest of Damascus (1400/1401): B. de Mignanelli's 'Vita Tamerlani' (1416)," *Oriens* 9 (1956), pp. 226–27.

42. Ibn Taghribirdi, *Nujum*, vol. 6, p. 66.

43. Michael Cooperson, "Biographical Literature," in *The New Cambridge History of Islam*, vol. 4, *Islamic Cultures and Societies to the End of the Eighteenth Century* (Cambridge, 2010), pp. 470–72.

44. Cooperson, "Biographical Literature," p. 460.

45. Walter J. Fischel, "Ibn Khaldûn's 'Autobiography' in the Light of External Arabic Sources," in *Studi orientalistici in onore di Giorgio Levi Della Vida* (Rome, 1936), vol. 1, pp. 289–90.

46. Shatzmiller, *L'Historiographie Mérinide*, p. 52.

47. Ibn Taghribirdi, *Nujum*, vol. 6, p. 108.

48. Fischel, *Ibn Khaldun in Egypt*, pp. 28–29; Abdesselam Cheddadi, *Ibn Khaldûn: L'homme et le théoricien de la civilisation* (Paris, 2006), p. 179. On the influence of Ibn Khaldun on al-Maqrizi, see Anne F. Broadbridge, "Royal Authority, Justice and Order in Society: The Influence of Ibn Khaldun on the Writings of al-Maqrizi and Ibn Taghribirdi," *Mamluk Studies Review* 7, pt. 2 (2003), pp. 231–45.

49. Ibn Taghribirdi, *Nujum*, vol. 6, p. 756.

50. Al-Maqrizi, *Al-Mawa'iz wa-l-i'tibar bi-dhikr al-khitat wa'l-athar* (Bulaq, 1854), vol. 2, p. 214.

51. Muhammad Al-Sakhawi, *Al-Daw' al-lami'* (Cairo, 1934–36), vol. 8, p. 233.

52. Cheddadi, *Ibn Khaldûn*, pp. 137–38, 179.

53. On Ibn Hajar, see Jonathan P. Berkey, *The Transmission of Knowledge in Medieval Cairo: A Social History of Islamic Education* (Princeton, 1992), passim.

54. Ahmad Ibn Hajar, *Inba al-ghumr bi-abna' al-umr* (Cairo, 1971), vol. 1, pp. 339–40; Ibn Hajar, *Raf al-'isr 'an qudat Misr* (Cairo, 1957, 1961), vol. 2, pp. 343–48; Fischel, *Ibn Khaldun in Egypt*, p. 29. On Ibn Hajar attending the lectures, see al-Sakhawi, *Daw'*, vol. 4. p. 148.

55. Ibn Hajar, *Raf' al-'isr fi qudat Misr*, vol. 2, pp. 343–48.

56. Ibn Hajar, *Inba*, vol. 3, p. 248.

57. On scholarly rancour in medieval Cairo, see Anne Broadbridge, "Academic Rivalry and the Patronage System: al-'Ayni and al-Maqrizi," *Mamluk Studies Review* 3 (1999), pp. 85–107.

58. Al-Sakhawi, *Daw'*, vol. 4, pp. 145–49. On the comprehensive scope of al-Sakhawi's malignity, see Ulrich Haarmann, "Auflösung und Bewahrung der klassischen Formen arabischer Geschichtsschreibung in der Zeit der Mamluken," *Zeitschrift fur deutschen Morgenländischen Gesellschaft* 121 (1971), p. 60.

59. Al-Sakhawi, *Daw'*, vol. 4. pp. 145–49.

60. Franz Rosenthal, *A History of Muslim Historiography* (Leiden, 1968), pp. 263–529.

61. Ali Oumlil, *L'Histoire et son discours: essai sur la méthodologie d'Ibn Khaldoun* (Rabat, 1982), pp. 135–36.

62. Ibn Taghribirdi, *Manhal*, vol. 7, pp. 205–9.

Chapter Six. The Sufi Mystic

1. On Sufism, see Carl W. Ernst, *The Shambhala Guide to Sufism* (Boston, 1997); Knysh, *Ibn 'Arabi*; Knysh, "Sufism," in Robert Irwin, ed., *The New Cam-*

bridge History of Islam, vol. 4, *Islamic Cultures and Societies to the End of the Eighteenth Century* (Cambridge, 2010), pp. 60–104; Lloyd Ridgeon, ed., *The Cambridge Companion to Sufism* (Cambridge, 2015).

2. Michael Cook, *Commanding Right and Forbidding Wrong in Islamic Thought* (Cambridge University Press, 2010), p. 459.

3. *Muq.*, vol. 3, pp. 94–99.

4. René Pérez, Introduction to Ibn Khaldun, *La Voie et la loi: ou le mâitre et le jurist, Shifa' al-sa'il li-tahdhib al-masa'il* (Arles, 1991), p. 75.

5. Pérez, Introduction, pp. 72–73.

6. *Muq.*, vol. 1, p. 222.

7. *Muq.*, vol. 3, p. 76.

8. *Muq.*, vol. 3, p. 81.

9. *Muq.*, vol. 3, pp. 102–3.

10. *Muq.*, vol. 2, p. 86.

11. *Muq.*, vol. 3, p. 167.

12. *Muq.*, vol. 1, pp. 224–26.

13. *Muq.*, vol. 3, p. 102.

14. *Muq.*, vol. 2, pp. 223–24.

15. *Muq.*, vol. 2, pp. 187–88; vol. 3, p. 92.

16. Knysh, *Ibn Arabi*, p. 128.

17. *Muq.*, vol. 3, pp. 87, 92.

18. Knysh, *Ibn 'Arabi*, pp. 191–95.

19. Fromherz, *Ibn Khaldun*, p. 115.

20. Fromherz, *Ibn Khaldun*, pp. 126–27.

21. Carole Hillenbrand, "al-Ghazzali," in Meisami and Starkey, *Encyclopedia*, vol. 1, p. 252.

Chapter Seven. Messages from the Dark Side

1. Michel Foucault, *The Order of Things: An Archaeology of the Human Sciences* (London, 1970), p. 17.

2. A. J. Arberry, trans., *The Koran Interpreted* (London, 1955), vol. 2, p. 362.

3. *Muq.*, vol. 3, pp. 160–61.

4. Arberry, *Koran Interpreted*, p. 363. (The "whisperer" is Satan.)

5. *Muq.*, vol. 3, pp. 104–5.

6. *Muq.*, vol. 3, p. 163.

7. *Muq.*, vol. 3, pp. 170–71.

8. *Muq.*, vol. 3, p. 159.

9. *Muq.*, vol. 3, pp. 178–79.

10. *Muq.*, vol. 1, p. 191; vol. 3, p. 167–68.

11. Rosenthal, "Introduction," in *Muq.*, vol. 1, p. lxxii.

12. Armand Abel, "La place des sciences occultes dans la décadence," in R. Brunschvig and G. E. Von Grunebaum, eds., *Classicism et déclin culturel dans l'histoire de l'Islam* (Paris, 1958), pp. 291–318.

13. Theodor Adorno, "Theses against Occultism," *Telos* (Spring, 1974), p. 9.

14. *Muq.*, vol. 3, pp. 158–59.

15. *Muq.*, vol. 3, p. 159.

16. *Muq.*, vol. 3, p. 113.

17. *Muq.*, vol. 3, p. 161.

18. *Muq.*, vol. 3, p. 156.

19. *Muq.*, vol. 3, p. 157.

20. Maribel Fierro, "Batinism in al-Andalus: Maslamah b. Qurtubi Author of the *Rutbat al-hakim* and the *Ghayat al-hakim*," *Studia Islamica* 84 (1996), pp. 87–112.

21. Paul Kraus, *Jābir ibn Hayyān: Contribution à l'histoire des idées scientifiques dans l'Islam* (Paris, 1942), 2 vols.

22. *Muq.*, vol. 3, p. 228.

23. *Muq.*, vol. 3, p. 245.

24. *Muq.*, vol. 2, pp. 319–26.

25. *Muq.*, vol. 2, p. 324.

26. *Muq.*, vol. 3, p. 174.

27. *Muq.*, vol. 3, p. 172.

28. *Muq.*, vol. 3, p. 172.

29. *Muq.*, vol. 3, p. 174.

30. *Muq.*, vol. 3, pp. 177–78.

31. *Muq.*, vol. 3, p. 181.

32. On the *Ikhwan*, see Yves Marquet, *La Philosophie des Ihwan al-Safa* (Algiers, 1975); S. H. Nasr, *An Introduction to Islamic Cosmological Doctrines* (London, 1978), pp. 25–104; Ian R. Netton, *Muslim Neoplatonism: An Introduction to the Thought of the Brethren of Purity (Ikhwan al-Safa')* (Edinburgh, 1991).

33. *Muq.*, vol. 2, pp. 422–23; cf. vol. 1, p. 195. On the same idea in Christian and Jewish thought, see Arthur O. Lovejoy, *The Great Chain of Being: A Study of the History of an Idea* (New York, 1936).

34. Ibn Taghribirdi, *Nujum,* vol. 6, pp. 141–42.

35. Ibn Taghribirdi, *Manhal,*vol. 5, pp. 171–73; Ilker Evrim Binbaş, *Intellectual Networks in Timurid Iran: Sharaf al-Din 'Ali Yazdi and the Islamicate Republic of Letters* (Cambridge, 2016), pp. 114–19.

36. Lewis Namier, *Conflicts: Studies in Contemporary History* (London, 1942), p. 70.

37. M'barek Redjala, "Un texte inédit de la *Muqaddima*," *Arabica* 22 (1975), pp. 322–23.

38. *Muq.*, vol. 3, pp. 117–18.

39. *Muq.*, vol. 2, p. 80.

40. *Muq.*, vol. 2, p. 281.

41. *Muq.*, vol. 2, p. 353.

42. *Muq.*, vol. 2, pp. 38–39, 46.

43. *Muq.*, vol. 1, p. 17.

44. David Hume, *Treatise on Human Nature* (London, 1734–37), bk. 1, pt. 3, sec. 4.

45. *Muq.*, vol. 1, pp. 184–245.

46. *Muq.*, vol. 2, p. 156.

47. *Muq.*, vol. 2, pp. 156–200.

48. *Muq.*, vol. 2, pp. 225–27, 229–31. On the obscure figure of al-Bajarbaqi, see Knysh, *Ibn 'Arabi*, p. 303n.

49. Madeleine Fletcher, "Al-Andalus and North Africa in Almohad Ideology," in Salma Khadra Jayyusi, ed., *The Legacy of Muslim Spain* (Leiden, 1992), pp. 241–42.

50. *Muq.*, vol. 2, p. 219.

51. *Muq.*, vol. 2, p. 196.

52. *Muq.*, vol. 2, pp. 195–96. On Mahdist prophecies, see Cheddadi, *Ibn Khaldûn*, pp. 358–62; Jean Pierre Filiu, *Apocalypse in Islam* (Berkeley, 2011).

53. Allen J. Fromherz, *The Almohads: The Rise of an Islamic Empire* (London, 2010), p. 76.

54. *Muq.*, vol. 3, pp. 262–63.

55. *Muq.*, vol. 2, pp. 200–203; cf. pp. 219–20.

56. On *malahim* more generally, see Paul Casanova, "Le Malhamat dans l'islam primitif," in *Revue de l'Histoire des Religions* 61 (1910), pp. 151–61; Casanova, *Mohammed et la fin du monde* (Paris, 1911); Armand Abel, "Changements politiques et littérature eschatologique dans le monde musulman," *Studia Islamica* 2 (1954), pp. 23–43; Abel, "Un hadith sur la prise du Rome dans la tradition escatologique de l'Islam," *Arabica* 5 (1958), pp. 1–14. Toufic Fahd, *La Divination arabe* (Paris, 1987), pp. 224–28.

57. *Muq.*, vol. 1, p. 235 and n., p. 238.

58. On Ibn al-Banna's career as a mathematician, occultist, and visionary, see Cheddadi, *Ibn Khaldun*, pp. 65–70.

59. *Muq.*, vol. 1, p. 204.

60. Khalidi, *Islamic Historiography*, pp. 45, 118.

61. *Muq.*, vol. 1, p. 219; cf. vol. 2, p. 202.

62. *Muq.*, vol. 1, pp. 216–18.

63. *Muq.*, vol. 1, p. 221.

64. *Muq.*, vol. 1, p. 221.

65. *Muq.*, vol. 1, p. 221.

66. *Muq.*, vol. 1, pp. 238–45, vol. 3, pp. 182–98. On the *za'iraja* see also Fahd, *La Divination*, pp. 243–45.

67. *Muq.*, vol. 3, p. 227.

68. *Muq.*, vol. 3, p. 184.

69. *Muq.*, vol. 3, p. 110.

70. *Muq.*, vol. 3, pp. 103–4.

71. *Muq.*, vol. 1, pp. 212–13.

72. Tom Hutchinson, in *Times*, November 26, 1988, p. 35.

73. Isaac Asimov, *Foundation, Foundation and Empire, Second Foundation* (New York, 2010), p. 17.

74. On Asimov's trilogy and its debt to Toynbee, see Michael Dirda, Introduction to *Foundation, Foundation and Empire, Second Foundation* (New York, 2010).

Chapter Eight. Economics before Economics Had Been Invented

1. *Muq.*, vol. 1, pp. 249–52.

2. *Muq.*, vol. 2, pp. 274–75.

3. *Muq.*, vol. 1, pp. 81–82.

4. *Muq.*, vol. 2, p. 272.

5. *Muq.*, vol. 2, p. 284.

6. *Muq.*, vol. 2, p. 274.

7. *Muq.*, vol. 2, p. 275.

8. *Muq.*, vol. 2, p. 313.

9. Warren Schulz, "Mansa Musa's Gold in Mamluk Cairo: A Reappraisal of a World Civilization Anecdote," in J. Pfeiiffer, S. Quinn, and E. Tucker, eds., *Post-Mongol Central Asia and the Middle East: Studies in History and Historiography in Honour of Professor John E. Woods* (Wiesbaden, 2006), pp. 428–47.

10. *Muq.*, vol. 2, pp. 54–60.

11. *Muq.*, vol. 2, p. 317.

12. *Muq.*, vol. 2, pp. 343–44.

13. *Muq.*, vol. 2, pp. 334–35.

14. *Muq.*, vol. 2, p. 312.

15. *Muq.*, vol. 2, p. 285.

16. *Muq.*, vol. 2, p. 277.

17. *Muq.*, vol. 2, p. 293.

18. *Muq.*, vol. 2, p. 294.

19. *Muq.*, vol. 2, p. 292.

20. *Muq.*, vol. 2, p. 339.

21. *Muq.*, vol. 2, p. 286.

22. *Muq.*, vol. 2, pp. 89–96.

23. *Muq.*, vol. 2, p. 282.

24. *Muq.*, vol. 2, pp. 89–96.

25. *Muq.*, vol. 2, pp. 259–60.

26. Friedrich Engels in *Die Neue Zeit*, 1894/5, quoted in Ernest Gellner, *Muslim Society* (Cambridge, 1981), p. 46.

27. Subhi Y. Labib, "Al-Asadi und sein Bericht über Verwaltungs- und Geldreform im 15 Jahrhundert," *Journal of Economic and Social History of the Orient* 8 (1965), pp. 312–16; John L. Meloy, "The Privatization of Protection: Extortion and the State in the Circassian Mamluk Period," *Journal of Economic and Social History of the Orient* 47 (2004), pp. 195–212.

Chapter Nine. What Ibn Khaldun Did for a Living: Teaching and Writing

1. Al-Sakhawi, *Daw'*, vol. 4, pp. 148–49.

2. Charles Pellat, ed. and trans., *The Life and Works of Jahiz* (Berkeley and Los Angeles, 1969), pp. 113–14.

3. *Muq.*, vol. 3, pp. 300–305.

4. *Muq.*, vol. 3, pp. 316–17.

5. *Muq.*, vol. 3, p. 298.

6. *Muq.*, vol. 1, pp. 58–60.

7. *Muq.*, vol. 3, pp. 392–98.

8. Robert Irwin, *The Penguin Anthology of Classical Arabic Literature* (London, 2006), p. 355.

9. *Muq.*, vol. 3, p. 341; cf. pp. 366–67.

10. *Muq.*, vol. 3, p. 396.

11. *Muq.*, vol. 3, p. 411.

12. *Muq.*, vol. 2, p. 402.

13. *Muq.*, vol. 3, pp. 336–37.

14. *Muq.*, vol. 3, pp. 415–20.

15. *Muq.*, vol. 3, pp. 332–39.

16. *Muq.*, vol. 3, p. 342.

17. *Muq.*, vol. 3, p. 340.

18. *Muq.*, vol. 3, p. 393.

19. *Muq.*, vol. 3, p. 340.

20. J. W. Burrow, *Gibbon* (London, 1985), pp. 97–98.

21. Vincent Monteil, "Introduction" to Ibn Khaldun, *Discours sur l'histoire universelle* (Beirut, 1967), vol. 1, p. xxx.

Chapter Ten. The Strange Afterlife of the *Muqaddima*

1. Ahmed Abdesselem, *Ibn Khaldun et ses lecteurs* (Paris, 1983), pp. 17–37.

2. Bernard Lewis, "Ibn Khaldun in Turkey," in *Islam in History*, pp. 233–36; Cornell Fleischer, "Royal Authority, Dynastic Cyclism and 'Ibn Khaldunism' in Sixteenth-Century Ottoman Letters," *Journal of Asian and African Studies* 18 (1983), pp. 198–219.

3. Barthélémy d'Herbelot, *Bibliothèque orientale* (The Hague, 1772–79), vol. 3, p. 414.

4. Joseph von Hammer-Purgstall, "Notice sur l'Introduction à la connaissance de l'histoire, célèbre ouvrage d'Ibn Khaldoun," *Journal Asiatique*, 1st ser., vol. 1 (1822), pp. 267–78; vol. 4, pp. 158–61. On Hammer-Purgstall, J. Fück, *Die Arabischen Studien in Europa bis in den Anfangdes 20. Jahrhunderts* (Leipzig, 1955), pp. 158–66; Robert Irwin, *For Lust of Knowing: The Orientalists and Their Enemies* (London, 2006), pp. 150–52; Alain Messaoudi, "Hammer-Purgstall," in François Pouillon, ed., *Dictionnaire des orientalistes de langue française* (Paris, 2012), pp. 509–10.

5. Hammer-Purgstall, *Uber den Verfall des Islam nach den ersten drei Jahrhunderten der Hidschrat* (Vienna, 1812), p. 360.

6. On Montesquieu, see Alain Grosrichard, *Structure du sérail* (Paris, 1979); Jean Goldzink, "Montesquieu," in *Dictionnaire*, pp. 742–44.

7. Rifa'a Rafi' al-Tahtawi, *An Imam in Paris: Account of a Stay in France by an Egyptian Cleric (1826–1831)* (London, 2011), p. 296.

8. Al-Tahtawi, *An Imam in Paris*, pp. 189–90.

9. Antoine-Isaac Silvestre de Sacy, *Chrestomathie arabe* (Paris, 1806), vol. 1, pp. 370–411; vol. 2, pp. 279–336.

10. On Silvestre de Sacy, see J. Fück, *Die Arabischen Studien*, pp. 140–57; Robert Irwin, *For Lust of Knowing*, pp. 141–46; Sylvette Larzul, "Silvestre de Sacy," in *Dictionnaire*, pp. 953–55.

11. Rosenthal, "Introduction," in *Muq.*, vol. 1, p. c.

12. Fück, *Die Arabischen Studien*, pp. 152–53; Irwin, *For Lust of Knowing*, pp. 148–49; Messaoudi, "Quatremère," in *Dictionnaire*, pp. 840–41.

13. On De Slane, see Messaoudi, "De Slane," in *Dictionnaire*, p. 959.

14. Hodgson, *Venture*, vol. 2, p. 283n.

15. On Gautier, see Yves Lacoste, *Ibn Khaldun: The Birth of History and the Past of the Third World* (London, 1984), pp. 69, 71, 75–78, 122; Florence Deprest, "Gautier," in *Dictionnaire*, pp. 546–47.

16. On Marçais, see Messaoudi, "Marçais," in *Dictionnaire*, pp. 683–34.

17. Alastair Horne, *A Savage War of Peace: Algeria 1954–1962* (London, 1977), pp. 110–11, 117; Jean-Louis Triaud, "Monteil," in *Dictionnaire*, pp. 740–42.

18. Vincent Monteil, "Introduction," in Ibn Khaldun, *Discours sur l'histoire universelle* (Beirut, 1967–68), vol. 1, p. 15; cf. Monteil, "Ibn Khaldoûn, sociologue et historien (1332–1406)," *Revue Historique* 237 (1967), p. 344.

19. On Von Kremer, see Fück, *Die Arabischen Studien*, pp. 187–89; Abdesselem, *Ibn Khaldun et ses lecteurs*, pp. 43–44.

20. Toynbee, *A Study*, vol. 3, pp. 321–22.

21. Albert Hourani, "Toybee's Vision of History," in Hourani, *Europe and the Middle East* (London, 1980), p. 146.

22. Edward Gibbon, *Autobiography of Edward Gibbon* (London, 1907), pp. 158–59.

23. Toynbee, *A Study*, vol. 10, p. 108.

24. Toynbee, *A Study of History*, vol. 10, p. 3.

25. Robert Irwin, "Toynbee and Ibn Khaldun," *Middle Eastern Studies* 33 (1997), pp. 461–79.

26. E. H. Carr, *What Is History?* (London, 1961), p. 43 and n.

27. The main assessments of Ibn Khaldun appear in *A Study*, vol. 3, pp. 321–28 and vol. 10, pp. 84–87.

28. Toynbee, *A Study*, vol. 9, p. 175; cf. vol. 10, p. 87.

29. Gibb, *Arabic Literature: An Introduction* (Oxford, 1926), pp. 154–55.

30. Gibb, "The Islamic Background," pp. 23–31.

31. Albert Hourani, *A History of the Arab Peoples* (London, 1991), p. 4.

32. Gibb, *Speculum* 35 (1960), pp. 139–42.

33. Azmeh, *Ibn Khaldun in Modern Scholarship*, pp. 51–52.

34. T. S. Eliot, *Four Quartets* (London, 1959), p. 19.

35. Hodgson, *Venture*, vol. 2, p. 55n.

36. Hodgson, *Venture*, vol. 2, pp. 478–84.

37. Cheddadi, *Ibn Khaldûn*, p. 9.

38. Stephen Dale, *The Orange Trees of Marrakesh: Ibn Khaldun and the Science of Man* (Cambridge, MA, 2015), p. 8.

39. Robert Brunschvig, *La Berbérie orientale sous les Hafsides*, 2 vols. (1940).

40. Bernard Lewis, "The Decolonisation of History," in Lewis, *Islam in History: Ideas, People, and Events in the Middle East*, 2nd ed. (Chicago and La Salle, IL, 1993), p. 45.

41. Yves Lacoste, *Ibn Khaldun; The Birth of History and the Past of the Third World* (London, 1984), p. 5. For a review of the book, see Bernard Lewis, "The Decolonisation of History," in *Times Literary Supplement*, August 1968, p. 853.

42. Muhsin Mahdi, *Ibn Khaldun's Philosophy of History* (Chicago, 1957).

43. Lacoste, *Ibn Khaldun*, pp. 159–60.

44. Mahdi, *Ibn Khaldun's Philosophy of History*, pp. 193–94n.

45. Mahdi, *Ibn Khaldûn's Philosophy of History*, p. 68.

46. Ernest Gellner, in *Philosophy*, vol. 36 (1961), pp. 255–56.

47. L. P. Hartley, *The Go-Between* (London, 1953), p. 1.

48. Gellner, *Anthropology and Politics: Revolutions in the Sacred Grove* (Oxford, 1995), pp. 195–96; cf. Gellner, *Muslim Society* (Cambridge, 1981), p. 86, in which Ibn Khaldun's positivism and lack of moralising is compared to that of Durkheim.

49. Gellner, *Saints*, pp. 5–6.

50. Gellner, *Muslim Society*, p. 74.

51. Gellner, *Muslim Society*, p. 77.

52. Ibn Khaldun, *Voyage*, p. 191.

53. Gellner, *Muslim Society*, p. 29.

54. For astringent criticisms of Gellner's approach to Ibn Khaldun, see Daniel Varisco, "Ernest Gellner: Idealized to a Fault," in Varisco, *Islam Observed: The Rhetoric of Anthropological Reprsentation* (New York, 2005), pp. 53–80.

55. Crone, *Slaves on Horses*, pp. 89–91.

56. Brunschvig, *La Berberie orientale*, vol. 2, p. 391.

57. Mark Sedgwick, *Muhammad Abduh* (Oxford, 2010), p. 17.

58. Mohammad Abdullah Enan, *Ibn Khaldun, His Life and Works* (Lahore, 1941), pp. 4, 115–17.

59. Enan, *Ibn Khaldun*, pp. 168–82.

60. Cheddadi, *Ibn Khaldûn*, pp. 489–94.

61. Enan, *Ibn Khaldun*, p. 170.

62. Aziz alAzmeh, *Ibn Khaldun in Modern Scholarship: A Study in Orientalism* (London, 1981); Azmeh, *Ibn Khaldun, an Essay in Reinterpretation* (London, 1982).

63. Michael Brett, review of Azmeh's two books on Ibn Khaldun, *Bulletin of the School of Oriental and African Studies* 46, pp. 345–47.

64. Abdesselam Cheddadi, *Le Voyage d'Occident et d'Orient* (Paris, 1980); Cheddadi, *Ibn Khaldoun revisité* (Casablanca, 1999).

65. Cheddadi, *Ibn Khaldûn*, p. 212.

66. Stephen Frederick Dale, *The Orange Trees of Marrakesh: Ibn Khaldun and Science of Man* (Cambridge, MA, 2015); cf. Dale, "Ibn Khaldun: The Last Greek and the First *Annaliste* Historian," *International Journal of Middle East Studies* 38 (2006), pp. 431–51; Robert Irwin review of *The Orange Trees of Marrakesh*, in *Times Literary Supplement*, April 1, 2016, p. 24.

67. Ibn Khaldun, *Voyage*, p. 233.

68. *Muq.*, vol. 3, pp. 139–41.

69. Dale, *Orange Trees*, pp. 77, 88.

70. Dale, *Orange Trees*, p. 3.

71. *Muq.*, vol. 1, p. 90.

72. *Muq.*, vol. 1, p. 210.

73. *Muq.*, vol. 1, p. 175.

74. P. G. Wodehouse, "Indian Summer of an Uncle," in Wodehouse, *Jeeves and the Yule-Tide Spirit* (London, 2014), p. 268.

75. Bensalem Himmich, *The Polymath* (Cairo, 2004), p. 228.

76. Bruce B. Lawrence, "Introduction," in Lawrence, ed., *Ibn Khaldun and Islamic Ideology* (Leiden, 1984), p. 5.

77. Robert Irwin, *For Lust of Knowing.*

78. Michael Brett, "Problems in the Interpretation of the History of the Maghreb in the Light of Some Recent Publications," *Journal of African History* 13 (1972), p. 490.

Chapter Eleven. Ending Up

1. H.A.L. Fisher, *A History of Europe* (London, 1938), vol. 1, p. vii.

2. Fisher, *A History of Europe*, vol. 1, p. ix.

3. Fisher, *A History of Europe*, vol. 3, p. 1219.

4. *Arab Human Development Report 2004* (New York, 2005), p. 145.

5. http://www.businessinsider.com/mark-zuckerberg-the-muqaddimah-2015-6.

6. *Muq.*, vol. 3, p. 481.

THE WORKS OF IBN KHALDUN

There are numerous editions of the *Muqaddima*, beginning with that of Etienne Marc Quatremère, *Prolégomènes d'Ebn-Khaldoun*, 3 vols. (Paris, 1858). But there is no critical Arabic edition of the *Muqaddima* that takes proper account of the variant manuscripts and therefore Rosenthal's translation should be used in lieu of this: Ibn Khaldûn, *The Muqaddimah: An Introduction to History*, translated by Franz Rosenthal, 3 vols. 2nd ed. (1967, London; reprinted in Princeton, NJ, 1980). Rosenthal's introduction provides an excellent survey of Ibn Khaldun's life, works, and manuscripts. There is also a one-volume abridgement by N. J. Dawood of Rosenthal's translation with an introduction by Bruce B. Lawrence, as well as Rosenthal's original introduction. See also Ibn Khaldun, *Le Livre des exemples*, 2 vols., translated by Abdesselam Cheddadi (Paris, 2002). This has been handsomely published by Gallimard, in the Bibliothèque de la Pléiade. The first volume in this well-edited and annotated publication comprises both a translation of the *Al-Ta'rif* and of the *Muqaddima*, while the second volume contains a translation of that part of the *'Ibar* that deals with the history of the Arabs and Berbers in the Maghreb.

Two other French translations of the *Muqaddima* are of historic interest. William MacGuckin De Slane's was published under the title *Prolégomenes historiques d'Ibn Khaldoun*, 3 vols. (Paris, 1862, 1865, 1868) and that of Vincent Monteil appeared as *Discours sur l'histoire universelle*, 3 vols. (Beirut, 1967–68).

The *Kitab al-'Ibar* has been published in 7 volumes edited by Y. A. Daghir (Beirut, 1992). William de Slane's *Ibn Khaldoun: Histoire des Berbères et des dynasties musulmanes de l'Afrique septenrionale*, 4 vols. (Algiers, 1952–56) is a partial translation. Ibn Khaldun, *Peuples et nations du monde*, 2 vols. (Arles, 1986) contains selected translations by Abdeesselam Cheddadi from the *Muqaddima* and the *'Ibar*. The selections from the *'Ibar* in the first volume deal with the earliest Arabs, the Himyarites, the kings of Babylon, the story of Moses, the Greeks, the Romans, and the Byzantines. The second volume contains selected episodes from the history of the Prophet, the Umayyads, the 'Abbasids, and the Arabs and Berbers of the Maghreb.

There is a well-edited edition of Ibn Khaldun's autobiography: *Al-Ta'rif bi-Ibn Khaldun wa-rihlatahu gharban wa sharqan,* edited by Muhammad Tawit al-Tanji (Cairo, 1951). There is also a partial translation of the *Ta'rif*: Ibn Khaldun, *Le Voyage d'Occident et d'Orient,* translated by Abdesselam Cheddadi (Paris, 1980).

Ibn Khaldun's *Shifa' al-sa'il li tadhhib al-masa'il* was edited and published by Ignace Abdo Kalifé (Beirut, 1959). The translation of the *Shifa'* by René Pérez as *La Voie et la loi* (Arles, 1991) contains a most useful and perceptive introduction.

General Bibliography

Abdesselem, Ahmed. *Ibn Khaldun et ses lecteurs* (Paris, 1983).

Abel, Armand. "Changements politiques et littérature eschatologique dans le monde musulman." *Studia Islamica* 2 (1954), pp. 23–43.

———. "La place des sciences occultes dans la décadence." In *Classicism et déclin culturel dans l'histoire de l'Islam,* edited by R. Brunschvig and G. E. Von Grunebaum (Paris, 1958), pp. 291–31.

———. "Un hadith sur la prise du Rome dans la tradition escatologique de l'Islam." *Arabica* 5 (1958), pp. 1–14.

Adorno, Anselm. *Itinéraire d'Anselme Adorno en Terre Sainte (1470–1471).* Edited and translated by Jacques Heers and Georgette de Groer (Paris, 1978).

Adorno, Theodor. "Theses against Occultism," *Telos* (1974), pp. 7–12.

Arab Human Development Report 2004 (New York, 2005).

Arabian Nights: Tales of 1001 Nights. Translated by Malcolm Lyons, 3 vols. (London, 2008).

Arié, Rachel. *L'Espagne Musulmane au temps des Nasrides (1232–1492)* (Paris, 1973).

Ayalon, David. *Gunpowder and Firearms in the Mamluk Kingdom: A Challenge to a Medieval Society* (London, 1956).

———. "The Position of the Yāsa in the Mamlūk Sultanate." *Studia Islamica* 36 (1972).

al-Azmeh, Aziz. *Ibn Khaldun, an Essay in Reinterpretation* (London, 1982).

———. *Ibn Khaldun in Modern Scholarship: A Study in Orientalism* (London, 1981).

Benchekroun, Mohammed B. A. *La Vie intellectuelle Marocaine sous les Mérinides et les Wattasides* (Rabat, 1974).

Berkey, Jonathan P. *Popular Preaching and Religious Authority in the Medieval Islamic Near East* (Seattle and London, 2001).

———. *The Transmission of Knowledge in Medieval Cairo: A Social History of Islamic Education* (Princeton, 1992).

Berque, Jacques. "Ibn Khaldoun et les Bédouins." In Berque, *Maghreb, histoire et société* (Algiers, 1974), pp. 48–52.

Binbaş, Ilker Evrim. *Intellectual Networks in Timurid Iran: Sharaf al-Din 'Ali Yazdi and the Islamicate Republic of Letters* (Cambridge, 2016).

Bosworth, Edmund. "Mirrors for Princes." In *Encyclopedia of Arabic Literature*, edited by Julie Scott Meisami and Paul Starkey, 2 vols. (London and New York, 1998), vol. 2, pp. 527–29.

Braudel, Fernand. *The Mediterranean and the Mediterranean World in the Age of Philip II.* Translated by Siân Reynolds, 2 vols. (London, 1972).

Bresc, Henri and Annliese Nef. *Idrisi; La première géographie de l'Occident* (Paris, 1999).

Brett, Michael. "The Flood of the Dam and the Sons of the New Moon." In *Mélanges offerts à Mohammed Talbi* (Tunis, 1993), pp. 55–67.

———. "Problems in the Interpretation of the History of the Maghreb in the Light of Some Recent Publications." *Journal of African History* 13 (1972), pp. 489–506.

———. Review of Aziz al-Azmeh's two books on Ibn Khaldun. *Bulletin of the School of Oriental and African Studies* 46 (1983), pp. 345–47.

Brett, Michael and Elizabeth Fentress. *The Berbers* (Oxford, 1996).

Brett, Michael and Werner Forman. *The Moors: Islam in the West* (London, 1980).

Broadbridge, Anne F. "Academic Rivalry and the Patronage System: al-'Ayni and al-Maqrizi." *Mamluk Studies Review* 3 (1999), pp. 85–107.

———. "Royal Authority, Justice and Order in Society: The Influence of Ibn Khaldun on the Writings of al-Maqrizi and Ibn Taghribirdi." *Mamluk Studies Review* 7, pt. 2 (2003), pp. 231–45.

Brunschvig, Robert. *La Berbérie orientale sous les Hafsides: des origines à la fin du XVe siècle.* 2 vols. (Algiers, 1940, 1947).

Burke, Peter. *Vico* (Oxford, 1985).

Burrow, J. W. *Gibbon* (London, 1985).

Cahen, Claude. "Quelques mots sur les hilaliens et le nomadisme." *Journal of the Economic and Social History of the Orient* 11 (1960), pp. 130–33.

Campanini, Massimo. "Al-Ghazzali." In *History of Islamic Philosophy*, pt. 1, edited by Seyyed Hossein Nasr and Oliver Leaman (London, 1996), pp. 258–74.

Carr, E. H. *What Is History?* (London, 1961).

Casanova, Paul. "Le Malhamat dans l'islam primitif." In *Revue de l'Histoire des Religions* 61 (1910), pp. 151–61.

———. *Mohammed et la fin du monde* (Paris, 1911).

Chatwin, Bruce. *The Songlines* (London, 1987).

Cheddadi, Abdesselam. *Ibn Khaldûn: L'homme et le théoricien de la civilisation* (Paris, 2006).

Cheddadi, Abdesselam. *Ibn Khaldoun revisité* (Casablanca, 1999).

Chejne, Anwar G. *Muslim Spain, Its History and Culture* (Minneapolis, 1974).

Cole, Donald P. "Bedouin and Social Change in Saudi Arabia." *Journal of Asian African Studies* 16 (1981), pp. 128–40.

Cook, Michael. *Commanding Right and Forbidding Wrong in Islamic Thought* (Cambridge University Press, 2010).

Cooperson, Michael. "Biographical Literature." In *The New Cambridge History of Islam*, vol. 4, *Islamic Cultures and Societies to the End of the Eighteenth Century* (Cambridge, 2010), pp. 458–73.

Crone, Patricia. *Medieval Islamic Political Thought* (Edinburgh, 2004).

———. *Pre-Industrial Societies* (Oxford, 1989).

———. *Slaves on Horses: The Evolution of the Islamic Polity* (Cambridge, 1980).

Dakhlia, Jocelyne. "Un miroir de la royauté au Maghreb: la ville d'airan." In *Genèse de la ville islamique en al-Andalus et au Maghreb occidental*, edited by Patrice Cressier and Mercedes García Arenal (Madrid, 1998), pp. 17–36.

Dale, Stephen Frederick. "Ibn Khaldun: The Last Greek and The First *Annaliste* Historian." *International Journal of Middle East Studies* 38 (2006), pp. 431–51.

———. *The Orange Trees of Marrakesh: Ibn Khaldun and the Science of Man* (Cambridge, MA, 2015).

Deprest, Florence. "Gautier." In *Dictionnaire des orientalistes de langue française*, edited by François Pouillon (Paris, 2012), pp. 456–57.

Dickson, H.R.P. *The Arab of the Desert: A Glimpse into Badawin Life in Kuwait and Sa'udi Arabia* (London, 1949).

Dirda, Michael. Introduction to *Foundation, Foundation and Empire, Second Foundation*. Bound as one (New York, 2010).

Dols, Michael W. *The Black Death in the Middle East* (Princeton, NJ, 1977).

Dunlop, D. M. *Arab Civilization to AD 1500* (London, 1971).

Enan, Mohammad Abdullah. *Ibn Khaldun, His Life and Works* (Lahore, 1941).

Ernst, Carl W. *The Shambhala Guide to Sufism* (Boston, 1997).

Fahd, Toufic. *La Divination arabe* (Paris, 1987).

Fakhry, Majid. *Averroes (Ibn Rushd): His Life, Works and Influence* (Oxford, 2001).

Fernandes, Leonor. *The Evolution of a Sufi Institution in Mamluk Egypt: The Khanqah* (Berlin, 1988).

Fierro, Maribel. "Batinism in al-Andalus: Maslamah b. Qurtubi Author of the *Rutbat al-hakim* and the *Ghayat al-hakim*." *Studia Islamica* 84 (1996), pp. 87–112.

Filiu, Jean Pierre. *Apocalypse in Islam*. Translated by M. B. DeBevoise (Berkeley, 2011).

Fischel, Walter J. "A New Latin Source on Tamerlane's Conquest of Damascus (1400–1401) (B. de Mignanelli's Vita Tamerlani 1416)." *Oriens* 9 (1956), pp. 201–32.

———. *Ibn Khaldūn and Tamerlane: Their Historic Meeting in Damascus, 1401 A. D. (803 A. H.): A Study Based on Arabic Manuscripts of Ibn Khaldūn's "Autobiography," with a Translation into English, and a Commentary* (Berkeley and Los Angeles, 1952).

———. *Ibn Khaldun in Egypt: His Public Functions and His Historical Research* (Berkeley and Los Angeles, 1967).

———. "Ibn Khaldûn's 'Autobiography' in the Light of External Arabic Sources." In *Studi orientalistici in onore di Giorgio Levi Della Vida*. 2 vols. (Rome, 1936), vol. 1, pp. 287–308.

Fisher, H.A.L. *A History of Europe*. 2nd ed., 3 vols. (London, 1938).

Fleischer, Cornell. "Royal Authority, Dynastic Cyclism and 'Ibn Khaldunism' in Sixteenth-Century Ottoman Letters." *Journal of Asian and African Studies* 18 (1983), pp. 198–219.

Fletcher, Madeleine. "Al-Andalus and North Africa in Almohad Ideology." In *The Legacy of Muslim Spain*, edited by Salma Khadra Jayyusi (Leiden, 1992), pp. 235–58.

Foucault, Michel. *The Order of Things: An Archaeology of the Human Sciences*. Anonymous translation (London, 1970).

Fromherz, Allen James. *The Almohads: The Rise of an Islamic Empire* (London, 2010).

———. *Ibn Khaldun, Life and Times* (Edinburgh, 2001).

Fück, J. *Die Arabischen Studien in Europa bis in den Anfangdes 20. Jahrhunderts* (Leipzig, 1955), pp. 158–66.

Fudge, Bruce. "Underworlds and Otherworlds in *The Thousand and One Nights*." *Middle Eastern Literatures* 15 (2012), pp. 257–72.

Garcin, Jean-Claude. *Les Mille et Une Nuits et l'Histoire* (Paris, 2016).

———. "The Regime of the Circassian Mamluks." In *The Cambridge History of Egypt: Volume One, Islamic Egypt, 640–1517*, edited by Carl Petry (Cambridge, 1998), pp. 290–317.

Gautier, Émil-Félix. *L'Islamisation de l'Afrique du Nord: Les siècles obscures du Maghreb* (Paris, 1927).

Gellner, Ernest. *Anthropology and Politics: Revolutions in the Sacred Grove* (Oxford, 1995).

———. *Muslim Society* (Cambridge, 1981).

———. *Saints of the Atlas* (London, 1969).

Ghrab, Saad. *Ibn 'Arafah et le Malikisme en Ifriqiya au VIII/XIVe siècles*. 2 vols. (Tunis, 1996).

Gibb, Hamilton. *Arabic Literature: An Introduction* (Oxford, 1926).

———. "The Islamic Background of Ibn Khaldun's Political Theory." In Gibb, *Studies on the Civilization of Islam* (Boston, 1962).

———. Review of Rosenthal's translation of the *Muqaddimah*. In *Speculum* 35 (1960), pp. 139–42.

Gibbon, Edward. *Autobiography of Edward Gibbon* (London, 1907).

Goldzink, Jean. "Montesquieu." In *Dictionnaire des orientalistes de langue française*, edited by François Pouillon (Paris, 2012), pp. 742–44.

Grosrichard, Alain. *Structure du sérail* (Paris, 1979).

Grunebaum, Gustave E. von. *Medieval Islam* (Chicago, 1946).

Gutas, Dmitri. *Greek Thought, Arabic Culture: The Graeco-Arabic Translation Movement in Baghdad and Early 'Abbasid Society (2nd–4th/8th–10th Centuries)* (London, 1988).

Haarmann, Ulrich. "Auflösung und Bewahrung der klassischen Formen arabischer Geschichtsschreibung in der Zeit der Mamluken." *Zeitschrift fur deutschen Morgenländischen Gesellschaft* 121 (1971).

Hammer-Purgstall, Joseph von. "Notice sur l'Introduction à la connaissance de l'histoire, célèbre ouvrage d'Ibn Khaldoun." *Journal Asiatique*, 1st ser., vol. 1 (1822) pp. 267–78; vol. 4, pp. 158–61.

———. *Uber den Verfall des Islam nach den ersten drei Jahrhunderten der Hidschrat* (Vienna, 1812).

Hamori, Andras. "An Allegory from the *Arabian Nights*: The City of Brass." In Hamori, *The Art of Medieval Arabic Literature* (Princeton, NJ, 1974), pp. 145–63.

Herbelot, Barthelémi d'. *Bibliothèque orientale*. 4 vols. (The Hague, 1772–79).

Herbert, Frank. *The Children of Dune* (London, 1976).

———. *Dune* (London, 1966).

———. *Dune Messiah* (London, 1971).

Hillenbrand, Carole. "Al-Ghazzali." In Meisami and Starkey, *Encyclopedia*, vol. 1, pp. 252–53.

Himmich, Bensalem. *Al-'allama* (Beirut, 1997). Translated by Roger Allen as *The Polymath* (Cairo, 2004).

———. *Khalduniyya fi daw' falsafat al-ta'rikh* (Cairo, 1998). Translated in French as *Ibn Khaldûn: Un philosophe de l'histoire* (Rabat, 2006).

Hodgson, Marshall. *The Venture of Islam: Conscience and History in a World Civilization*. 3 vols. (Chicago and London, 1977).

Holt, P. M. *The Age of the Crusades: The Near East from the Eleventh Century to 1517* (Harlow, Essex, 1986).

———. "The Structure of Government in the Mamluk Sultanate." In *The Eastern Mediterranean Lands in the Period of the Crusades*, edited by Holt (Warminster, Wiltshire, 1977), pp. 44–61.

Hookham, Hilda. *Tamburlaine the Conqueror* (London, 1962).

Horne, Alastair. *A Savage War of Peace: Algeria 1954–1962* (London, 1977).

Hourani, Albert. *A History of the Arab Peoples* (London, 1991).

———. "Toybee's Vision of History." In Hourani, *Europe and the Middle East* (London, 1980), pp. 135–60.

Huizinga, Jan. *The Waning of the Middle Ages: A Study of the Forms of Life, Thought and Art in France and the Netherlands in the Fourteenth and Fifteenth Centuries*. Translated by F. Hopman (London, 1955).

Hume, David. *Treatise on Human Nature* (London, 1734–37).

Husayn, Taha. *Étude analytique et critique de la philosophie sociale d'Ibn Khaldoun* (Paris, 1917).

Ibn 'Arabshah, Ahmed. *Fakihat al-khulafa' wa mufakahat al-zurafa'*. Edited by Ayman 'Abd al-Jabir al-Buhayri (Cairo, 2001).

———. *Tamerlane or Timur the Great Amir*. Translated by J. H. Sanders (London, 1936).

Ibn al-Furat, Muhammad. *Ta'rikh al-duwal wa'l-muluk*. Edited by Qutantin Zurayq, 9 vols. (Beirut, 1936–42).

Ibn Hajar, Ahmad. *Inba' al-ghumr bi-abna' al-umr*. Edited by Hasan Habashi, 3 vols. (Cairo, 1971).

———. *Raf al-'isr 'an qudat Misr.* 2 vols. (Cairo, 1957, 1961).

Ibn Jubayr, Muhammad. *The Travels of Ibn Jubayr.* Translated by R.J.C. Broadhurst (London, 1952).

Ibn Taghribirdi, Abu al-Muhasin. *Al-Manhal al-safi wa al-mustawfi ba'd al wafi.* 9 vols. (Cairo, 1994).

———. *Al-Nujum al-Zahira fi muluk Misr wa-al-Qahira.* Publications in Semitic Philology (Berkeley, 1915–60), vols. 5–7, 12, 14, 17–19, 22.

Irwin, Robert. *The Alhambra* (London, 2004).

———. *For Lust of Knowing: The Orientalists and Their Enemies* (London, 2006). Published in the United States as *Dangerous Knowledge: Orientalism and Its Discontents* (New York, 2007).

———. "Gunpowder and Firearms in the Mamluk Sultanate Reconsidered." In *The Mamluks in Egyptian and Syrian Politics and Society,* edited by M. Winter and A. Levanoni (Leiden, 2004), pp. 114–39.

———. *The Penguin Anthology of Classical Arabic Literature* (London, 2006). First published as *Night and Horses and the Desert: An Anthology of Classical Arabic Literature* (London, 1999).

———. "The Privatisation of 'Justice' under the Circassian Mamlūks." *Mamluk Studies Review* 6 (2002), pp. 63–70.

———. Review of Stephen Dale, *The Orange Trees of Marrakesh,* in *Times Literary Supplement,* April 1, 2016, p. 24.

———. "Toynbee and Ibn Khaldun." *Middle Eastern Studies* 33 (1997), pp. 461–79.

———. "Tribal Feuding and Mamlūk Factions in Medieval Syria." In *Texts, Documents and Artefacts: Islamic Studies in Honour of D. S. Richards,* edited by C. F. Robinson (Leiden, 2003), pp. 251–64.

Kennedy, Hugh. *The Court of the Caliphs: The Rise and Fall of Islam's Greatest Dynasty* (London, 2004).

———. *An Historical Atlas of Islam* (Leiden, 2002).

Khalidi, Tarif. *Islamic Historiography: The Histories of Mas'udi* (New York, 1975).

Khaneboubi, Ahmed. *Les Institutions gouvernmentales sous les Merinides (1258–1465)* (Paris, 2008).

Knysh, Alexander D. *Ibn 'Arabi in the Later Islamic Tradition: The Making of a Polemical Image in Medieval Islam* (Albany, NY, 1998).

———. "Ibn al-Khatib." In *The Cambridge History of Arabic Literature: The Literature of Al-Andalus,* edited by Maria Rosa Menocal, Raymond P. Scheindlin, and Michael Sells (Cambridge, 2000).

———. "Sufism." In *The New Cambridge History of Islam,* edited by Robert Irwin, vol. 4, *Islamic Cultures and Societies to the End of the Eighteenth Century* (Cambridge, 2010), pp. 60–104.

Kosei, Morimoto. "What Ibn Khaldun Saw: The Judiciary of Mamluk Egypt." *Mamluk Studies Review* 6 (2002), pp. 109–31.

Kraus, Paul. *Jābir ibn Hayyān: Contribution à l'histoire des idées scientifiques dans l'Islam.* 2 vols. (Paris, 1942).

Labib, Subhi Y. "Al-Asadi und sein Bericht über Verwaltungs- und Geldreform im 15 Jahrhundert." *Journal of Economic and Social History of the Orient* 8 (1965), pp. 312–16.

Lacoste, Yves. *Ibn Khaldun: The Birth of History and the Past of the Third World.* Translated by David Macey (London, 1984). First published as *Ibn Khaldoun: naissance de l'histoire passé du tiers-monde* (Paris, 1966).

Larzul, Sylvette. "Silvestre de Sacy." In *Dictionnaire des orientalistes de langue française,* edited by François Pouillon (Paris, 2012), pp. 953–55.

Lawrence, Bruce B. "Introduction: Ibn Khaldun and Islamic Ideology." In *Ibn Khaldun and Islamic Ideology,* edited by Lawrence (Leiden, 1984), pp. 2–13.

Lawrence, T. E. *Seven Pillars of Wisdom: The Complete 1922 "Oxford" Text* (Fordingbridge, Hampshire, 2004).

Leaman, Oliver. *An Introduction to Classical Islamic Philosophy* (Cambridge, 1985).

Lewis, Bernard. "The Decolonisation of History." *Times Literary Supplement,* August 1968, p. 853.

———. "Ibn Khaldun in Turkey." In *Islam in History; Ideas, People, and Events in the Middle East.* 2nd ed. (Chicago and La Salle, IL, 1993), pp. 233–36.

———. "Islamic Concepts of Revolution." In Lewis, *Islam in History; Ideas, People, and Events in the Middle East.* 2nd ed. (Chicago and La Salle, IL, 1993), pp. 311–20.

Little, Donald Presgrave. *An Introduction to Mamluk Historiography: An Analysis of Arabic Annalistic and Biographical Sources for the Reign of al-Malik an-Nasir Muhammad ibn Qala'un* (Wiesbaden, 1970).

López, Emilio Molina. *Ibn al-Jatib* (Granada, 2001).

Lovecraft, H. P. *Lovecraft, The Complete Fiction.* Edited by T. Joshi (New York, 2008).

Lovejoy, Arthur O. *The Great Chain of Being: A Study of the History of an Idea* (New York, 1936).

Lyons, Malcolm C. *The Arabian Epic: Heroic and Oral Storytelling.* 3 vols. (Cambridge, 1995).

Mahdi, Muhsin. *Ibn Khaldûn's Philosophy of History: A Study in the Philosophic Foundation of the Science of Culture,* 2nd ed. (Chicago, 1964).

Mahfouz, Naguib. *The Harafish.* Translated by Catherine Cobham (New York, 1993).

al-Maqrizi, Ahmed ibn 'Ali. *Kitab al-suluk.* 3 vols. (Cairo, 1956–73).

———. *Mamluk Economics: A Study and Translation of al-Maqrizi's Ighathah.* Edited and translated by Adel Allouche (Salt Lake City, 1994).

———. *Al-Mawa'iz wa-l-i'tibar bi-dhikr al-khitat wa'l-athar.* 2 vols. (Bulaq, 1854).

Marquet, Yves. *La Philosophie des Ihwan al-Safa* (Algiers, 1975).

Marzolph, Ulrich, and Richard van Leeuwen. *The Arabian Nights Encyclopedia.* 2 vols. (Santa Barbara, CA, 2004).

Massoud, Sami G. *The Chronicles and Annalistic Sources of the Early Mamluk Circassian Period* (Leiden, 2007).

al-Mas'udi, 'Ali ibn al-Husayn. *Meadows of Gold: The 'Abbasids.* Translated by Paul Lunde and Caroline Stone (London, 1989).

———. *Muruj al-dhahab wa-ma'adin al-jawhar.* 9 vols. (Paris, 1861–77).

———. *Les prairies d'or.* Translated by Barbier de Meynard and Pavet de Corneille, 2nd corrected ed. by Charles Pellat, 5 vols. (Paris, 1966–79).

Meloy, John L. "The Privatization of Protection: Extortion and the State in the Circassian Mamluk Period." *Journal of Economic and Social History of the Orient* 47 (2004), pp. 195–212.

Menocal, María Rose. *The Ornament of the World: How Muslims, Jews, and Christians Created a Culture of Tolerance in Medieval Spain* (New York, 2002).

Messaoudi, Alain. "De Slane." In *Dictionnaire des orientalistes de langue française,* edited by François Pouillon (Paris, 2012), p. 959.

———. "Hammer-Purgstall." In *Dictionnaire des orientalistes de langue française,* edited by François Pouillon, 2nd ed. (Paris, 2012), pp. 509–10.

———. "Quatremère." In *Dictionnaire des orientalistes de langue française,* edited by François Pouillon (Paris, 2012), pp. 840–41.

Monteil, Vincent. "Ibn Khaldoûn, sociologue et historien (1332–1406)." *Revue Historique* 237 (1967), pp. 339–58.

Namier, Lewis. *Conflicts: Studies in Contemporary History* (London, 1942).

Nasr, S. H. *An Introduction to Islamic Cosmological Doctrines.* 2nd ed. (London, 1978), pp. 25–104.

Nasser, Nassif. "Le maître d'Ibn Khaldun: al-Abili." *Studia Islamica* 20 (1964), pp. 103–15.

Netton, Ian R. *Muslim Neoplatonism: An Introduction to the Thought of the Brethren of Purity (Ikhwan al-Safa')* (Edinburgh, 1991).

Norris, H. T. *Saharan Myth and Saga* (Oxford, 1972).

Oumlil, Ali. *L'Histoire et son discours: essai sur la méthodologie d'Ibn Khaldoun* (Rabat, 1982).

Pellat, Charles, ed. and trans. *The Life and Works of Jahiz* (Berkeley and Los Angeles, 1969).

Penman, Jim. *Biohistory: Decline and Fall of the West* (Newcastle upon Tyne, 2015).

Pérez, René. Introduction to Ibn Khaldun, *La Voie et la loi: ou le maître et le jurist, Shifa' al-sa'il li-tahdhib al-masa'il.* Translated by René Pérez (Arles, 1991).

Pinault, David. *Story-Telling Techniques in the Arabian Nights* (Leiden, 1992).

Poncet, J. "Le mythe de catastrophie hilalienne." *Annales Economies, Societés, Civilisations* 22 (1967), pp. 1099–120.

Redjala, M'barek. "Un texte inédit du Muqaddima." *Arabica* 22 (1975), pp. 320–23.

Ridgeon, Lloyd, ed. *The Cambridge Companion to Sufism* (Cambridge, 2015).

Robinson, Chase F. *Islamic Historiography* (Cambridge, 2003).

Rosenthal, Franz. *A History of Muslim Historiography* (Leiden, 1968).

———. "Ibn Khaldun in His Time." In *Ibn Khaldun and Islamic Ideology,* edited by Bruce B. Lawrence (Leiden, 1984).

Roughi, Ramzi. *The Making of a Mediterranean Emirate: Ifriqiyya and Its Andalusis, 1200–1400* (Philadelphia, 2011).

Russell, Bertrand. *A History of Philosophy* (London, 1946).

al-Sakhawi, Muhammad. *Al-Daw' al-lami'.* 12 vols. (Cairo, 1934–36).

Sedgwick, Mark. *Muhammad Abduh* (Oxford, 2010).

Serjeant, R. B. Review of Rosenthal's translation of the *Muqaddima* in *Bulletin of the School of Oriental and African Studies,* vol. 24 (1961), pp. 143–44.

Schulz, Warren. "Mansa Musa's Gold in Mamluk Cairo: A Reappraisal of a World Civilization Anecdote." In *Post-Mongol Central Asia and the Middle*

East: Studies in History and Historiography in Honour of Professor John E. Woods, edited by J. Pfeiffer, S. Quinn, and E. Tucker (Wiesbaden, 2006), pp. 428–47.

Shatzmiller, Maya. *L'historiographie Merinide: Ibn Khaldūn et ses contemporains* (Leiden, 1982).

———. *The Berbers and the Islamic State: The Marinid Experience in Pre-Protectorate Morocco* (Princeton, NJ, 2000).

Shboul, Ahmed. *Al-Masʿudi and His World* (London, 1979).

Silvestre de Sacy, Antoine-Isaac. *Chrestomathie arabe.* 2nd revised ed. 2 vols. (Paris, 1806).

Stetkevych, Jaroslav. *The Zephyrs of Najd: The Poetics of Nostalgia in the Classical Arabic Nasib* (Chicago, 1993).

al-Tahtawi, Rifaʿa Rafiʿ. *An Imam in Paris: Account of a Stay in France by an Egyptian Cleric (1826–1831).* Translated by Daniel L. Newman. 2nd ed. (London, 2011).

Talbi, M. "Ibn Khaldun." In *The Encyclopedia of Islam.* 2nd ed. Edited by H.A.R. Gibb et al., 13 vols. (Leiden, 1960–2009), vol. 3, pp. 825–31.

Tales of the Marvellous and News of the Strange. Translated by Malcolm Lyons (London, 2014).

Thesiger, Wilfred. *Arabian Sands* (London, 1959).

Toynbee, Arnold. *A Study of History.* 2nd ed. 12 vols. (London, 1935).

Trevor-Roper, Hugh. "Ibn Khaldoun and the Decline of Barbary." In Trevor-Roper, *Historical Essays* (London, 1957).

Triaud, Jean-Louis. "Monteil." In *Dictionnaire des orientalistes de langue française,* edited by François Pouillon (Paris, 2012), pp. 740–42.

Valéry, Paul. "The Crisis of the Mind." In Valéry, *History and Politics,* translated by Denise Foliot and Jackson Mathews (London, 1963).

Varisco, Daniel. "Ernest Gellner: Idealized to a Fault." In Varisco, *Islam Observed: The Rhetoric of Anthropological Reprsentation* (New York, 2005), pp. 53–80.

Webb, Peter. *Imagining the Arabs: Arab Identity and the Rise of Islam* (Edinburgh, 2016).

Wiseman, John. *SAS Survival Guide* (Glasgow, 1993).

INDEX

✦✦✦

'Abd al-'Aziz, 31, 36
'Abduh, Muhammad, 190
al-Abili, Muhammad ibn Ibrahim, 26–27, 68, 99, 137, 150, 154, 197
Abu 'Abd Allah, 30, 34–35
Abu Faris, 93
Abu Hammu II, 35, 37, 39, 41
Abu 'Inan Faris, 27–29, 95, 109
Abu Ishaq, 28
Abu'l-Abbas, 35, 60, 84
Abu'l-Faraj al-Isfahani, 156–57
Abu'l-Hasan 'Ali, 25–26, 27, 31, 58, 142, 153
Abu'l-Hasan al-Mustansir, 89
Abu Muslim ibn Khaldun, 123
Abu Nuwas, 3
Abu Salim, 30, 31
Adorno, Anselm, 25
Adorno, Theodor, 121
al-Afghani, Jamal al-Din, 190
al-Akhlati, Husayn, 127–28
alchemy, 17, 59, 76–77, 122, 123–25
Alexander the Great, 14, 17, 21, 34, 59, 60, 66, 77
'Ali, 49, 57, 70, 95, 108, 132
Altunbugha al-Jubani al-Yalbughawi, 'Ala al-Din, 88, 92, 93, 157
'Amar ibn 'Abdullah, 33–34
Amir ibn Muhammad ibn Ali, 39
Anurshirwan, 59, 60, 66
Aristotle, 41, 67, 68, 69, 76–78, 121, 184, 196, 199; Alexander and, 34, 59–60, 97; on mistakes, 207
'asabiyya (group solidarity), 19, 45–48, 56, 63, 69, 70, 90, 95, 97, 117, 135, 187, 189–90;

European translations of, 167, 171; pejorative sense of, 207; Toynbee on, 175. See also 'isaba
al-'Asadi, 151–52
al-Ash'ari, Abu al-Hasan, 78–79
Asimov, Isaac, 141, 200
astrology, 71, 77, 98–99, 115, 121–23, 125, 127, 129, 135–37, 148–49, 170; Ibn Khaldun's sign, 170
Averroes (Ibn Rushd), 68–70, 75, 184, 196
Ayalon, David, 62
al-'Ayni, Badr al-Din, 106–7, 127
al-Azmeh, Aziz, xi, 180, 193–94, 195, 199

Bahram ibn Bahram, 60
al-Bajarbaqi, 133
Banu Fadl, 57, 90–91
Banu Hilal, 7, 52–53, 158, 175–76
Banu Muzni, 35
Banu Sulaym, 7, 27, 52–53, 175
Barquq, 62, 88–92, 96, 104, 127, 129, 133, 142
al-Batha ibn Abi 'Amr, 28
Baybars al-Jashankir, 89
Baybars al-Mansuri, 88
Berkey, Jonathan P., 6
al-Bistami, Abu Yazid, 114, 140
Black Death, 8–9, 17, 27, 64, 71, 101, 149
Braudel, Fernand, 22
Brethren of Purity (Ikhwan al-Safa'), 71, 117, 126
Brett, Michael, 194, 203
Brunschvig, Robert, 61, 182, 189
al-Buni, Ahmad, 111, 121, 125–26
Burkhardt, Jacob, 171